Birds in Roman Life and Myth

This book explores the place of birds in Roman myth and everyday life, focusing primarily on the transitional period of 100 BCE to 100 CE within the Italian peninsula.

A diverse range of topics is considered in order to build a broad overview of the subject. Beginning with an appraisal of omens, augury, and auspices – including the 'sacred chickens' consulted by generals before battle – it goes on to examine how Romans farmed birds, hunted them, and kept them as pets. It demonstrates how the ownership and consumption of birds were used to communicate status and prestige, and how bird consumption mirrored wider economic and social trends. Each topic adopts an interdisciplinary approach, considering literary evidence alongside art, material culture, zooarchaeology, and modern ornithological knowledge. The inclusion of zooarchaeology adds another dimension to the work and highlights the value of using animals and faunal remains to interpret the past.

Studying the Roman view of birds offers great insight into how they conceived of their relationship with the gods and how they stratified and organised their society. This book is a valuable resource for bird lovers and researchers alike, particularly those studying animals in the ancient world.

Dr Ashleigh Green is a graduate of The University of Melbourne and a fellow of the State Library of Victoria. Her research interests include the study of birds in the classical world, and more generally what human-animal studies can tell us about societies both past and present. She was the 2021 recipient of the Australasian Society for Classical Studies Early Career Award and a 2022 Virtual Fellow for the Centre for the History of Emotions.

Global Perspectives on Ancient Mediterranean Archaeology
Series editor: Jeremy Armstrong
University of Auckland
Gijs Tol
University of Melbourne

The series' remit embraces a broad span of time from the Mediterranean Bronze Age through the Byzantine period (c. 3200 BCE–1453 CE). Although nominally focused on the Mediterranean Sea and areas which immediately border it, the series also welcomes studies on areas slightly further afield which are linked to the Sea by cultural, social, economic, religious, or political connections, and where the Mediterranean zone is directly relevant. A guiding principle of the series is the inclusive appreciation of all available material from a particular area, time, and culture, even if the primary emphasis is on the archaeological aspects. Finally, as suggested by its name, the series is particularly interested in publishing works which adopt a broad comparative and cross-cultural approach, as well as those which bring together concepts and themes more common in the study of archaeology from elsewhere in the world (most notably the Pacific and Australasia) with those from the Old World.

Birds in Roman Life and Myth
Ashleigh Green

For more information about this series, please visit: https://www.routledge.com/ Global-Perspectives-on-Ancient-Mediterranean-Archaeology/book-series/GPAMA

Birds in Roman Life and Myth

Ashleigh Green

LONDON AND NEW YORK

First published 2023
by Routledge
4 Park Square, Milton Park, Abingdon, Oxon OX14 4RN

and by Routledge
605 Third Avenue, New York, NY 10158

Routledge is an imprint of the Taylor & Francis Group, an informa business

British Library Cataloguing-in-Publication Data
A catalogue record for this book is available from the British Library

ISBN: 978-1-032-16286-7 (hbk)
ISBN: 978-1-032-16289-8 (pbk)
ISBN: 978-1-003-24790-6 (ebk)

DOI: 10.4324/9781003247906

Typeset in Times New Roman
by MPS Limited, Dehradun

For my parents

Contents

Figures

Note from the Series Editors

Dear Readers,

We are very pleased to introduce the new Routledge/Taylor & Francis Group book series, 'Global Perspectives on Ancient Mediterranean Archaeology', through this inaugural volume, Dr. Ashleigh Green's *Birds in Roman Life and Myth*.

As noted in the series' description, the series' remit embraces a broad span of time from the Mediterranean Bronze Age through the Byzantine period (c. 3200 BCE–1453 CE). Although nominally focused on the Mediterranean Sea and areas which immediately border it, the series also welcomes studies on areas slightly further afield which are linked to the Sea by cultural, social, economic, religious, or political connections, and where the Mediterranean zone is directly relevant. As will be apparent from the volume before you, while the series will obviously have a strong focus on the presentation and discussion of archaeological material, both new and historical, it also explicitly encourages the union of archaeological and historical material wherever possible and appropriate. A guiding principle of the series is the inclusive appreciation of all available material from a particular area, time, and culture, even if the primary emphasis is on the archaeological aspects. Finally, as suggested by its name, the series is particularly interested in publishing works which adopt a broad comparative and cross-cultural approach, as well as those which bring together concepts and themes more common in the study of archaeology from elsewhere in the world (most notably the Pacific and Australasia) with those from the Old World.

Both the series editors and board members sincerely hope that you enjoy and appreciate this first volume in the series, and we look forward to bringing you other volumes which will deepen and expand our understanding of both the ancient Mediterranean world and our modern, global relationship to it.

Jeremy Armstrong & Gijs Tol
Series Editors
'Global Perspectives on Ancient
Mediterranean Archaeology'

Acknowledgements

This book evolved from a PhD thesis submitted at The University of Melbourne in 2020. I completed this course with the assistance of an Australian Postgraduate Award and the Australian Government Research Training Program Scholarship. I first had the idea to write about birds in ancient Rome at the end of 2015. I had been reading about birds in ancient Greece and Egypt, and was disappointed when I could not find an equivalent work on Rome. With the deadline approaching to submit a PhD proposal, I put forward the idea to write about *Birds in Roman Life and Myth* – a nod to John Pollard's 1977 publication, *Birds in Greek Life and Myth*. The original plan was, to say the least, ambitious. Initial discussions with my primary supervisor Frederik Vervaet and my secondary supervisors Tamara Lewit and James Chong-Gossard helped me to refine my scope and break the topic into manageable pieces. At this early stage I also reached out to Jeremy Mynott, whose work had been so influential to me. He was kind enough to provide feedback on some early drafts and remained in contact as the years progressed. This monograph represents the end of a long journey, the culmination of many years of hard work and collaboration.

I wish to acknowledge the efforts of all my supervisors for their keen insight and high standards that always kept me striving for perfection as the thesis took shape. I thank Frederik Vervaet for his boundless support and rigorous evaluations; Tamara Lewit for her generosity and insight; and James Chong-Gossard, who was also my Honours supervisor, for his encouragement and incisive advice. I must also thank Professor Tim Parkin, who joined as a supervisor halfway through my PhD journey when my primary supervisor went on long-service leave. I could not have asked for a more generous or supportive group of people to guide me through this process. In this vein I wish also to acknowledge the entire staff at the School of Historical and Philosophical Studies at The University of Melbourne – not only my supervisors, but also Louise Hitchcock, Hyun Jin Kim, Gijs Tol, and finally Andrew Turner, who has been a mentor to me since my undergraduate days. I also thank my fellow graduate students: Dan Qing Zhao, Julia Pelosi-Thorpe, Donna Storey, and the rest of the cohort at the School of Historical and Philosophical Studies for advice and support rendered throughout my years as a student.

The University of Melbourne was generous enough to award funding so I could travel to Italy to complete essential research, without which this book would be incomplete. I am indebted to the Robert Anderson Trust for facilitating a month of research in London. On my travels, I attended the ICAZ Bird Working Group Meeting, held at The University of Sheffield in 2018. I am grateful to everyone at the conference for being so welcoming, and many parts of this book refer to research that was shared and discussed there. I thank Historic England for allowing me to access their zooarchaeology reference collection, and I thank Naomi Sykes and The University of Exeter for inviting me to present some of my research in 2018. Continued contact and collaboration with the HumAnE Bioarchaeology Centre at The University of Exeter has proven invaluable, and I continue to be impressed by the research they produce.

The publication process was aided by the Australasian Society for Classical Studies. I am deeply grateful to the Society for awarding me 2021 Early Career Award to help with publication costs. I thank Ron Ridley for reading the manuscript in its entirety and providing advice and feedback, as well as for his friendship and support. I thank series editors Gijs Tol and Jeremy Armstrong for their patience and guidance throughout this process, and I thank Edward Blume-Poulton for providing images and always being so supportive of my work.

Finally, I thank my friends and family. I thank Maddie Haywood for her friendship and for sharing her love of birds with me. I thank Jan Ryrie for always being an inspiration to me. I thank my sister Jasmine for being such a tremendous source of support throughout my years as a student, and I send all my love to my nieces Lily and Emilia. To my parents, I give my sincerest thanks. I thank my father, who took me to the library every Saturday when I was a child, and I thank my mother, who encouraged my love of learning and always supported me to pursue my dreams. As the thesis took shape, they were the ones who humoured me as I set about reconstructing my very own *templum* and building a flock of chickens so I could practice taking auspices. This book is dedicated to them.

Abbreviations List

Ael	Aelian
NA	*De natura animalium*
VH	*Varia Historia*
Aen. Tact	Aeneas Tacticus
Aesch	Aeschylus
Ag	*Agamemnon*
PV	*Prometheus Vinctus*
Supp	*Supplices*
AJArch	*American Journal of Archaeology*
AJPhil	*American Journal of Philology*
Amer. Acad. Rome	*Memoirs of the American Academy at Rome*
Anc. Soc	*Ancient Society*
Anth. Pal	*Anthologia Palatina*
Antip. Sid	Antipater Sidonius
Apollod	Apollodorus mythographus
Bibl	*Bibliotheca*
App. Verg	*Appendix Vergiliana*
Apul	Apuleius
Met	*Metamorphoses*
Ap. Rhod	Apollonius Rhodius
Argon	*Argonautica*
Ar	Aristophanes
Av	*Aves*
Aratus, *Phaen*	Aratus, *Phaenomena*
Arist	Aristotle
Gen. an	*De generatione animalium*
Hist. an	*Historia animalium*
Mete	*Meteorologica*
[Arist.]	Pseudo-Aristotle
De mirab	*De mirabilibus auscultationibus*
Artem	Artemidorus Daldianus
On	*Oneirocritica*
Ath	Athenaeus

August	Augustine
CD	*De civitate Dei*
Doct. christ	*De doctrina Christiana*
Aur. Vict	Aurelius Victor
Caes	*Caesares*
Or	*Origo gentis Romanae*
Caes	Caesar
BCiv	*Bellum Civile*
BGall	*Bellum Gallicum*
Cass. Dio	Cassius Dio
Cato, *Agr*	Cato, *De agricultura* or *De re rustica*
Catull	Catullus
Cic	Cicero (Marcus Tullius)
Att	*Epistulae ad Atticum*
Brut	*Brutus* or *De Claris Oratoribus*
Div	*De divinatione*
Fam	*Epistulae ad familiares*
Fin	*De finibus*
Flac	*Pro Flacco*
Leg	*De legibus*
Nat. D	*De natura deorum*
Off	*De officiis*
QFr	*Epistulae ad Quintum fratrem*
Rep	*De republica*
Sen	*De senectute*
Tusc	*Tusculanae disputationes*
CIL	*Corpus Inscriptionum Latinarum*
CJ	*Classical Journal*
Columella, *Rust*	Columella, *De re rustica*
CPhil	*Classical Philology*
CQ	*Classical Quarterly*
Dig	*Digesta*
Dio Chrys. *Or*	Dio Chrysostomus, *Orationes*
Diod. Sic	Diodorus Siculus
Dion. Hal	Dionysius Halicarnassensis
Ant. Rom	*Antiquitates Romanae*
Enn. *Ann*	Ennius, *Annales*
Eur	Euripides
Hel	*Helena*
Festus, *Gloss. Lat*	Festus, *Glossaria Latina*
Frontin	Frontinus
Str	*Strategemata*
Fronto, *Ep*	Fronto, *Epistulae*
G & R	*Greece and Rome*
Galen, *Alim. Fac*	Galen *De Alimentis Facultatibus*

Gell	Aulus Gellius
NA	*Noctes Atticae*
Harv. Stud	*Harvard Studies in Classical Philology*
Hes	Hesiod
Op	*Opera et Dies*
Theog	*Theogonia*
Hom	Homer
Il	*Iliad*
Od	*Odyssey*
Hor	Horace
Ars P	*Ars poetica*
Carm	*Carmina* or *Odes*
Epist	*Epistulae*
Epod	*Epodi*
Sat	*Satirae* or *Sermones*
Isid	Isidorus
Etym	*Etymologiae*
JRA	*Journal of Roman Archaeology*
JRS	*Journal of Roman Studies*
Juv	Juvenal
Sat	*Satirae*
Livy, *Per*	Livy, *Periochae*
Luc	Lucan
Phars	*Pharsalia*
Luc	Lucian
Anach	*Anacharsis*
Lucr	Lucretius
Macrob	Macrobius
Sat	*Saturnalia*
Mart	Martial
Nemes	Nemesianus
OJA	*Oxford Journal of Archaeology*
Ov	Ovid
Am	*Amores*
Ars am	*Ars amatoria*
Fast	*Fasti*
Met	*Metamorphoses*
Pont	*Epistulae ex Ponto*
Rem. am	*Remedia amoris*
Tr	*Tristia*
Paus	Pausanias
Petron	Petronius
Sat	*Satyrica*

Philostr	Philostratus
Imag	*Imagines*
VA	*Vita Apollonii*
Pl	Plato
Leg	*Leges*
Plt	*Politicus*
Plaut	Plautus
Asin	*Asinaria*
Aul	*Aulularia*
Capt	*Captivi*
Cas	*Casina*
Mil	*Miles gloriosus*
Poen	*Poenulus*
Plin	Pliny (the Elder)
HN	*Naturalis historia*
Plin	Pliny (the Younger)
Ep	*Epistulae*
Pan	*Panegyricus*
Plut	Plutarch
Mor	*Moralia*
De fort. Rom	*De fortuna Romanorum*
De frat. amor	*De fraterno amore*
De soll. an	*De sollertia animalium*
Quaest. Rom	*Quaestiones Romanae*
Vit	*Vitae Parallelae*
Alc	*Alcibiades*
Alex	*Alexander*
Ant	*Antonius*
Brut	*Brutus*
Cic	*Cicero*
Fab	*Fabius Maximus*
Luc	*Lucullus*
Mar	*Marius*
Marc	*Marcellus*
Rom	*Romulus*
Ti. Gracch	*Tiberius Gracchus*
Porph	Porphyry
Abst	*De abstinentia*
Prop	Propertius
Prudent	Prudentius
Sen	Seneca (the Elder)
Con. ex	*Controversiarum excerpta*
Controv	*Controversiae*
Suas	*Suasoriae*

Sen	Seneca (the Younger)
Apocol	*Apocolocyntosis*
Constant	*De constantia sapientis*
Ep	*Epistulae*
QNat	*Quaestiones naturales*
Serv	Servius
Aen	*Commentaria in Vergilii opera*
SHA	Scriptores Historiae Augustae
Alex. Sev	*Alexander Severus*
Heliogab	*Heliogabalus*
M. Ant	*Marcus Aurelius Antoninus* (Caracalla)
Marc	*Marcus*
Max	*Maximinus*
Pert	*Pertinax*
Pesc. Nig	*Pescennius Niger*
Prob	*Probus*
Sev	*Severus*
Tyr. Trig	*Tyranni Triginta*
Verus	*Lucius Verus*
Sil	Silius Italicus
Pun	*Punica*
Soph	Sophocles
Phil	*Philoctetes*
Stat	Statius
Silv	*Silvae*
Suet	Suetonius
Aug	*Divus Augustus*
Calig	*Gaius Caligula*
Claud	*Divus Claudius*
Dom	*Domitianus*
Galb	*Galba*
Tib	*Tiberius*
Vesp	*Divus Vespasianus*
Vit	*Vitellius*
Tac	Tacitus
Ann	*Annales*
Hist	*Historiae*
TAPA	*Transactions of the American Philological Association*
Ter	Terence
De monog	*De monogamia*
Theoc	Theocritus
Id	*Idylls*
Tib	Tibullus
Val. Max	Valerius Maximus

Varro, *Ling*	Varro, *De lingua Latina*
Rust	*De re rustica*
Veg	Vegetius
Mil	*De re militari*
Vell. Pat	Velleius Paterculus
Verg	Virgil
Aen	*Aeneid*
Ecl	*Eclogues*
G	*Georgics*
Vitr	Vitruvius
de Arch	*de Architectura*
Xen	Xenophon
Cyr	*Cyropaedia*
Mem	*Memorabilia*
Xen Ephes	Xenophon of Ephesus
Zonar	Zonaras

Introduction

Legend has it that in the year 753 BCE, the twin sons of Mars, Romulus and Remus, fought over who should be king of their new settlement on the banks of the Tiber. To resolve the matter, the brothers agreed to defer to the wisdom of birds. At dawn they rose and each took auspices. Six heavenly vultures appeared to Remus, but twelve appeared to Romulus, communicating to all that Jupiter had chosen his king. Thus was the city of Rome founded, made firm by auspices, and approved by birds.[1]

This story is familiar to anyone with even a passing interest in Roman history, but seldom do we pause to consider how strange it is. Why would the Romans' founding myth stress the importance of ritual birdwatching? More than that, why were vultures considered 'sacred birds', and why did they furnish the signs necessary for the founding of the City? Why did Jupiter communicate through the movement of birds at all? Histories of augury and auspices stress the importance of these birdwatching rituals to the functioning of the state and the military, but fail to interrogate the birds themselves. Equally, while we can all picture the magnificent eagle that was the symbol of the Roman army and the companion of Jupiter, we fail to consider the real eagles that inspired this symbolism. All too easily, birds fade into the background when we study history, and the natural world becomes a simple backdrop against which human drama conducts itself. This book seeks to address this by placing birds at the centre of the grand narrative that is the fall of the Republic and the rise of the Empire. The Italian peninsula is home to hundreds of bird species, many of them migratory, and Romans responded to them in unique and interesting ways. Everywhere we look in Roman history, there are birds. Rome's armies marched beneath the outspread wings of eagles; imperial tables overflowed with exotic fowl; urban populations feasted on the world's first flocks of commercially and intensively raised chickens; pet parrots and ravens talked to their owners in Latin, caged songbirds filled houses with music, and children played with pigeons and battled cockerels. Following the mythic precedent set by Romulus, nothing of importance was ever done in Rome without first asking the birds. Mighty generals consulted caged hens before marching into battle and magistrates took auspices from wild birds before

DOI: 10.4324/9781003247906-1

conducting the day's public business. Studying the Roman view of birds can give us tremendous insight into how they conceived of their relationship with the gods and how they stratified and organised their society. This book aims to examine the distinctive ways the Romans used, observed, thought about, and lived with birds.

Interest in the study of birds in the ancient world dates back to Sir D'Arcy Wentworth Thompson's pioneering work, *The Glossary of Greek Birds,* first published in 1895 and revised in 1936. This book inspired multiple works after it and remains a pinnacle reference tool today. Dedicated studies considered birds in ancient Greece and Egypt, though none focused solely on Rome.[2] The investigation of birds in the Roman world tended to be dominated by literary and philological studies that mainly sought to catalogue birds in literature.[3] In other works, the place of birds in Roman art and culture comprised just a small part of larger studies focusing on other animals.[4] Recently, classicist and ornithologist Jeremy Mynott published two important books on birds in the ancient world that are particularly noteworthy for their methodologies and breadth of research. The first, *Birdscapes* (2009), contains one chapter on ancient history, but more importantly it outlines in general terms how the study of birds can be used to understand the past. His latest publication, *Birds in the Ancient World* (2018), collates and interprets classical literature on birds in a way that is accessible to both the academic and casual readers. It is a thorough and engaging text, but it is intended to provide a general overview on the subject, meaning there is ample room for further investigation, especially on Rome alone. In particular, this book is focused on collating and interpreting art and literature, necessarily leaving aside zooarchaeological findings.

The inclusion of zooarchaeology is perhaps the most important addition that can be made to the study of birds in the ancient world. The works of Geoffrey Kron and Michael MacKinnon show how enlightening zooarchaeology is for understanding and reconstructing Roman agriculture, while also demonstrating how it can be used to make social and cultural inferences.[5] For birds alone, it must be noted that they are generally underrepresented in the archaeological record because excavators in the nineteenth and early twentieth centuries were primarily interested in museum pieces and threw out small bones as a matter of course.[6] However, more recent excavations and the development of new methods for interpretation have enormously improved the evidence pool available to us. Dale Serjeantsen is widely considered the great pioneer of archaeo-ornithology, and credit must duly be paid to her for showing how studying the relationship between humans and birds can aid our understanding and reconstruction of past societies, their beliefs, and their values.[7] Umberto Albarella, Chiara Corbino, Fay Worley, and Polydora Baker are among the most significant zooarchaeologists working to reconstruct bird-human relations using faunal assemblages.[8] In her book *Beastly Questions*, Naomi Sykes lays out how faunal assemblages can be used to interpret past societies. She defines zooarchaeology as the study of animals, their remains, representations, and associated material culture in order to examine how people in past societies behaved and thought, arguing that we must move beyond simple catalogues of animal bones at archaeological sites to provide meaningful interpretations.[9] Recognition of the fact that people in every cultural context use animals to communicate social meaning is key in the works of some of the most prominent anthropologists such as Jack Goody, Arjun Appadurai, and Claude Lévi-Strauss. It was Lévi-Strauss who coined the expression that animals are 'good to think', and therefore imbued with diverse social import.[10] Further to this, Mynott expresses the more pointed idea that 'birds are good to think with'. Coining his own term, 'ornithomorphism', he shows that across cultures 'we all of us use birds freely, if unconsciously, as symbols in everyday life and in the language of analogy and metaphor'.[11] This Roman ornithomorphism is explored throughout this book, in order to understand how birds were used to communicate ideas, values, and social differences.

While there has been ample research on birds in classical Greece, ancient Egypt, and the ancient world in a general sense, to date there has been no comparable study that solely considers birds in ancient Rome. The primary purpose of this publication is to fill this gap in the literature and provide a solid foundational text that will demonstrate the richness of this field and its potential for future research. It takes a broad approach, focusing on four topics the author deems most important to bird-human relations in ancient Rome. These topics are:

- Omens, augury, and auspices (Chapters 1 and 2)
- Birds in Roman agriculture (Chapter 3)
- Wildfowling and bird-catching (Chapter 4)
- Birds kept for pleasure or as pets (Chapter 5)

The first chapter concerns the great Roman institution of augury and auspices. It examines how and why birds were regarded as messengers of divine will in the Republican period. The second chapter follows on from this theme to look at the curious 'sacred chickens' that were used in military auspices, cataloguing how they eventually came to be the dominant auspicial bird, a process culminating in their use by Augustus to help secure the principate. The third chapter outlines Roman aviculture and poultry farming techniques, while the fourth chapter catalogues how Romans hunted birds for pleasure, profit, and subsistence. These two chapters are especially concerned with understanding why and how an appetite for exotic and fattened birds took such a strong hold in the late Republic and early Empire. They consider the social implications surrounding the consumption of different farmed or hunted birds. The final chapter looks at how birds provided pleasure, whether as pets, ornamental features, songsters, or garden visitors.

This book focuses primarily on the period of late Republic to early Empire. The reason for this is that Roman uses of birds undergo a dramatic shift at this time, reflecting the nature of the transitional period. Time periods before and after are also considered in order to illustrate broad trends, but in rough terms the period of 100 BCE to 100 CE is most important. Given how vast the Roman Empire was, this book attempts to limit itself to Rome and the Italian peninsula, though regional differences throughout the Empire are considered, particularly in regard to Roman Britain since a great deal of zooarchaeological evidence comes from this region. In sum, the first two chapters are intended to reveal how Romans conceived of their relationship with the gods and how birds affected political and religious processes. The latter three are investigated for the social truths they can reveal; namely, how owning, eating, or otherwise exploiting birds expressed social stratification and inequality. This focus on inequality is in keeping with the latest trends in the field of human-animal relationships, which target the social, rather than strictly economic, uses of animals and how they could advertise social difference.[12] Diet is often used to construct and express identity, and may particularly express the presence of inequality. For birds, there were different markers that expressed power, wealth, and status. Whether a bird was wild or domestic, fattened or unfattened, exotic or common, available seasonally or year-round, could all express power through acts of consumption or possession.[13]

In terms of evidence, this book takes a multidisciplinary approach in an attempt to overcome the various shortcomings of each individual strand of evidence. Artistic representations of birds are valuable for interpreting symbolism and general attitudes towards various species.[14] It is all too easy, however, to call reliability into question, as art may have an ambiguous symbolic meaning or serve a particular purpose that is difficult for the modern eye to discern. Care must be taken not to interpret birds in art in a way that is too straightforward. For instance, the peacock was a powerful symbol in art and on coinage, but its presence in art does not necessarily indicate its commonality or presence in everyday life, comparable to the way a lion may be used in art and poetry even in contexts where the animal was not present. Images of animals may travel before the animals themselves, and we must remember that art does not always reflect reality.

When it comes to faunal remains there are myriad survival issues. Bird bones are fragile and delicate. In cases where the literature attests the eating of small passerines, it can be difficult to confirm this by looking at faunal assemblages, since the tiny bones are often irrecoverable, or easy to overlook. Issues with survival are among the reasons that the field of zooarchaeology shows a preference for investigating mammals, and why archaeo-ornithology is comparatively niche. In cases where faunal assemblages are successfully recovered, interpretation is always shadowed by questions of whether they accurately reflect avian presence at a site. Nevertheless, zooarchaeology affords us the opportunity to investigate environment and subsistence in a unique way, and shows how humans interacted with birds on an intimate, day-to-day basis. Refuse dumps reveal how birds were butchered and eaten.

They can reveal sex ratios and the presence or absence of certain species in certain contexts. Physical evidence of meat distribution and consumption does much to reveal cultural values, and in general terms shows how Roman lives were intertwined with the wild and domestic birds with which they lived.

The majority of evidence is derived from Roman literature. This is problematic because it offers an elite perspective that does not necessarily reflect common practice. In the case of augury and auspices, we notably struggle to reconstruct augural lore of the early Republic since we are relying on authors writing hundreds of years after the fact. A critical and circumspect approach is necessary to avoid mistakes that come from taking authors at face value, and attention must always be paid to the context in which works were written. Most attention is paid to the period of the late Republic, as our sources chiefly spring from this time. On this point, Jerzy Linderski is the undisputed expert on augural law, and his works collate and interpret many obscure sources.[15] When looking at the place of birds in augural law in particular, this book attempts to follow his rigorous methodology, especially when grappling with the fact that augural law was a subject of mystery and debate to many of the ancient authors themselves. Some of our key sources for information and misinformation about birds come from the works of Aristotle (384–322 BCE), Pliny the Elder (25–79 CE), and Aelian (c.170–230 CE). Though Aristotle is of course Greek, the latter two Roman authors draw upon his works, making his writings relevant to this discussion. Pliny and Aelian record a heady miscellany of bird lore that is equally valuable and difficult to use; their works benefit enormously from corroboration with other strains of evidence. When it comes to birds and agriculture, the works of Cato (c.234–149 BCE), Varro (116–27 BCE), and Columella (4–70 CE) provide a great deal of information on traditional farming practices and approaches to land management, but it must be acknowledged that these works come from a skewed elite perspective and contain many omissions. Written primary sources are also rendered somewhat dubious by the moralising bent of authors lamenting the debasement of the present and yearning for the 'Good Old Days' – regardless of whether such a golden past ever existed.[16] Nevertheless, they are invaluable for investigating the world of intensive farming to supply the urban and luxury markets.

As noted above, current scholarship on birds in Rome relies heavily on literature and often focuses on cataloguing or classifying birds in place of interpreting their significance. This book posits that an accurate and meaningful interpretation of textual sources is dependent on the inclusion of zooarchaeology as well as ornithology. The decision to include ornithology and faunal remains means that this book is primarily concerned with how Roman people lived with, interacted with, and thought about real birds that had some tangible presence in their lives. Purely mythological constructions such as the phoenix and the Stymphalian birds are put to one side to focus on more practical topics like fowling. In considering aspects of myth and religion that involve birds (particularly in auspices), this book posits that they are best understood by comparing depictions and descriptions in Roman art and literature with the natural behaviour of birds. For example, it considers the myth of Romulus and Remus with its flocks of circling vultures according to how vultures naturally fly and flock, and how their unique diets might explain why these birds were chosen to send the sign that founded Rome. MacKinnon lays out the diverse ways that zooarchaeology is used in the study of Roman history, as part of a larger edited volume that demonstrates how human and natural histories are intertwined, and how they may successfully be studied together.[17] Science allows us to interpret history in new and exciting ways. The science of zooarchaeology and the science of ornithology are here employed together. One cannot effectively study birds and their place in Roman life without first understanding birds themselves. Romans were, after all, reacting to the natural behaviour and appearance of birds, so the natural behaviour and appearance of birds ought to be understood and used when interpreting the past.

The use of ornithology does have some drawbacks, especially when it comes to the task of identifying birds in literature. The picture is necessarily complicated by the fact that our modern systems of identification using scientific means, aided by our ready access to identification guides that summarise behaviour and plumage variation to a highly precise and accurate degree, are at odds with the ancient experience of viewing birds from a distance, with birds named in general terms and names often varying across time and place. On the one hand, accurate identification is essential to reconstructing how Romans interacted with birds, but on the other hand it can be exceptionally difficult to pair Latin names with discrete species. The works of Filippo Capponi and Jacques André represent the best attempts to match Latin names with individual birds, while Mynott rightly cautions against concrete identification.[18] This book tries to fall somewhere in between insisting on certain identifications while remaining aware that ancient categorisation is nowhere near as clear cut as our modern minds would like. For example, *hirundo* might refer to the barn swallow (*Hirundo rustica*), but this word and the Greek *chelidon* (χελιδών) could also refer to birds similar in behaviour and silhouette, including the house martin (*Delichon urbica*), red-rumped swallow (*H. daurica*), sand martin (*Riparia riparia*), and crag martin (*Ptyonoprogne rupestris*). Even the swift (*Apus apus*), though not a part of the swallow family, is somewhat similar in appearance and could fall under the umbrella term of *hirundo*.[19] Care must always be taken to pay attention to context when translating, and care must also be taken not to force modern identification when it will not fit. Conversely, there are times when a more rigorous identification is called for. In the augural context, the words *corvus* and *cornix* – raven and crow – are often translated haphazardly into English despite the Romans distinguishing very carefully between the two, as they delivered different signs in different ways at auspices.

Further, common mistranslations can render some Latin passages non-sensical. *Pica* is often translated as magpie, when in fact it refers to the Eurasian jay (*Garrulus glandarius*) in most contexts. Wild magpies that mimic human speech sound fanciful (Plin. *HN* 10.118–19), but the passage reads correctly when translated as jay. The book adheres to standard translations throughout, but makes amendments to reflect correct identification where appropriate.

The same problems occur when trying to identify birds in art, especially in paintings. In some cases, the images have simply faded too much for definite identification to be possible. In other cases, such as when a nondescript brown bird may be seen, it is not desirable to quibble down to exact species, since Romans may have categorised it simply as *passer,* without recourse to the subtle plumage variations only visible up close that would allow us to call it *Passer Italiae* or *Passer domesticus.* Despite this, it must be said that Romans, in general, depict birds in art with a remarkable degree of accuracy, which helps immensely in interpreting literary passages. Again, the rule of thumb is to make judgements according to context. This book does not aspire to be an identification guide, but it does strive to be as accurate as possible according to the information available in order to make the inclusion of modern ornithological knowledge effective.

In sum, this book examines birds in their assigned roles of divine messengers, heralds, hunting quarries, domestic flocks, and companion animals. It argues that Roman relations with birds in these capacities can only be understood if art and literature are cross-checked against modern ornithological knowledge and faunal assemblages. Finally, it asserts that taking a 'bird's-eye view' of history is an effective method for interpreting and understanding cultural beliefs and social stratification.

Notes

1 This story is retold in slightly varying forms in the following sources: Aur. Vict. *Or.* 23; Cass. Dio 16.46; Dion. Hal. *Ant. Rom.* 1.86; Livy, 1.7; Luc. *Phars.* 7.337; Ov. *Fast.* 4.817ff; Plut. *Vit. Rom.* 9; Plut. *Quaest. Rom.* 93; Suet. *Aug.* 95.

2 Pollard (1977) looks at birds in the Greek world, drawing mainly upon Thompson's research while providing a more reader-friendly experience. W. Geoffrey Arnott's *Birds in the Ancient World from A to Z* (2007) is perhaps the most comprehensive and thorough work of reference for those interested in birds in the classical world; however, Arnott follows Thompson's precedent of listing birds alphabetically according to their Greek names, a decision that makes the book somewhat inaccessible to casual readers, and necessarily places the Greek perspective at the forefront. Houlihan (1986) catalogues birds found in Egyptian art and hieroglyphs while recounting their importance in both religious and secular life. Of particular note is Baillieul-LeSuer (2012), a collaborative effort on birds in ancient Egypt that demonstrates how different strands of evidence can be combined to draw conclusions about the past. It collects data from language, mummies, art, and ornithology, and could be considered a model for how to combine different sources of evidence on birds in order to investigate ancient societies.

3 Martin (1914) looks at birds in Latin poetry. Krauss (1930) provides an analytical interpretation of bird omens and prodigies recorded in Roman literature. André (1967) and Capponi (1979) catalogue and identify birds by their Latin names. These are slightly outdated but still excellent works of reference. Johnson (1968) looks at farming and aviculture.

4 Keller (1920) investigates the place of animals and birds in classical life, while Toynbee (1973) contains a sizeable chapter on birds in Roman art and entertainment. See also Jennison (1937).

5 Kron (2008), (2014), (2015), (2017); MacKinnon (2004), (2007), (2013), (2014), (2018). For zooarchaeology in the Roman period more generally, Joris Peters (1998) is indispensable.

6 Watson (2002) 358.

7 Serjeantsen (2009).

8 See Albarella et al. (2020) and Albarella et al. (2022) for two special editions of *Quaternary International* that bring together a wide range of papers on the archaeology of bird-human interactions.

9 Sykes (2014) 1.

10 Lévi-Strauss (1963).

11 Mynott (2009) 267.

12 Arbuckle and McCarty (2014) 2; Morris (2011) 1.

13 For comparison, Obermeier (2019) investigates the symbolic power of consuming certain birds and other animals in the Middle Ages.

14 See Tammisto (1997) for a thorough investigation of birds in art.

15 See Linderski (1986a) for a comprehensive appraisal of augural law.

16 Lewit (1991) 67.

17 MacKinnon (2018).

18 André (1967); Capponi (1979); Mynott (2018).

19 Green (2019).

1 Omens, Augury, and Auspices

Introduction

Human societies across the ancient Mediterranean, and indeed all over the world, have traditionally accorded supernatural divinatory powers to birds.[1] The Greek word for bird, *ornis* or *oionos,* was also the word for omen, just as the word for bird in Latin, *avis,* could mean an omen.[2] The ancients considered birds to be the principal agents by which the gods conveyed their wills, close to the heavens and therefore close to heavenly counsel.[3] The ability to prophesy via birds is listed among the forbidden knowledge given to mankind by Prometheus, the titan whose liver was daily torn out by a vulture.[4] They were winged messengers, not necessarily wise in their own right, but the most fitting creatures to be utilised by the gods.[5] According to Cicero, birds were the most divine and appropriate gifts for gods.[6] Ovid tells us:

> You birds, the solace of the countryside, you haunters of the woods, you harmless race that build your nests and warm your eggs under your plumes, and with glib voices utter sweet tunes, you were untouchable once; but all that avails not, because you are accused of chattering, and the gods opine that you reveal their thoughts. Nor is the charge untrue; for the nearer you are to the gods, the truer are the signs you give, whether by wing or voice. Long time immune, the brood of birds was slaughtered then at last, and the gods gloated on the guts of the talebearing fowls.[7]

Birds were close to the gods, pleasing as sacrifices, and many Roman gods from Cupid to Mercury sported wings so that divinity itself was created in the image of a bird. How did birds come to be seen this way? Why were they held in such esteem, and why was this esteem prevalent across the ancient Mediterranean world? Plutarch offers one explanation, claiming that it is not merely a bird's ability to fly, but its own inherent cleverness and speedy responses to environmental phenomena that made it sensitive to the directives of deities (*Mor. De soll. an.* 975A). There was a recognition of birds' sensitivities to weather and the changing of seasons, with migration being

DOI: 10.4324/9781003247906-2

the most obvious example of this. On this point, and before we treat Roman augury in detail, a distinction must be made between the types of divination that involve birds.

On the one hand, there are signs which can be derived from a bird's own natural behaviour and perceived intelligence. On the other hand, there are signs which are derived from a controlling deity's supposed influence on a bird, over which the bird has no control. We may call these two categories, respectively, natural and superstitious divination. Into the category of natural divination fall the signs which are entirely appropriate to take as predictors of the future. Birds were important markers of time in ancient societies, making seasons known by their arrival or departure. Chaffinches were said to be cleverer than man at foretelling the future, for they knew when winter was coming (Ael. *NA* 4.61). The swallow is a famous harbinger of spring, signalling the end of winter with its return.[8]

The crying of migrating cranes told the farmer when it was time to sow.[9] Even the barnyard cock was elevated to the rank of prophetic animal. Pliny recounts that a rooster's habit of heralding sunrise by crowing makes him something of an astronomer, with a knowledge of celestial movements exceeding man's (*HN* 10.24). Though this seems exaggerated in our eyes, one cannot underestimate the importance of cock-crow to pre-industrial societies. As Hermann Dembeck points out, while there were many measures of time in the ancient world, from sundials to hourglasses, these were silent. The rooster woke the community each morning, heralding sunrise like an alarm clock.[10] For the sailor, bird behaviour could help him predict the weather. Migrating cranes only flew in favourable conditions, so if a pilot saw cranes turning back from the sea he knew contrary winds were blowing and that he should return to shore.[11] Theophrastus also informs us that cranes departing early forebode an early winter, and a late winter if they lingered, which is an entirely sensible assumption (*Hist. pl.* 6.4.38). A particularly hot summer could result in a shortage of food that would cause atypical behaviour in birds such as an owl hunting in the daytime. Prolonged wet weather might interrupt breeding patterns, all of which could be interpreted by a shrewd farmer.[12] It was said many hoopoes crying in the fields portended a good harvest, ostensibly because the birds knew there was food for them (Horapollo 2.92). Weather even has an effect on birdsong, as sound carries further during certain meteorological conditions. For example, birds will cease to sing in strong wind, while a calm morning enables audibility and encourages strident singing.[13] Audibility is better at night than during the day, and for diurnal birds, singing in the morning can be up to twenty times more effective in terms of coverage than singing at midday.[14] Waterfowl will seek shelter from rough water and adverse weather by moving closer to a lee shore, and some will even roost ashore when it is particularly bad.[15] In his *Georgics*, Virgil writes a passage describing all the signs of fair and foul weather given by birds and displays an awareness that a bird's prescience is natural rather than supernatural in origin:

Not, methinks, because [birds] have wisdom from on high, or from Fate a larger foreknowledge of things to be; but because when the weather and fitful vapours of the sky have turned their course, and Jove, wet with the south winds, thickens what just now was rare, and makes rare what now was thick, the phases of their minds change, and their breasts now conceive impulses, other than they felt when the wind was chasing the clouds. Hence that chorus of the birds in the fields, the gladness of the cattle, and the exulting cries of the ravens.[16]

It was not only time and weather that birds presaged. They were useful in warfare, and observing them could lead to victory. Frontinus records:

In the Etruscan war, the consul Aemilius Paulus was on the point of sending his army down into the plain near the town of Vetulonia, when he saw afar off a flock of birds rise in somewhat startled flight from a forest, and realized that some treachery was lurking there, both because the birds had risen in alarm and at the same time in great numbers. He therefore sent some scouts ahead and discovered that ten thousand Boii were lying in wait at that point to meet the Roman army. These he overwhelmed by sending his legions against them at a different point from that at which they were expected.[17]

For ancient farmers, sailors, and soldiers, it was prudent to watch birds in order to determine whether an undertaking would be favourable or not. Viewed through ancient eyes, birds do seem to possess a prescience and a knowledge of time that is divine, mystical, and above all useful. Even sceptics like Virgil do not scorn the wisdom of birds, though they might question the source of such wisdom and call it natural understanding rather than divine inspiration. It is likely that early observations of bird behaviour spawned the many superstitions that came to surround birds. If a swallow can herald springtime, what else can it tell us? If a crane can tell us a storm is approaching, can another kind of bird act as a weather prophet? Is it possible, in fact, to *ask* the birds what they know?

Hence the category of superstitious divination, one that is inevitably much broader. This relies on the belief that a god or gods can and will control the behaviour of a bird to send messages to humans, and that such messages can be reliably interpreted. Prophesying via birds was a tradition common across Greece, Italy, and the Near East, but no culture developed, codified, or regulated it as rigorously as the Romans.[18] Thus, the great institution of augury and auspices was formed, which we shall interpret according to the idea that the natural behaviour of birds still has bearing on how signs were given and interpreted. The above catalogue of various bird behaviours is intended to impress that the natural movement of birds, their habits, and their place in the environment is essential to understanding how the Romans interpreted them as divinatory signs. Many erudite scholars have written about Roman augury, and this chapter intends to build on their work by investigating it from a different perspective. Beginning with an overview of the key concepts related to the study, this chapter goes on to ask *how* the Romans divined using birds, *where* such divination took place, and *which* birds were chosen as key messengers. In this way it is hoped that birds may help us to understand the complex social and legal rules surrounding augury and auspices.

Roman Augury and Auspices

The power of a Roman magistrate *cum imperio* was chiefly defined by two inextricably interconnected prerogatives: *imperium* and *auspicium,* as expressed in the term *imperium auspiciumque.* The former was his power to command, the latter his ability to ask the gods for permission to use that power. It must be stressed that taking auspices was not an attempt to see the future, like crystal-gazing, but rather an appraisal of divine will pertaining to a proposed action.[19] *Auspicium* was inherent in full *imperium*, allowing magistrates to exercise their authority in a coordinated fashion.[20] The word *auspicium* is derived from *avis* and *spectio*, and literally means 'watching birds', so it should come as no surprise that taking auspices involved, among other things, observing bird behaviour. Though the discipline as a whole was overseen by augurs, only magistrates had *spectio* and therefore the ability to take *auspicia publica,* which were an essential precursor to any public action. The auspices of the magistrates were divided into *minora,* belonging to the lesser magistrates, and *maiora,* belonging to the greater magistrates (consuls, praetors, censors, and a number of other non-annual magistrates *cum imperio*). This meant that the same omen would be given greater or lesser weight depending on who saw it.[21] This practice of birdwatching (or perhaps skywatching) was ancient, even more ancient than the founding of the City, and is amply recorded in Rome's histories and the stories of her mythic founding.[22]

Festus records that there were five types of *omina*.[23] Out of the three most important, two involved birds, though the strongest of all were *signa ex caelo* (signs from the sky), which manifested as thunder and lightning.[24] This is unsurprising given that the augural deity was Jupiter, sky god of thunder and lightning. Next in importance came the *signa ex avibus* (signs from birds), the present subject of our investigation. The augural birds were divided into two categories, *oscines* (singers) and *alites* (fliers), although Isidore of Seville implies that most birds delivered portents through *both* flight patterns and cries. He, however, is interpreting augural lore in the sixth and seventh centuries CE, long after augury had ceased to be practised.[25] The more reliable Cicero, who was himself an augur, says:

> The Divine Will accomplishes like results in the case of birds, and causes those known as *alites*, which give omens by their flight, to fly hither and

thither and disappear now here and now there, and causes those known as *oscines*, which give omens by their cries, to sing now on the left and now on the right.[26]

Then came the *auspicia ex tripudiis*, the auspices taken from observing the feeding patterns of chickens. The final categories of omen named by Festus are auspices *ex quadrupedibus*, which came from the odd behaviour of mammals, and *ex diris*, which drew conclusions based on odd occurrences and accidents that seemed portentous. The last two categories held less weight and importance than the first three.

Roman divination was further divided into two classes: impetrative, where signs were formally sought out, and oblative, where unsolicited signs were sent from heaven.[27] The Roman impetrative auspices were more developed than those of the Greeks.[28] Far from being intuitive or mystical, the business of taking auspices was narrowly demarcated and described as *disciplina, ars, scientia,* or law: the so-called *ius augurium* or *ius in auspiciis*.[29] The business of formally soliciting signs from Jupiter and interpreting those signs was managed by augurs.[30] Augurs formed one of the four major Roman colleges of priests, and they traced their origins back to Romulus, who is credited as being the first augur. For the Romans, the very founding of their City began with the observation of birds. According to the famous myth, Rome was founded when Romulus and his twin brother Remus quarrelled over who should be king. Romulus declared: "'There is no need for contest. Great faith is put in birds. Let us try the birds'",[31] leading to the brothers taking auspices to settle the matter. A common version of this legend relates that six vultures appeared to Remus on the Aventine Hill, but twelve appeared to Romulus on the Palatine, communicating to all that Romulus should be king.[32] In Ennius' version it is described thus:

> Meanwhile the white sun [the moon] had set into the depth of night. Then struck by rays the shining light showed itself openly and at once on high from far away a beautifully winged leftward flight advanced. Just as the golden sun arises, there comes descending from the sky a dozen blessed bodies of birds, settling themselves on fine and favorable seats. Thus Romulus sees that given to himself alone, approved by auspices, were the base and bulwark of a kingdom.[33]

This passage, of course, offers us more insight into the ritual of *auspicium* in the early second century BCE than the rites of 753 BCE. The intended audience of Ennius' *Annales* was most likely the *nobiles*, making it a useful illustration of the great importance and prestige that was attached to birdwatching. Here, augury is lauded for its place in affirming the strength of Roman politics and aristocratic values, conferring unassailable legitimacy upon both the founder and the City.[34] Another mythical story that stresses the importance of augurs and their art takes place in the reign of Tarquin the Elder:

But since this was a matter in which Romulus had obtained the sanction of augury before acting, it was asserted by Attus Navius, a famous augur of those days, that no change or innovation could be introduced unless the birds had signified their approval. The king's ire was aroused by this, and he is reported to have said, in derision of the science, "Come now, divine seer! Inquire of your augury if that of which I am now thinking can come to pass." When Attus, having taken the auspices, replied that it would surely come to pass, the king said, "Nay, but this is what I was thinking of, that you should cleave a whetstone with a razor. Take them, and accomplish what your birds declare is possible!" Whereupon, they say, the augur, without a sign of hesitation, cut the whetstone in two (...) however this may be, auguries and the augural priesthood so increased in honour that nothing was afterwards done, in the field or at home, unless the auspices had first been taken: popular assemblies, musterings of the army, acts of supreme importance – **all were put off when the birds refused their consent.**[35]

These passages exemplify the centrality of birds to Roman augury, making an investigation of birds pertinent to understanding the social and legal powers and prerogatives of augurs and magistrates. The position of augur was one of privilege and great influence, and only a few men in the state could serve at any one time. Cicero tells us that Romulus created one augur for each of the three tribes. Two more were added by Numa to make five (Cic. *Rep.* 2.9.1). Livy has it that only four augurs existed in 300 BCE, and posits that two posts were vacant, making six augurs the usual number, though it is just as likely that four in total was the true number.[36] Whatever the truth, after the Ogulnian Law of 300 BCE, the College was served by four patricians and five plebeians, making nine in total.[37] New members were admitted for life, and from 103 BCE onwards they were elected by the assembly of seventeen tribes, taken from candidates put forward by two College members.[38] Suffice to say that, especially in the early days, these learned men would have spent a lot of time observing and thinking about birds. One of their major duties was observing birds on behalf of the *res publica.*[39] The pre-eminence of the College meant that the citizen body was very interested in bird omens too. The extensive use of augural terms and allusions to augural omens in Plautus' comedic plays (c. 254–184 BCE) demonstrates how the taking of auguries and auspices was fixed in the habits and beliefs of the people of Rome.[40] And, of course, private auspices existed too. While public auspices – auspices that pertained to matters of state – were the prerogative of magistrates, every person had the right to take auspices pertaining to his or her own affairs.[41] Citizens often consulted the birds before private matters of importance, with nuptial auspices appearing to be the most widely practised form of private auspices.[42] In both public and private spheres, auspices were taken to feel confident of the gods' goodwill, and to stay alert to any hostility (Val. Max. 2.1.1). In Plautus' words, 'I go out with clear auspices, a bird on my left' (*Epidicus* 183). The Romans made divination integral to political, religious, and personal matters in a way that was utterly distinct in the ancient world (Polyb. 6.56).[43]

It is important now to contextualise some of the general rules that governed the actual taking of auspices. When a magistrate took auspices pertaining to some public action, they were valid for one day only, and related only to the timing of the proposed action, not to its substance.[44] If a negative result was received, an auspicant could simply return the next day and ask again (Livy 9.38.15–39). A day was defined as twenty-four hours, from one midnight to the next (Macrob. *Sat.* 1.3.7). The best time to take auspices varied according to what kind of sign one was searching for,[45] but the Romans preferred to take auspices *ex avibus* at dawn, partly according to the principle that auspices should be taken at the beginning of things, and partly for the practical reason that auspices had to be taken before public business could begin.[46] Dawn is indeed the best time to observe birds, when they are seen and heard most easily. The dawn chorus is a familiar phenomenon, and given the reliance on *oscines*, it would ensure you would at least hear a sign.[47] It must also be noted that perfect silence was necessary for auspices to be taken without fault.[48] The silence was so important that Cicero says an expert was required to determine when it had been obtained (*Div.* 2.71). The reason for this pedantry is probably because silence would make it easier to determine the type and provenance of bird cries. Taking auspices at dawn also meant that public business could begin immediately without a waste of daylight hours.[49] If omens were bad, activity was delayed, but once positive signs were received, public business could commence without interruption for the rest of the day.[50]

So much for the public *auspicia*, performed by magistrates to facilitate the running of state with divine approval. What of the rites of augurs? When an augur consulted the birds, it was to perform a rite known as *augurium*, not *auspicium*. It was through this that they 'inaugurated' and invested people, places, and ceremonies with divine approval. An *augurium* was binding, and in these cases the deity's verdict *did* pertain to substance. If a negative answer was received, the question could not be repeated, and if a positive answer was given, then the effects of *inauguratio* could only be undone through a ritual of *exauguratio*. Livy (1.55.3) tells us that the *fanum Termini* enclosed within the temple of Capitoline Jupiter testifies to this principle. It was an inaugurated place, and when an *exauguratio* was attempted, the birds did not consent. Their refusal was final and binding, and so the sanctuary stayed. It is but one example of how birds and augural principles literally shaped the city of Rome. In addition to performing these rites, augurs were also responsible for maintaining the integrity of the discipline as a whole. They could be called upon to assist a magistrate when he took auspices, and to help with interpretation given his greater understanding of the lore. He could also announce oblative signs observed either by himself or others that seemed to pertain to the welfare of the state.[51] They also delineated sacred spaces in the earth and in the sky. There were five types of terrestrial space which augurs could demarcate: *Romanus, Gabinus, peregrinus, hosticus, incertus*. By definition, all inaugurated spaces were laid out by them.[52] We should also distinguish between the duties of the Augural College and that of individual augurs. The College was a monolith, a body of experts that had a duty to uphold the augural law that governed the observation and interpretation of auspices (Cic. *Nat. D.* 1.122). It was consulted on augural law and passed decrees or issued responses to questions posed by magistrates and the Senate. The College was most often consulted on matters of *vitium*, or 'ritual fault', and it was the College's duty to determine whether auspices had been nullified through *vitium*.[53] They also worked to remove *religio*, or a ritual obstacle to action. As individuals, they could take *auguria*, assist magistrates, and inaugurate priests and *templa*.[54] An augur could also issue responses, which were treated separately to College responses, and they had the right of making a binding announcement – a *nuntiatio* – of oblative omens. By pronouncing the formula *alio die* (another day), they could cancel the public business of the day, and this is recorded as occurring chiefly at popular assemblies.[55] Like birds, augurs could be considered intermediaries in the communication between gods and humans.[56]

Auspices in the Late Republic

Cicero was elected augur in 53 BCE on the motion of Hortensius and Pompey.[57] He considered this a great honour that he cited as the pinnacle of his distinguished career (Cic. *Fam.* 4.5.5). His *De Divinatione* is thus a valuable source on the state of augury and auspices in the first century BCE. It is generally thought that this text indicates that the elite were sceptical about augury, prodigies, and divination, but it must be noted that the text is firmly split in two, with one book arguing for the validity of auspices, and one arguing against it.[58] Cicero fails to give us a clear conclusion, and merely sets out the two arguments. We probably cannot divine his real thoughts on the subject from this text, but the argument in favour of scepticism at the very least shows that there was doubt and discourse surrounding the institution at this time.[59] The *De Legibus* (2.13, 32–3) sees Cicero affirm his support for augury and other traditional Roman practices, and he certainly took his duties as an augur seriously. His personal correspondence refers to the day-to-day activities of augurs. He mentions that a meeting of the Senate was postponed after the College confirmed a negative omen reported by a *pullarius* (*Fam.* 10.12.3). After the death of his daughter Tullia, he asked his friend Atticus to excuse him from augural meetings (*Att.* 12.13.2; 12.15). In public writings, he never tired of boasting of an augur's powers and responsibilities. Shortly after his appointment, he declared the *ius augurum* was the greatest and most important authority in the state, and furthermore that this was an indisputable fact, and not something he said merely because he was an augur (*Leg.* 2.31–2). He describes augurs as 'the interpreters of

Jupiter Best and Greatest' (*Leg.* 2.20) and claims that a good augur should always use his skills to aid the state when it needs him (*Leg.* 3.43). Elsewhere he calls auspices and the Senate the two foundations of the Republic (*Rep.* 2.17).

In spite of this praise, we cannot ignore the sceptical arguments he makes in many of his writings. Frank discussion of this scepticism seems to be a product of his day. By the late Republic, the major religious offices were almost purely political and there was widespread doubt among the aristocracy about the actual existence of gods.[60] Linderski points out that Caesar's *De Bellico Gallico* and *De Bello Civili,* which were addressed to educated upper classes, do not mention auspices, omens, or *haruspices*. While the idea of divine favour was important for securing the support of the masses, when it came to his political rivals Caesar chose to highlight his personal qualities and his own martial skill.[61] Cicero betrays the Augural College for what it really was – a tool of the *senatus auctoritas*.[62] He thought it wise to continue maintaining the Augural College for the sake of the Republic.[63] Augury was an institution of the state, essential to smooth and legitimate governance; the true validity of omens and the wisdom of birds was a secondary concern. Augural law was so interwoven with the fabric of state it was simply impossible to imagine Rome without it.[64]

It is unsurprising that the ability to act as the interpreter of Jupiter's will on behalf of the state was found only among the most distinguished statesmen and was in turn bestowed by the power of other distinguished statesmen. Certainly, Cicero had the gift of foresight, but it came from his political experience and not from birds:

> And therefore I take it not from the flight of the *alites,* nor the left-hand cry of the *oscines,* as our discipline would have it, nor even from *tripudia sollistima* or *sonivia,* for I have other signs which I must observe, no more certain perhaps, but less difficult to see and less prone to error. The divining of signs to me is observed in two categories, one of which derives from the behaviour of Caesar himself, and the other from the general nature of political conditions.[65]

It is evident that augury in the late Republic had very little to do with watching birds, and everything to do with watching one's political opponents with great care. The strongest defence Cicero accords to augury is the way it can check abuses of *auspicium.* Disputes over omens and validity of auspices were common, and the power of an individual augur was great indeed, since he could postpone and negate a magistrate's wishes by pronouncing the formula *alio die*.[66] In the *Philippics*, Cicero abuses Antony for violating the auspices while he was an augur. Over the matter of Dolabella's election to consulship, the auspices changed with Antony's mind: 'So long as *you* wish, Dolabella's consulship is flawed; then, the moment your wishes change, he was elected with the auspices in order'.[67] Cicero has Cato praise a famous augur, Fabius Maximus, by saying: 'And, although an augur, he dared to say that whatever was done for the safety of the Republic was done under the best auspices, and that whatever was inimical to the Republic was against the auspices'.[68] So much for the wisdom of birds, and the wisdom of gods; it was man who decided what was best for himself or the Republic, what counted as favourable or unfavourable auspices. By the late Republic, augury was a shadow of its former self, and much lore about birds was lost in the need to simplify and control the formulae for political purposes. It is a fact that Cicero does not shy away from:

> Now let us examine augury as practised among foreign nations, whose methods are not so artificial as they are superstitious. They employ almost all kinds of birds, we only a few; they regard some signs as favourable, we, others. Deiotarus used to question me a great deal about our system of augury, and I him about that of his country. Ye gods! How much they differed! So much that in some cases they were directly the reverse of each other. He employed auspices constantly, we never do except when the duty of doing so is imposed by a vote of the people. Our ancestors would not undertake any military enterprise without consulting the auspices; but now, for many years, our wars have been conducted by proconsuls and propraetors, who do not have the right to take auspices. Therefore they have no *tripudium* and they cross rivers without first taking the auspices. What, then, has become of divining by means of birds? It is not used by those who conduct our wars, for they have not the right of auspices. Since it has been withdrawn from use in the field I suppose it is reserved for city use only![69]

If we examine the evidence, it is possible to track the decline of bird divination. Cicero says that augurs only paid attention to a few birds, and a passage from Seneca corroborates this: 'But why is this privilege to give auspices of important events assigned to a very few birds, an eagle, or a raven, while the cries of the other birds are without prophetic meaning?'.[70] This was not the case in earlier days. We know the Etruscans, who influenced the Roman art, fastidiously studied birds and wrote complex identification guides.[71] These guides, though lost, must have been comparable in intricacy and detail to the Piacenza liver, which outlines how to correctly divine from the liver of a sacrificial animal.[72] It is likely that these Etruscan books detailed how to identify birds, what their behaviour meant, whether they were lucky or unlucky, and in which quadrants of the sky they should ideally be seen or heard.[73] The discovery of Etruscan tombs richly decorated with images of birds also intimates that these birds, by species or position in the artwork, were deeply symbolic.[74] The Tomb of the Augurs depicts a man with a curved *lituus* watching birds above the heads of wrestlers.[75] Nancy de Grummond reminds us that among the few words of Etruscan that survive are the words for falcon (*capys*), eagle (*antar*), crane (*gnis*), and hawk (*arak*),

Figure 1.1 Detail from The Tomb of the Augurs, Tarquinia, c. 510 BCE.

Source: Photo by Prisma/Universal Images Group via Getty Images.

indictive of their augural system.[76] The meaning of an eagle snatching up and replacing a cap on the head of Tarquinius Priscus was interpreted by his wife, showing that avian prodigies were significant in the Etruscan political context (Livy 1.34.8–9). The Tomb of the Augurs in Tarquinia depicts an augur interpreting the flight of birds (Figure 1.1).[77]

Writing under the Empire, Seneca outlines the difference in Roman and Etruscan beliefs:

> This is the difference between us and the Etruscans, who have consummate skill in interpreting lightning: we think that because clouds collide lightning is emitted; they believe that clouds collide in order that lightning may be emitted. Since they attribute everything to divine agency, they are of the opinion that things do not reveal the future because they have occurred, but that they occur because they are meant to reveal the future. Whether it is displaying their purpose or their consequences they none the less occur on the same principle. "But how do things indicate future events unless they are sent to do so?" In the same way as birds provide favourable or unfavourable auspices even though they are not, in this respect, moved in order to appear to us. "But god moved them," he says. You make god too unoccupied and the administrator of trivia if he arranges dreams for some people, entrails for others. None the less, such things are carried out by divine agency, even if the wings of birds are not

actually guided by god nor the viscera of cattle shaped under the very axe. The roll of fate is unfolded on a different principle, sending ahead everywhere indications of what is to come, some familiar to us, others unknown. Whatever happens, it is a sign of something that will happen. Chance and random occurrences, and without a principle, do not permit divination. Whatever has a series of occurrences is also predictable.[78]

We ought not to take Seneca's stern and sensible Stoic view as the norm; the dissenting voice of this piece is probably closer to the average Roman's beliefs, but it illustrates how far removed Roman divination was from Etruscan principles by the late Republic and early Empire. Out of the many notable Etruscan birds, Roman augural birds dwindled to a mere handful, with the most important being vultures, eagles, crows, ravens, woodpeckers, owls, and chickens, all of which shall be treated in individual detail later on. Of course, superstition and symbolism were attached to every bird, but these birds seem to be the most charismatic for the Romans, and the most important augural signs came from them.

Templa

It is clear that birdwatching was a fundamental part of the Roman political system. Birds were called upon to convey the gods' consent in almost every decision of state importance. It becomes prudent to ask *how* they delivered messages, and in what way different birds and their behaviour were interpreted by augurs and magistrates. The first step is to consider where the rite took place: namely, a *templum*. A *templum* referred to a section of the sky observed by magistrates or augurs. It was the field of vision in which birds or lightning could be seen. There was also a secondary *templum in terris,* a quadrangular space on earth delimited and inaugurated by an augur that was reserved for observing signs.[79] Many official state functions had to take place in a *templum,* including meetings of the Senate. Temples (*aedes*) and shrines (*aedes sacra*) were often built within the space marked out as a *templum,* which explains why our word 'temple' is derived from *templum.*[80] The importance of being able to see every part of the sky meant that any building that obscured the *templum* could be torn down (Cic. *Off.* 3.16). When marking out the sky for observation, the *templum* was divided into four parts with a *lituus,* a curved augural wand. The sections were: 'in front' (*pars antica*), 'behind' (*pars posterior*), 'on the left' (*in sinistrum*), and 'on the right' (*in dextrum*). This ritual, with its complexity and obsession with orientation, was probably influenced by the Etruscan belief system – the *lituus* is even an Etruscan wand.[81] When taking impetrative auspices, a magistrate first pitched a tent on a particular place known as the *auguraculum.* In Rome, there were three *auguracula*: one on the citadel (the *Arx*), one on the Quirinal hill, and one on the Palatine.[82] The tent itself was referred to as a *tabernaculum.* According to Festus (11 L), it was made of skins. The expression *tabernaculum capere* – 'to pitch a tent' –

came to refer to the whole ceremony of auspication, not just the erection of the structure.[83] Presumably the *tabernaculum* would ensure only the desired portion of the sky was available for the auspicant to view, and when augural chickens were consulted, the tent served to stop them from absconding once freed from their cage. In the field, every Roman military camp would establish a temporary *templum,* or *auguratorium,* in the middle of the camp (Serv. *Aen.* 4.200). A tent was erected within the boundary so the magistrate could consult the augural chickens in relative privacy (Tac. *Ann.* 2.13, 15.30). Not all in-augurated places were *templa* – the *pomerium,* for example, which marked the boundary of the city and the limits of the city auspices, was an inaugurated space, but not a *templum.*[84] The military camp, on the other hand, is an example of a *templum* that did not need to be inaugurated.

Now we may consider how birds were observed in *templa* and how they delivered signs. It is well-documented that when birds appeared, the right-hand side was considered favourable among the Greeks.[85] The opposite was true for Romans, which many find surprising given the reputation of the *sinistra,* or sinister left hand. It is in fact likely that confusion with Greek principles caused the left side to lose its lucky significance. But despite this difference, both cultures considered the same quarter of the sky lucky – the east. The Greeks looked north when divining, facing the seat of the gods in the celestial heavens, so a bird flying to the right headed towards the rising sun of the auspicious east, while a bird flying left went towards the darkness of the inauspicious west (Hom. *Il.* 12.238ff.).

It must be acknowledged that there is some discrepancy in our sources that makes it difficult to prove Roman orientation when taking auspices, so we shall lay out the evidence here. Some claimed one should look south.[86] Others said east.[87] To put this conclusively to rest, we must examine the excavated *templum* at Bantia (modern-day Banzi in southern Italy). This is the only surviving example we have of a *templum in terris* that was designed for auspices *ex avibus.* Interestingly, it seems it was used exclusively for birds, indicating that thunder and lightning were observed in a different space. The Banzi *templum* has been reliably dated to the last century of the Republic and was originally interpreted and reconstructed by Mario Torelli.[88] It was rectangular, with the sides oriented to the cardinal directions. The shorter sides ran from north to south and the slightly longer sides from east to west. Three rows of three *cippi,* limestone pillars, marked its boundaries. These nine stones were between thirty and fifty centimentres high, roughly thirty centimentres in diameter, and arranged in a rectangle around nine metres long.[89] Each *cippus* was inscribed in such a way that they could only be read by someone looking east.[90] The *templum* in the sky should be understood as a mental projection of this terrestrial *templum,* meaning that the quadrangular sections marked out by the *cippi* correspond to the regions of the sky through which the birds flew.[91] The inscriptions existed to help the auspicant determine the meaning of the signs he saw or heard.

On the western side of the *templum,* a large, square, limestone slab was excavated, quite distinct from the circular *cippi*. Examining this layout allowed Jerzy Linderski to solve the confusion surrounding Roman orientation. He proved that an auspicant sat on this slab and looked east, turning his back on the unfortunate west.[92] Father Jove, meanwhile, was envisioned as sitting in the north and looking south. One description runs thus: 'From the seat of the gods looking south, on the left-hand sides are the eastern parts of the world, and on the right-hand the western, so that left-hand auspices appear to be better than right-hand auspices'.[93] In this way, the most favourable part of the sky becomes the northeast, for this makes a left-hand sign for the god looking south and a left-hand sign for the auspicant looking east, the best one could hope for. This system of orientation accounts for seemingly paradoxical situations described by Cicero, where a sign is simultaneously left and right, for a bird in the southeast would be a left-hand sign for Jupiter and a right-hand sign for the auspicant. This also accords with the way most early Roman temples were situated facing south with an unobstructed view; they were built on *templa,* meant for watching birds.[94]

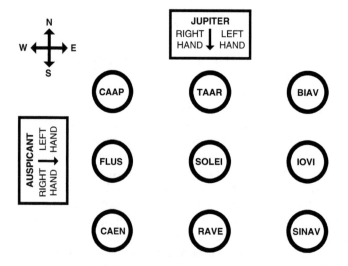

Figure 1.2 Reconstruction of the Bantia *templum.*

Mario Torelli, the original excavator of the site, gives us the following expansions of the inscriptions on the *cippi:*

Northern line:
Northwest: **C**(ontraria) **A**(ve) **A**(ugurium) **P**(estiferum) – the bird contrary, an evil augury.
North: **TAAR** – unknown. Interpreted as a neutral sign.
Northeast: **B**(ene) **I**(uvante) **A V**(e) – the bird most helpful.

Middle line:
West: **FLUS**(ae) – dedicated to an Oscan deity native to the region, who corresponds to Flora.
Centre: **SOLEI** – dedicated to the sun.
East: **IOVI** – dedicated to Jupiter.

Southern line:
Southwest: **C**(ontraria) **A**(ve) **EN**(ubra) – the bird contrary, forbidding.[95]
South: **R**(emore) **A VE** – the bird delaying.
Southeast: **SIN**(istra) **A V**(e) – the bird left-hand.[96]

This is a reliable reconstruction, and it corresponds with testimony from literary sources, though there is one mistake. Linderski objects to the reconstruction of the SINAV inscription in the southeast, pointing out that *sinistra ave* is unsatisfactory. An auspicant looking east would behold the southwest on his right, not his left, and this was not as strong or favourable as the northeast. He proposes the alternative of *sinente ave* – the 'bird allowing'.[97] Not as strong as the bountifully propitious northeast, but still a positive answer. Meanwhile, the *remore ave* of the south is the bird delaying, which does not say no, but merely advises the auspicant to try again another time.[98] The 'neutral' northern position probably represents the *avis arcula* mentioned in Festus, a bird which prohibits action, but which is not threatening.[99] One might then expect the southwest to be the least auspicious, since it makes a right-hand sign for god and man, but it is not dire, only 'inhibitory' (Paulus ex Festo 67 L). The northwest, meanwhile, which is a left-hand sign for man and a right-hand sign for Jupiter, is the domain of the contrary bird which not only forbids the action, but threatens calamity.

This augural system has a great deal in common with haruspicy, for the arrangement of the sky corresponds closely to the arrangement of significant regions on sacrificial livers interpreted by *haruspices*.[100] Livers were divided into sixteen sections, for the sixteen astrological houses of the heavens.[101] The liver's propitious half was to the east, and the unpropitious to the west. Similarly, when interpreting lightning, Etruscans deemed flashes in the west inauspicious, and flashes in the east auspicious. This was because the propitious divinities were thought to reside in the east and the infernal in the west. The northeast was the seat of the heavenly divinities, the south was the seat of the earthly, and the northwest the seat of the infernal.[102]

In this *templum* we see the Romans observed half as many heavenly seats as the Etruscans, dividing the sky into eight parts around a central point. Looking east along the central *cippus*, we see the centre is the sun, while the west is dedicated to a deity of earth and nature, Flusa/Flora, and the east to the sky god Jupiter. The north/south axis in both cultures seems to indicate the strength of the sign, and the east/west axis is its auspiciousness. In the simplest terms possible, north was strong, south was weak, east was good, and west was bad. Our ancient sources insist that auspices and the science of augury were not

Etruscan in origin.[103] The only form of divination that the Romans considered Etruscan in origin was extispicy (the examination of entrails), which remained the preserve of the Etruscan *haruspices* throughout Roman history.[104] Despite this, the similarity of the systems is striking, and the observation of and obsession with boundaries has always been an Etruscan trait.[105] We should conclude, then, that although the observation of birds ultimately became a Roman speciality, it is likely that it had common origins with Etruscan lore.[106]

With all this said we can reconstruct the *templum* to the fullest:

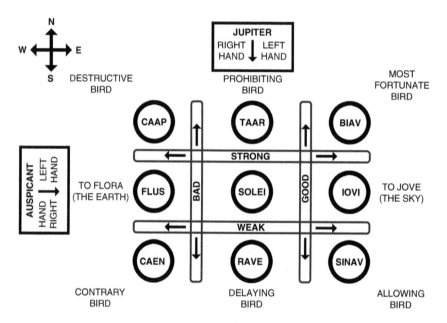

Figure 1.3 Full reconstruction of the Bantia *templum*.

We can see that every point has a different level of auspiciousness assigned to it except for the central *cippus,* since no bird can spontaneously appear in the centre of the *templum.* This central *cippus* stands instead for the sun at its

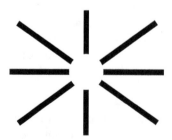

Figure 1.4 The *templum* as a compass?

noonday zenith. If we draw eight lines from the central *cippus* fanning outward to each of the *cippi* surrounding it, we create something that appears to be a perfect compass.

When Pliny gives instructions for making a compass, he calls for a line to be drawn running from north to south, and a line lying transversely across this from east to west. Upon this was drawn an X, with all points crossing at a centre point called the *umbilicus*. The *umbilicus* stood for the sun at noon, fixed and unchanging, while the positions of sunrise and sunset differed each day.[107] He then explains how noting the position of the sun at dawn in relation to the compass allowed one to track the times of the solstices, equinoxes, and slow changing of the seasons. The northeast point marks where the sun rises on the summer solstice, the longest day of the year. Naturally, the southeast marks the point at which the sun rises on the winter solstice, the shortest day. This allows us to account for the augural system. The strength accorded to the north/south axis corresponds to the strength of the sun at the summer solstice versus the winter solstice, while the fortuitousness of the sign along the east/west axis corresponds to sunrise and sunset. The central labelled *sol* marker shows us how everything in auspices literally revolved around the sun and the movement of the heavens. This alignment to cardinal and solsticial points is observed in many ancient edifices, and could be mapped out using simple observation, as Pliny demonstrates.[108] We can compare this to Vitruvius, who recommends building temples along cardinal points, and in particular says that a temple and the statue of the god within should ideally look west so that a supplicant can look east when they make their approach, though he makes allowances for cases where this is not practical; however, he stresses that the altars should look east (*De arch.* 4.5.1, 4.9.1).[109]

It is intriguing that this compass shape also looks like a star with eight points – three above, three below, and one on either side, with the 'sun' at the centre. According to Festus, inaugurated spaces were marked by a bronze star.[110] It is likely that this 'star' was actually a representation of the *templum* grid itself. A Republican *aes signatum* from c. 260 BCE shows two augural hens feeding with two eight-pointed stars between them.

Rudi Thomsen speculates that this coin is connected to a naval victory in the First Punic War since chickens would have provided the favourable auspices needed to go into battle.[111] The fact that they are feeding in an auspicial capacity is expressed through the stars, which we can interpret as basic representations of *templa*.

Studying the archaeological site at Banzi also gives us an opportunity to review some of the literature on augury. The famous augur Messalla wrote that the reason the Aventine Hill alone of Rome's seven hills was not included in the *pomerium* (and therefore excluded from the urban auspices) was because this was where the unlucky Remus took auspices. It was *quasi avibus obscenis ominosum* – 'as if it were made ominous by inauspicious birds', so even when the *pomerium* was expanded in the Republic,

Figure 1.5 Republican *aes Signatum*, c. 260 BCE; Sutherland (1974) 29.
Source: Photo by Edward Blume-Poulton.

it remained unwelcome (Gell. *NA* 13.14.6). It was not until Claudius made a further extension in 49 CE that the hill was finally included within the boundary.[112] But curiously, in Ennius' account of the myth, the oldest of the sources, he places Romulus on the Aventine and Remus on the *mons Murcus,* a second peak of the hill. He is unique in recounting such place-ment. Otto Skutsch argues that in the period after Ennius, Romulus began to be associated exclusively with the Palatine, and so it became tradition that he took auspices there as well.[113] It is also recorded that after the augural contest, Romulus threw his cornel lance from the Aventine to the Palatine, where it grew into a sacred tree, possibly just after auspices had been taken (Serv. *Aen.* 3.49). Using the Banzi *templum* as a model, Lisa Marie Mignone makes the case that the Aventine was traditionally held to be the site where Romulus took auspices. Ennius described the twelve birds descending on Romulus' left in the northeast part of the sky. If we map this onto the topography of Rome, we find that a figure looking east on the Aventine would indeed find the Palatine Hill to his left, in the northeast.[114] The mythical *auguraculum* was therefore originally on the Aventine in the southwest, with birds flying over the Palatine on Romulus' left, in the northeast, marking that hill as the site of the City. The Aventine was ex-cluded from the *pomerium* like all the hills and valleys beside the Palatine in the early days, and continued to be excluded even as the *pomerium* ex-panded. In succeeding centuries, the need to explain its ongoing exclusion led to the augur Messalla saying it was *quasi* – 'as if' – the hill was made ominous by Remus' failed auspices, since the unlucky brother's *auguraculum* was still assigned to the Aventine.

This business of birds being lucky in certain parts of the sky is complicated by the fact that there were right-hand and left-hand birds; that is, some birds were seen as lucky if they appeared on the auspicant's left, as we would expect, while some were considered lucky only if they appeared on the right. Knowledge of whether a bird was left-hand or right-hand was at the forefront of public consciousness, and Plautus gives us several humorous examples of characters applying augural formulae to everyday life:

> I have a favorable omen, a favorable sign: the birds let me go in any direction. The woodpecker and the crow on the left and the raven and the owl on the right recommend it; I've decided to follow your advice. But what's this? A woodpecker is tapping an elm? That cannot be due to chance![115]

The woodpecker and crow on the left are lucky but the situation is reversed for the owl and the raven. This reversal is substantiated by Cicero and Horace, so we may take Plautus at his word despite the humour intended here.[116] Since both the raven and the owl were more often birds of ill-omen (the owl especially), it may be that a bad bird in a bad part of the sky served to cancel out the offence. They were in the part of the sky accorded to them, making it favourable. In another Plautus passage, we see the cry of the raven on the left, the favourable side, treated as unlucky: 'It's not by chance that a raven was cawing to my left now; at the same time it was scraping the ground with its claws and croaking with its voice'.[117] The left-hand/right-hand distinction, the exceptions to these rules, and the way a sign could be *both* left and right at once no doubt caused much confusion, which was only exacerbated by the way the rules were reversed in Greek culture. By the Augustan age, Roman traditions were visibly slipping to accommodate the Greek, especially in literature. Ovid names 'left-hand birds' as birds of ill-omen (*Her.* 2.115). Horace claims a woodpecker on the left is unlucky, and a raven from the east lucky (*Carm.* 3.27.11–16). It is probable that these poets chose the Greek version deliberately, but the dissemination of such work would have caused confusion abroad.

Other intricacies of formula involve hierarchy, as we know there were many grades of auspices.[118] Those observed by a major magistrate supplanted those observed by a minor (Gell. *NA* 13.15.4). Thunder and lightning – the *auspicia maxima* – supplanted a sign given by a bird.[119] A lightning stroke could not be contradicted by any other sign (Sen. *QNat.* 2.34.1). So among birds themselves, species mattered: 'For example, if a *parra* [barn owl] or a *picus* [woodpecker] were to give a sign at auspices, and then an *aquila* [eagle] gave a contrary sign, the eagle's sign would prevail'.[120] If two signs of equal weight were observed, preference went to the one seen first, as Ovid tells us an augur would take his cue from the first bird he saw (Ov. *Fast.* 1.178–80). A stronger sign seen afterwards still prevailed, so this explains why an augur would jump up immediately after receiving the desired auspices, breaking his line of sight and ending the ritual. It left no time for Jupiter to change his mind and countermand the signal by sending a stronger, negative sign (Serv. *Aen.* 2.699). On the other hand, an auspicant receiving a negative sign might be inclined to remain in position, just in case Jupiter sent a contrary bird. A number of factors determined how strong a sign was, not only species, but the number of birds, the type of cry they emitted, where in the *templum* they flew in and out, how high or low they flew, what they perched on, whether they dropped something and what that was, their general behaviour, and so on, which we shall consider in finer detail shortly.[121]

We can only make guesses as to how such signs were further broken down, but in terms of numbers it seems likely that three was significant. The Romans considered three to be a magic number (Livy 22.9.7–11, 10; Plut. *Fab.* 4.4–5). Pliny declares odd numbers are favourable; later, that even numbers are bad (*HN* 28.23; 28.27). When interpreting the *oscines* – the birds who cry – the number of cries was important.[122] When interpreting the *alites* – the birds who fly – it is similarly prudent to assume the number of times a bird circled or entered into a particular quadrant of sky was significant, and also the number of birds seen. Nowhere is this more clearly illustrated than in the fact that Romulus' twelve vultures trumped Remus' six, even though his brother saw the sacred birds first.

We shall now consider the augural birds in individual detail.

Vultures

It is best to start with the *vultur*, since legend has it that the City owes its existence to this bird.[123] Among the Greeks, there was a famous tendency to confuse vultures with eagles, but the Romans were far more fastidious.[124] Vultures were pre-eminent in Roman augury, delivering the strongest signs an augur or auspicant could receive from a wild bird. They furnished Romulus with his perfect augury for the founding of the City, while Posidippus (*Ep.* 27) tells us that a vulture was a perfect omen for the birth of a child. We can deduce from this that vultures were particularly positive omens for beginnings, whether for people or places. How do we make sense of the vulture's importance in Roman augury? Some two thousand years ago, Plutarch grappled with this very question:

> Why do [the Romans] make most use of vultures in augury? Is it because twelve vultures appeared to Romulus at the time of the founding of Rome? Or is it because this is the least frequent and familiar of birds? For it is not easy to find a vulture's nest, but these birds suddenly swoop down from afar; wherefore the sight of them is portentous.[125]

Pliny states that there were black vultures and white vultures, which likely correspond to the cinereous vulture (*Aegypius monachus*) and the griffon vulture (*Gyps fulvus*), respectively. He describes the black vulture as the stronger, which fits with the cinereous vulture's larger size (*HN* 10.19). These imposing birds – among the largest birds found in the old world – are rare in Italy today, but they were widespread in the Roman period, with archaeological evidence showing that cinereous vultures lived close to Roman towns and forts, and possibly scavenged from refuse pits.[126] Pliny also speaks of the bearded eagle (*Gypaetus barbatus*), which was known to the Tuscans, who called it *ossifraga* – bone-breaker (Plin. *HN* 10.12). The name *ossifraga* comes from its habit of dropping bones onto rocks from a great height, after which it consumes the shattered fragments. Its range in the Italian peninsula is limited, however, and Romans placed it in the *aquila* category. For his part, Pliny says he does not believe a bird as strange as the bearded vulture exists and writes it off as a fabrication. We can therefore exclude the bearded vulture from auspices and assume that the cinereous and griffon vultures were the birds most beloved by the Romans.

What made vultures pre-eminent as augural birds was a matter of diet and behaviour as well as appearance. Vultures are obligate scavengers, meaning they feed exclusively on carrion.[127] They soar over enormous distances to find food, scanning the landscape with their powerful eyesight. When a vulture locates a potential meal, it will investigate by flying in a circle. This circling behaviour draws in other vultures to form a 'kettle', or group of vultures circling a body. Once they drop to begin feeding, the 'wake' works together to break the carcass open, watch for predators, and fend off competitors. It is thus normal behaviour for vultures to appear suddenly, in great numbers, and circle around a fixed spot before diving to the ground. These behaviours are all attested in augural lore.

As the largest birds with the biggest wingspans, vultures are difficult to ignore. It is said that the griffon vulture was valued by Etruscan augurs for its enormous wingspan, larger than that of the golden eagle, and more beautiful too.[128] Their size is a byproduct of their adaptation to a scavenging lifestyle, as it allows them to glide efficiently with minimal energy expenditure while searching for a body, then store enough energy to sustain themselves until the next meal. Their flight patterns are distinct. To avoid strenuous flapping, they gain height by circling upwards on columns of warm air called thermals. They then coast through the sky until they need to gain height again, at which point they locate another thermal.[129] Their dietary habits were accurately observed, for as Plutarch points out, they do no harm to living creatures, and are benign to crops, livestock, humans, and birds (Plut. *Quaest. Rom.* 93 286b). That last point was emphasised; they were considered the most righteous of flesh-eating birds because, unlike hawks and eagles, they did not eat other birds. In Aeschylus' words, 'How can a bird that eats birds be pure?' (*Supp.* 226). Since the bird harmed none, the Romans were encouraged to repay the kindness by refraining from harming vultures, though demand for cures and charms derived from vulture bodies often overrode this prerogative.[130]

Their scavenging was also considered in a positive light for the way it cleansed after death. The vulture was the personification of purity, an idea that now finds expression in the scientific name of the turkey vulture, *Cathartes*. This too is accurate. Vultures have highly acidic stomachs (pH = 1.0) that can kill most bacteria and viruses, allowing them to consume diseased and decaying bodies without getting ill. This helps to limit the transmission of pathogens in the wider environment, making them critical to human health as well as the health of ecosystems in general.[131] One recorded prodigy involves a calamitous lack of vultures to clean up after a plague: 'During a terrible plague in men and cattle alike, corpses lay exposed because Libitina was overwhelmed, but no vultures appeared'.[132] Proverbially, vultures were known for eating human corpses.[133] Specifically, they ate the dead on the battlefield (Hom. *Il.* 16.836; 18.271). Their diets implicitly connected them with warfare, and they were known to follow armies in anticipation of slaughter.[134] On an Etrusco-Corinthian jug from the early sixth century BCE, we see two vultures settling on a corpse after combat.[135] An anecdote from St Basil in the fourth century CE provides illumination for how the Romans interpreted such a phenomenon: 'Who foretells to vultures the deaths of men, when they are waging war upon themselves? You can see the innumerable flocks of vultures following the armies, and reasoning the outcome based on the preparations of arms'.[136] The vulture's pre-eminence in augury was possibly derived from soldiers trying to divine who would be victorious based on the number or behaviour of vultures lingering near the camps, waiting for the feast.

In what is usually called the first case of bird banding, Plutarch records that while the famous commander Marius (157–86 BCE) was waging war on Germanic tribes, two vultures were seen hovering above his armies as they

Figure 1.6 Pompeiian painting of a griffon vulture in a Nile scene. Despite their significance, vultures are rare in Roman art. Naples Archaeological Museum, inv. 8533.

Source: Photo by the author.

marched from victory to victory. One day, the soldiers caught the vultures in their nets. The blacksmith forged two bronze collars, fastened these around their necks, and released them. From then on, whenever the soldiers saw the vultures appear with their collars gleaming in the sun, they took it as an omen that they would be victorious, and that their beloved mascots would soon feast on the bodies of their slain enemies (Plut. *Vit. Mar.* 17.3). This is comparable to the way the Vikings marched under raven banners, which signalled to their enemies that their own favoured carrion bird would soon feast on their flesh.[137] But such symbolism could be turned against an army too. While Brutus and Cassius prepared for battle against Octavian and Antony, vultures and other carrion-feeding birds gathered around their army, a prodigy that apparently signalled their own corpses would soon feed the birds (Julius Obsequens 42).

Aelian writes of the Vaccaei, a tribe in the north-west of Spain. They believed vultures were sacred and offered up to them the bodies of warriors who had died nobly in battle. Those who died a cowardly death at home were granted no such honour and were burned instead (Ael. *NA* 10.22). We might compare this to Tibetan sky burials, where human bodies are dismembered and left out to be consumed by vultures. This was not a custom the Romans shared, but they had a similar relationship with the birds nonetheless, explicitly calling them 'sacred birds', as in Ennius. Their appearance before battle indicated they possessed powers of prescience and knew a battle was imminent. Men studied them in the hope they could divine the outcome. Vultures then purified battlefields afterwards and helped to limit the spread of disease.

Unsurprisingly, vultures also appear in magic and medicine. They were said to protect against serpents, although the black allegedly had less power in this respect than the white (Plin. *HN* 29.77). Burning vulture feathers acted as a fumigant against snakes, and carrying the heart of a vulture was a charm to protect against snakes, beasts, bandits, and the wrath of kings (Plin. *HN* 29.77). Reading Pliny's lore on vultures, we can detect a high amount of superstition in the recorded remedies. Five out of sixteen examples are concerned with the vulture as a magical charm. The rest include five ointments, four potions, one fumigant, and one remedy for bad breath, employing parts as diverse as the skull, brain, gall, feathers, blood, heart, lung, liver, and fat.[138] One of the most interesting lines concerns the directive to feed a sick patient a vulture that has dined upon a human corpse (Plin. *HN* 30.92). The remarkable find of ritually deposited vulture bones at Rome's Lapis Niger also indicates their use in ritual.[139] Vultures were viewed in similarly protective terms in Egypt. The words for mother and vulture were both *mw.t*, and Maat, a mother-goddess, was identified with the vulture. She sheltered kings beneath her mighty wings, which are so omnipresent and recognisable in Egyptian art, and the vulture Nekhbet symbolised Upper Egypt.[140] It was said the Egyptians believed all vultures were female and impregnated by the wind, a belief that migrated to Italy at a later date.[141]

Despite its reputation as auspicious, we do find instances of the vulture as a bird of ill-omen. In 209 BCE, one flew down into a shop in the crowded Forum at Privernum. This prodigy required immediate expiation (Livy 27.11.4). The previous year in Caere, a solitary vulture flew around Jupiter's temple. Livy counts this as a grim portent (27.33.3). Let us compare these incidents to Romulus' augury, and to Augustus' own tale that twelve vultures appeared to him when he took the auspices during his first consulship, a sign that indicated he would become emperor and found a new Rome (Suet. *Aug.* 95). In the first two instances, the omens were dire, unsolicited, and came from a single bird. In the latter two, the omens were positive, solicited, and conferred through a magical number of them. We can conclude that solitary vultures were inauspicious, and oblative signs from vultures were similarly unlucky. Vultures that appeared in great numbers (multiples of three) were positive, as were vultures that appeared when impetrative auspices were taken.

Eagles

Of all the birds, the mighty *aquila* is the one most readily associated with ancient Rome. A huge, unmistakable apex predator, the eagle was the bird of Father Jove, the Imperial family, and the Roman army. Due to its lack of a crest and the way it is usually painted, the Roman eagle is most readily identified as the golden eagle (*Aquila chrysaetos*). However, while calling eagles the strongest and most honourable of birds, Pliny lists six different types recognised by the Romans. The appearance of any eagle was thought to be Jupiter himself indicating his will to mankind (Plin. *HN* 10.6). Indeed, it may have been the white-tailed eagle (*Haliaeetus albicilla*) that furnished most sightings. Pliny tells us that in his day the white-tailed eagle could be found in towns and open country (Plin. *HN* 10.7). Modern observation bears this out, showing that it is primarily a scavenger that benefits from association with human settlements, while the more elusive golden eagle is a predator less inclined to settle in urban areas.[142]

The Egyptians considered the eagle to be a royal bird, as did the Greeks.[143] In Homer, the eagle sends signs directly from Zeus (*Il.* 8.345–52, 24.315–21). Augustus' soul was said to have been carried into the sky by an eagle.[144] Allegedly, the eagle became Jupiter's armour bearer because it cannot be killed by a thunderbolt (Plin. *HN* 2.146; 10.15). In art, along with the thunderbolt and sceptre, the eagle is one of the most common attributes of Jupiter.[145] The eagle was, in essence, the most trusted messenger of Jupiter, god of auspices. A popular image was that of Jupiter, either seated or standing, with an eagle at his feet looking up at him as if waiting for a command.[146] Eagles are often shown clutching lightning in their talons.[147] There is a sense, as we shall see, that the bird was sent directly from Jupiter's side to deliver auspices. Crucially, as well as accompanying Jupiter himself, it is common for the eagle to be depicted as standing at the foot of the emperor.[148]

Figure 1.7 Jupiter and his eagle, from Pompeii, House of the Dioscuri. Naples
Archaeological Museum, inv. 9551.

Source: Photo by the author.

Cicero gives us the tale of the omen that foretold Marius' return from
exile. In this retelling, Marius saw an eagle fighting a snake. The bird won
the battle and dropped the snake into the sea, and then, in typical fortunate fashion, turned its back on the west and flew away towards the east,
soaring high (Cic. *Div.* 1.106). The eagle appears in a number of other
doubtful stories that are still worth relating. It is said that in the regal
period an eagle flew down from an auspicious part of the sky, snatched the
cap from the head of Tarquin the Elder while he was on the road, soared
upwards, and then replaced it on his head as an omen of his future rule.[149]
In a story of suspiciously similar substance, an eagle stole some bread out
of Augustus' hand while he was on the road, flew up high, and returned it
to him (Suet. *Aug.* 94.7). Doubtless Augustus' story was modelled on the
first, but it shows how they envisioned divine favour. For an eagle to do
something so out of character, and to leave the target completely unharmed while also flying in and out of an auspicious quarter could be
nothing less than a message straight from Jupiter. Another message of
support came from an eagle dropping a white hen, unharmed, into
Augustus' wife Livia's lap while she was returning to her estate, on which
more later (Suet. *Galb.* 1).

There are many more examples to ponder. Eagles followed Brutus to Philippi, and foretold his defeat by deserting him upon arrival (Plut. *Vit. Brut.* 37.4). An eagle set upon by two ravens was likened to the princely eagle Octavian being attacked by, but ultimately defeating, the upstart ravens Brutus and Cassius (Suet. *Aug.* 96.1). Young Germanicus was led by eight eagles, and of course went on to lead eight legions on the Rhine (Tac. *Ann.* 2.17.2). The sight of an eagle in Rhodes caused the exiled Tiberius to hope he would return to Augustus' good graces (Suet. *Tib.* 14.4). The death of Augustus and his deification were prophesied by an eagle (Suet. *Aug.* 97.1). Three eagles were seen fighting in the year of the four emperors, obviously symbolising the imperial struggle.[150] An eagle snatched entrails from a sacrifice and hung them in an oak tree, thus foretelling Galba's rise (Suet. *Galb.* 4.2). An eagle kept pace with Vitellius' victorious army (Suet. *Vit.* 9). Domitian knew of his success when he saw an eagle (Suet. *Dom.* 6.2). From this catalogue of omens, we see a pattern emerging. The eagle – Jupiter's bird – became increasingly associated with the emperor and the imperial struggle. It almost always appears as an oblative sign, dropping out of the sky at its own leisure and not when called upon. Many (all?) of these stories are certainly fabricated, and they serve as part of imperial propaganda to assure the people that the king of gods and men approved of the empire and its emperor.

Figure 1.8 Eagle with the trappings of Jupiter. Pompeii, House of the Ephebe.
Source: Photo by the author.

The eagle is most famous as a military symbol. Pliny says in the time of Gaius Marius (104 BCE), five animals were used on the military standards: boars, eagles, wolves, minotaurs, and horses (*HN* 10.16). A few years earlier it had become practice to advance only the eagles into battle and leave the rest at the camp. Marius ended up abolishing the others and made the eagle the sole military ensign. Standards were simply known as *aquilae*. If an *aquila* was captured, it was a source of immense shame for the Romans, and much is made of the need to retrieve lost eagles. When Augustus persuaded the Parthians to return lost eagle standards in 20 BCE, he made a famous issue of coins, *signis receptis,* to celebrate the occasion.[151] The imagined loss of an eagle was even a prodigy that beset Gnaeus Pompeius: 'To Gnaeus, son of Pompey, the eagles of the ten legions appeared to drop the lightning bolts they held and fly into the sky. The young Pompey was himself defeated and killed as he fled'.[152] Similarly, in 43 BCE Octavian received an omen from the standards. Those standards of the legion left by Pansa as a garrison for Rome appeared as if wrapped in spiderwebs from long disuse. The same year, in Octavian's camp at dawn an eagle landed on a ridge above, was disturbed by several smaller birds, and flew away (Julius Obsequens 43).

In the archaeological context, it is interesting to note that finds of eagle remains increased in the Roman period in Britain.[153] Britain has two native eagles, the white-tailed eagle and the golden eagle. Both were caught and killed. They were particularly abundant on Roman military sites, where mass collection is evident.[154] As one example, the fort at South Shields, Newcastle, contained the remains of fourteen white-tailed eagles, thirteen of which were found at the commandant's house. Other sites showed butchery relating to the harvesting of wing feathers.[155] A.J. Parker offers an explanation for the abundance of eagle wings by citing possible uses as brushes, quill pens, or for fletching arrows.[156] However, given the symbolic importance of eagles to the Roman army, it is more likely that their collection was inspired by something less utilitarian. Ritual deposition or personal adornment are possible factors. One find from Cheriton Rd, Kent, shows that the ulna and radius had been carefully cut in a way that would preserve the wing feathers for use as a fan or brush.[157] A possible artistic representation of eagle feathers being used for personal display comes to us from the funeral stele of a gladiator called Aquilo, who is depicted wearing a crest of upright feathers. Exactly which bird the feathers came from is unclear, but with a name like Aquilo it would not be remiss to assume the gladiator did indeed wear eagle feathers.[158]

Many cultures around the world attribute special powers and properties to eagle feathers. They can be used as good luck charms or as decorative elements on ritual and martial items, including headdresses, weapons, and shields. They may act as status markers that indicate social standing or battle prowess.[159] Emma Durham points out that they are also used as a form of sympathetic magic. Soldiers may have coveted eagle feathers to bring them success in warfare.[160] According to Pliny, parts of the eagle could also be employed in medicine. Their gall was said to be effective at healing eye wounds and cataracts due to the belief that eagles could stare at the sun (Plin. *HN* 29.118, 123).

The eagle's association with victory was palpable. He was the very guardian spirit of the Roman legion.[161] Eagle symbolism has resounded through the ages, and the armies of Charlemagne, Peter the Great, Napoleon, Bismarck, and Hitler all marched beneath eagles.[162] The imperial eagle is one of the most powerful symbols of all time, and as an augural bird he was impressive beyond belief, deigning to appear only in times of great strife or victory as an oblative omen, and interacting only with royalty.

Ravens

The *corvus* is an exceedingly charismatic bird in Roman augury. Ravens were auspicious on the right and ill-omened on the left, but were generally viewed with less dread than the owl when appearing as inauspicious signs. In Plautus, when a raven croaks on his left the character Euclio is grateful for having heard it, as its warning gave him time to avert disaster (*Aulularia*, 669–73). Part of this mixed attitude may be due to a curious belief recorded by Pliny that 'Ravens seem to be the only birds that have an understanding of the meanings that they convey in auspices'.[163] While all other birds who acted as divine portents were controlled by deities and otherwise unaware of their actions, ravens knew of their own significance. They knew if they were delivering good or bad omens. It adds a sort of human dimension to them, and allows for the possibility of regarding them as smug or fearful when they delivered their portents. This might be why Horace calls on ravens to hold him to his word in this humorous declaration: 'If I lie, may my head be befouled by the white shit of ravens'.[164] In this we may see the Roman recognition of the unsurpassed intelligence of ravens. Crows, ravens, and related birds, the corvid family, are opportunistic omnivores that exhibit great intelligence due to their need for behavioural flexibility to pursue a diverse diet. When removed from their nests and hand-raised, they become strongly attached to humans and can be taught how to speak and perform tricks.[165]

Ravens gave powerful positive signs if they vocalised clearly on the right (Cic. *Div.* 1.12, 85). After *pullarii* falsified auspices, causing the Roman army to go into battle *contra auspicia,* the consul Papirius discovered the truth and expiated the sin by sending the guilty chicken-keeper to the front line. The unlucky man was struck through the chest with a javelin and Papirius declared the sin had been expiated. A raven cawed to him in agreement, and the army knew the gods were on their side (Livy 10.40.1–14). More often, however, the raven was the messenger of mischief and destruction.[166] In a list of evil portents, Livy states a raven perched on Juno's own couch in her temple (Livy 21.62.4). In another case a raven nested in Juno's temple (Livy 24.10.6). It is reported that ravens pecked and ate some of the gold off the Capitol (Livy 30.2.9). Ravens brawling to the left of Tiberius Gracchus as he was on his way to the Capitol made him pause, but his followers told him it would be shameful to turn back on their account, since he was too illustrious to listen to such creatures. He proceeded and was duly clubbed to death that same day.[167] Shortly before his fall from grace, Sejanus took auspices in his capacity as consul (31 CE). He did not see a single favourable sign. Instead, a great flock of ravens circled around him and cried from every direction. The confusion made it impossible to determine the exact provenance of the cries. They then settled on the jail in which Sejanus would shortly be imprisoned (Cass. Dio 58.5.7). Ravens and crows are opportunistic feeders, and their fondness for dead bodies did not go unnoticed by the Romans (Macrob. *Sat.* 7.5.11). It was a colloquial expression that a crucified criminal would make a feast for ravens.[168] Like vultures, ravens learned that marching armies meant fresh meat, and so followed them. Their appetite for human flesh combined with their ability to predict accurately when slaughter would occur undoubtedly had a hand in shaping their reputations.[169] A prodigy list records the following event:

> Sextus Titius, a tribune of the plebs, persisted in offering legislation for the distribution of land against the opposition of his colleagues; thereupon ravens, two in number, flying aloft fought so fiercely over the assembly as to tear each other with beak and claw. The *haruspices* declared that a propitiatory offering should be made to Apollo, and that action on the law which was being proposed should be abandoned.[170]

Another prodigy runs thus: 'As Mithridates was preparing for war against the allies of Rome, portents appeared to him. At Stratopedon, where the senate usually meets, ravens killed a vulture by striking it with their beaks'.[171] A happier incident deserves closer inspection. In 349 BCE, a Roman soldier called Valerius Corvus defeated a Gaul in single combat, allegedly because a raven appeared and pecked the face of his opponent. This show of divine favour through the assistance of the bird led to him adopting the name Corvus.[172] This myth has been combed extensively by historians, and not necessarily for auspicial lore. Gallic helmets often had animals fixed to the top, so it may be that this tale comes from Valerius capturing an enemy's helmet which had a raven fixed atop it.[173] An iron Celtic helmet from the second or third century BCE, found in Ciumesti (Romania), was crowned with a raven that had hinged wings that would 'flap' in battle. There is also the question of which deity was thought to have sent the raven. The bird was sometimes associated with Juno, Minerva, and Apollo, but not in connection with warfare. However, to send a raven would have been in character for the Celtic battle goddesses Badbh and Morrigan, to whom ravens were sacred, and it was said to be a lucky sign if a raven followed a warrior.[174] It is possible that this tale was meant as a co-option of the Celtic goddesses to demonstrate that the native gods were on the Romans' side.[175] Whatever the merit of that argument, it is undeniable that this myth uses accurate augural terminology. Jupiter often sent ravens as messengers. This raven conforms to our understanding of what constituted a positive sign, for it was said to come from the sky and landed firmly.

Valerius formally accepted this omen, said a prayer, and when the Gaul was defeated the bird flew east and was lost from sight (*ex conspectu elatus orientem petit*). The same flight pattern was accomplished by Romulus' vultures and an eagle sent to Marius.[176]

Ravens and crows were interred in graves in Iron Age and Roman Britain. Many of these showed signs of having feathers deliberately removed, perhaps for use in decoration or as charms. It is suggested that the helmets with metal ravens mounted on the top may have had feathers glued to their flapping wings – a more impressive sight than pieces of metal clattering against one's head.[177] It is uncertain why these birds were interred in the graves, but one possible explanation is that they were pets or animal familiars, tamed for companionship or ritual purposes.[178] Raven bones have been found in Roman camps in Britain, thought to be camp sacrifices to native gods.[179]

A raven's cry was important when taking auspices, possibly because it was capable of making such a wide variety of sounds. Isidorus claims that *corvi* were so named because they speak *a cordis voce* – from a voice in its chest, in unmistakable croaks and groans that rise gutturally from the chest (Isid. *Etym.* 12.4.13). Pliny states that it is especially bad if a raven gulps as it croaks, as if it were choking. Its ability to make watery sounds may be why it holds such widespread esteem as a weather prophet (Plin. *HN* 10.33). The following piece from Horace asks the raven to appear in the east and mentions its connection to rain explicitly.

> But on behalf of one for whom I, as an augur with second sight, feel concern, I shall rouse with my prayer the prophetic raven from the rising sun before that inspired bird, which forecasts imminent rainstorms, can fly back to the stagnant marshes.[180]

This association is recorded in Greek literature too. Both Theophrastus and Aratus state the raven can signify rain sent from Zeus.[181] Aristotle informs us that two ravens lived in the temple of Zeus at Pedasa in Caria, leading us to conjecture that their association with the god of thunder may be responsible for their status as harbingers of rain and storms (Arist. *De mirab.* 844b 8). Among the Norse the raven was a storm bird, as the raven god Odin's son was Thor the Thunderer. Even in the Bible the raven is associated with rainstorms in the tale of Noah's Ark, where it is said Noah first released a raven from the ark, and then a dove (Genesis 8:6–9).

Aelian states that Apollo afflicted the raven with thirst, and his croaking betrays this punishment (though he personally does not believe the tale).[182] He goes on to say: 'The raven must really be the most clamorous of birds and have the largest variety of tones, for it can be taught to speak like a human being. For playful moods it has one voice, for serious moods another, and if it is delivering answers from the gods, then its voice assumes a devout and prophetic tone'.[183] Ravens are indeed excellent mimics, and hand-reared birds can learn to speak an impressive variety of phrases. In fact, for the Romans, ravens and crows were the chief speaking birds, and were often tamed and taught phrases (Macrob. *Sat.* 2.4.29–30). It was not until the first century CE that they began to be supplanted by superior foreign talkers such as parrots. Their ability to communicate is extraordinary, with corvids having big brains relative to their body sizes, and an ability to vary meaning by changing intensity, pitch, sequence, and repetition.[184] However, this does not amount to delivering weather forecasts. In the wild, their natural vocalisations are usually used to share foraging information between individuals.[185] It appears that the belief that ravens were weather prophets must be partly blamed on the Romans' interpretation of ravens' communicative cries as indicative of thirst, or imitative of raindrops, and partly because the raven was caught in a folkloric web across Eurasia that tied the bird to rainstorms (Ael. *NA*, 6.19).

Overall, the Roman attitude towards ravens is more positive than that of the Greeks. The Greeks shunned ravens as portents of death. The birds allegedly prophesied the death of Alexander the Great and foretold disaster when they suddenly attacked the statue of Athena at Delphi and pecked away all the gold just as the Athenians were preparing to leave for their ill-fated Sicilian expedition.[186] Dreaming of ravens was said to foretell death (Artem. *On.* 4.32). The Roman tendency to tame and speak to ravens, and their blatant anthropomorphising of the intelligent birds may account for the grains of positivity in augural lore. In Augustan poetry, as Apollo became more important to the Romans as a god of augury, the raven was even consecrated to him due to the bird's own gift of prophecy.[187] We can consider the raven to be one of the *oscines,* a right-hand bird capable of giving positive and negative signs in equal measure with its large repertoire of distinct cries.

Crows

The *cornix* shared many similarities with the raven as an augural bird, but also many crucial differences. For one, the crow was a left-hand bird, and therefore had to be carefully distinguished from the right-hand raven. Fortunately, this was a simple task even at a distance for the Romans. The pure black carrion crow (*Corvus corone*) is a native only in Spain, north-western Europe, and Britain. The Italian crow was, and still is, the hooded crow (*Corvus cornix*), which has a jacket of grey feathers.[188] It, too, was thought to take its name from the sound it made, because it croaks – *coracinare* – in its throat (Isid. *Etym.* 12.7.43). The crow was associated with corpses, and Isidorus records that it showed a special fondness for eyes, seeking them out first when it alighted on a dead body.[189] He adds the detail that it was attentive to the concerns of humans and could show where ambush lay and predict the future – though, as a Christian writing retrospectively, he holds it a sin to believe that God would entrust His wisdom to mere crows (Isid. *Etym.* 12.7.44). A crow's age was proverbial, and it was believed they lived for many decades.[190]

Ovid dreamt he saw a black crow pecking the breast of a white heifer, and the crow was interpreted to represent an aged female procuress (Ov. *Am.* 3.5). Crows and ravens are indeed long-lived, sometimes living up to twenty years in the wild; not quite as long as the ancients claimed, but certainly longer than the average for smaller passerine birds.

This notion of longevity combined with their garrulous, intelligent natures, and their habit of living alongside humans in family groups of their own probably contributed to the idea that crows were knowledgeable and interested in human affairs. Propertius says certain truths may be divined by one who understands the beating wings of a crow (Prop. 4.1a.105). Virgil writes an example of a personal warning delivered by a crow: 'So, had not a crow on the left first warned me from the hollow oak to cut short, as best I might, this new dispute, neither your Moeris here nor Menalcas himself would be alive'.[191] Horace refers to the tale that a crow once tried to dress herself in the cast-off feathers of a peacock (Hor. *Epist.* 1.3.17–20). The lesson appears to be that despite attempts to beautify herself, she could not disguise her true, black feathers and only made a fool of herself. The crow, in broad terms, symbolised age, darkness, and misfortune, and to some extent femininity. The bird's appearance was portentous, but like all augural birds the interpretation depended on context.

Crows also had special significance as symbols of conjugal fidelity.[192] The Romans believed that they mated for life and remained faithful to their partners even in death. While it is true that ravens and crows are monogamous, and often raise broods with the same bird for years on end, the idea that they remained single if widowed is an exaggeration. Yet this explains why wedding guests earnestly hoped to see or hear crows when nuptial auspices were taken, and why a single crow was an evil omen at a wedding (Ael. *NA*, 3.9). Two or more crows meant family and a happy marriage. A single, unpaired crow was a widow, and it threatened the bride with widowhood.[193] Hera, equivalent to Juno, patroness of marriage, was sometimes shown in conference with crows (Ap. Rhod. *Argon.* 3.923–51). Like ravens, crows were seen as harbingers of storms (Plin. *HN* 18.363). In Virgil's words: 'Then the wicked crow calls down rain with her deep voice' (*G.* 1.388).

The crow gave signs through its cries, but their vocalisations were not considered as impressive as ravens'. However, Suetonius gives us this story about the demise of Emperor Domitian:

> A few months before he was killed, a crow perched on the Capitolium and cried "All will be well," an omen which some interpreted as follows: Recently a crow which was sitting on a Tarpeian rooftop, could not say "It is well," only declared "It will be."[194]

To the Roman ear, the cry of a crow sounded like '*cras! cras!*' – 'tomorrow! tomorrow!'. It was a shout of hope, a cry that better times were coming, which may be why it was thought to deliver this message.

In fable, it is said that the *cornix* was jealous of the greater significance of the raven, for crows were not particularly ominous for the Greeks.[195] The same may be said of the Romans, for although the crow was an important augural bird, it is evident it did not quite have the same charisma as the raven. Nevertheless, it was capable of delivering myriad omens through vocalisations and appearance, both positive and negative. A left-hand bird that was best seen in numbers, it was of particular interest to those taking private auspices, especially nuptial auspices.

Owls

Nocturnae aves – night birds – were the most fearful of all portents and inauspicious of birds. We might think of owls as wise, but to the Romans the owl was *avis turpissima*, the foulest bird, associated with death, night, evil spirits, and witches. The Athenians alone considered the owl venerable in the ancient world, since they likened her to Athena.[196] The goddess' bird was the little owl, still called the *Athene noctua*, and so identified today because ancient depictions of the bird are spotted and lack the tufted 'horns' of the larger varieties.[197] Minerva was also attached to this owl, and the tawny owl (*Strix aluco*) too, but owls were not revered by Romans as a result, and they

Figure 1.9 Fullers and the owl. Pompeii, fresco from a fuller's shop. Naples Archaeological Museum, inv. 9774.

Source: Photo by the author.

were certainly not subject to protective taboos.[198] Nevertheless, as long as it had no horns, an owl in art could indicate Minerva's presence or benediction. Graffito on a Pompeiian shop front gives us this delightful riff on the first line of the Aeneid – *fullones ululam ego cano non arma virumque* – 'I sing of fullers and the owl, not arms and a man'.[199] Minerva was the patron deity of fullers, which explains why the owl accompanied them.[200] This graffito is made more enigmatic by the fact that it was discovered outside the workshop of M. Fabius Ululitremus – Owl-Shaker – in the context of an image that depicted Aeneas himself.[201]

Fullers and the owl are linked by another piece of graffiti in Pompeii, which is even accompanied by a crude drawing of the creature: 'Greeting from Crescens to the fullers and his owl. (It is an owl)'.[202] The helpful phrase 'it is an owl' was apparently meant to clarify what the drawing represented. Small, hornless owls seem to have been tolerated, even liked by certain groups. In comparison to the plentiful images of hornless owls in Roman art, horned owls appear only infrequently. One rare example is an engraved onyx gemstone dated to between the first and third centuries CE that depicts an owl standing on a bowl that contains a poppy. Both the poppy and the owl symbolise death, making this a foreboding image.[203]

Proserpina's owl was the ghostly barn owl (*Tyto alba*), the *parra*, which Plautus names as a bird of ill omen. Horace declares, 'May evil people be

Figure 1.10 Owl surrounded by dead songbirds. Late third century CE, El Djem Archaeological Museum, Tunisia.

Source: Photo by Paul Williams, Alamy Stock Photo.

sped on their way by the omen of a screaming owl'.[204] However, a *parra* on the right hand became a lucky sign (Plaut. *Asin.* 260). In contrast to other owls, the barn owl does not hoot but lets out a bloodcurdling, humanlike scream that would doubtless terrify any innocent Roman walking home at night. The natural characteristics of owls as predatory, nocturnal, and eerie-sounding creatures with forward-facing, almost human eyes, make it easy to account for their poor reputation and association with death goddesses.[205] An owl appearing during the day was a particularly bad omen. What may have contributed to this dread of owls appearing during the day is the fact that an owl emerging in daylight is likely to be attacked by large numbers of small diurnal birds. This behaviour is called 'mobbing', and it is an instinctive response to drive out the threatening intruder. As early as the sixth century BCE, bird-catchers used this behaviour to their advantage, and would capture an owl to use as bait. They would place it in a tree, cover the branches with birdlime, and collect all the little birds that got caught while attacking the owl.[206]

A late third century CE owl mosaic from Thysdrus, El-Djem Tunisia, depicts mobbing in action. In it, an owl wearing a toga is surrounded by dead songbirds. Above the mosaic, a line reads *invidia rumpuntur aves, neque noctua curat* – 'the birds burst with envy, but the little owl cares not'. This floor mosaic was discovered in the bathhouse of Thysdrus in North Africa and displays the insignia of a local troupe of performers, the Telegenii. The mosaic seems to exhibit their status and immunity to attacks from those in the city who resented their influence.[207] This metaphorical image expresses the idea that other birds attacked decoy owls out of envy, a belief recorded in Aristotle (*Hist. an.* 609a). By contrast, Pliny believes the birds mob the owl because they hate it, and on this particular issue Pliny is correct (*HN* 10.39). The animosity of other birds towards the owl, not to mention the fact that they were prey to it, seemed to exacerbate the Romans' dislike. Nevertheless, this widespread cultural trend could not resist the predilections of a strange few who delighted in the company of owls. Aelian describes with mystified revulsion the ability of owls to charm fowlers, who end up carrying them on their shoulders as beloved pets (Ael. *NA* 1.29). We can compare this to the fullers' affection for their mascot bird, perhaps an indulgence of those engaged in such low-class work that was shunned by those of higher rank; they enjoyed the association with a reviled animal.

Out of all the owls, the most dreadful was the *bubo,* commonly identified as the Eurasian eagle-owl (*Bubo bubo*). Its fearsome size, great tufted horns and chilling hoot made it a monster to the Romans. These enormous birds had a connection to witches, as in Apuleius when the witch Pamphile transforms herself into a *bubo* (Apul. *Met.* 3.23). Pliny writes:

Night birds also have hooked talons, for instance the little owl, the eagle-owl and the tawny owl. All of these are dim-sighted in the daytime. The eagle-owl is a funereal bird, and is regarded as an extremely bad omen, especially at public auspices; it inhabits deserts and places that are not merely unfrequented but terrifying and inaccessible; a wierd creature of the night, its cry is not a musical note but a scream. Consequently, when seen in cities or by daylight in any circumstances it is a direful portent; but I know several cases of its having perched on the houses of private persons without fatal consequences. It never flies in the direction where it wants to go, but travels slantwise out of its course. In the consulship of Sextus Palpellius Hister and Lucius Pedanius (43 CE) an eagle-owl entered the very shrine of the Capitol, on account of which a purification of the city was held on March 7th in that year.[208]

The appearance of a *bubo* at the public auspices was undoubtedly the worst sign one could receive, and Pliny's rather reasonable aside that he has seen the *bubo* perch on private houses without any fatalities indicates that generally the *bubo* was believed to bring death wherever it went. Unlike the *parra,* which might give a positive omen on the right hand, the appearance of a *bubo* could not be positive under any circumstances. One can only imagine the sheer terror it must have caused ordinary people as well as statesmen, since it could threaten individuals and the state in private and public auspices alike. The *bubo* was used to presage the death of Dido (Verg. *Aen.* 4.462). Allegedly, it also presaged the assassination of Julius Caesar (Ov. *Met.* 15.791). Pliny records a second purification that took place on account of a *bubo* in 107 BCE during the consulship of Lucius Cassius Longinus and Gaius Marius. These extreme reactions to portentous birds are corroborated by Livy's list of prodigies as reproduced by Julius Obsequens, where *bubones* are common omens.[209] The year 135 BCE saw this dramatic scene: 'The cry of an eagle-owl was heard first in the Capitol, and then around the City. When a reward was offered, the bird was caught by a fowler and burned. Its ashes were scattered in the Tiber'.[210] In 134 BCE, though no owl is mentioned, there is a similarly disturbing scene that can probably be blamed on a *bubo*: 'At night on the Capitol a bird gave groans that sounded human'.[211] In 133 BCE a *bubo* was seen, as well as an *avis ignota.* Both 125 and 122 BCE record the sighting of a *bubo* on the Capitol. In 108, a 'firebird' and a *bubo* were seen in the City. In 104, one was seen outside the City. Here, no purification is recorded. In 99, a *bubo* was sighted and the City underwent purification. In 98, a *bubo* was seen on the Capitol and expiatory offerings were made. In 96 a *bubo* was caught and killed on the Capitol. In 92, a *bubo* was killed in the temple *Fortunae Equestris.*[212] In Tacitus we also have the prodigy of evil birds perching on the Capitol during Claudius' reign, which merited a lustration (Tac. *Ann.* 12.43.1). Purification after such a portent involved citizens and pontifices solemnly walking around the *pomerium.* In times of crisis, the sacred boundary of Rome had to be purified and strengthened.[213] The appearance of a *bubo* was such a terrible portent that it threatened the safety of Rome herself, and every effort was immediately made to avert calamity.

These reactions to owl omens reveal that Romans actively sought to kill owls that perched or hooted in the City as a method of expiation, and that a fowler might even be employed to do just that. Ordinary people beset by hooting owls employed similar methods to avert calamity, with Apuleius informing us it was common to kill an owl by nailing it to one's house, thereby expiating the evil they had presaged through their own suffering (Apul. *Met.* 3.23).[214] This explains why the following story featuring Augustus was an example of insolence:

> In the case of a soldier, he [Augustus] tolerated speech that was not merely free but brazen: when he was passing some restless nights at a villa where a little owl's hooting was disturbing his sleep, a soldier who was also a skilled bird-catcher caught the bird and brought it to Augustus, expecting a huge reward. The emperor praised him and ordered that he be given 1, 000 sesterces—at which point the soldier dared to say, "I'd rather see it live," and let the bird go. Who could not amazed that Caesar took no offense and let the defiant soldier off scot-free?[215]

Had it been a monstrous *bubo* and not a comparatively harmless *noctua* – little owl – perhaps Augustus would not have been so forgiving.

Varro notes that some owls have onomatopoeic names such as *bubo* and *ulula.* This allows us to nail down identifications, as an eagle-owl's hoot really does sound like a morbid rendition of the word *bubo.* As for *ulula,* it is often translated as 'screech owl'. This is misleading, for although colloquially and historically the barn owl was sometimes called a 'screech owl', strictly speaking there are no screech owls native to Europe; they are restricted to the Americas. To avoid confusion, the bird the Romans called *ulula* should be translated as 'tawny owl' (*Strix aluco*). Proof that the Roman *ulula* and our tawny owl are the same comes straight from the name: the tawny owl is the only European owl whose cry could match the onomatopoeic *ulula* sound. While the female makes a *ke-whit* sound, the male's call is a distinctive – and unsettling – ululating hoot. Pliny records that the learned Nigidius says owls have nine distinct cries.[216] We can safely count owls among the *oscines* that deliver portents through their voices. Any augur worth his salt would need to identify these different cries and the associated portents. Their nocturnal habits mean that it is far more likely the average Roman would hear an owl rather than see one, and the superstition surrounding them probably meant most people learned to identify different owls by ear. The bat was also included among the night birds as a consequence of its nocturnal habits and birdlike screams:

> The little owl, the tawny owl, the eagle-owl, the barn owl, the little horned owl, the long-eared owl and also the bat and any other kind of nocturnal bird all signify failure in regard to business enterprises ... The bat alone is auspicious for pregnant women. For it does not lay eggs like other birds

but is live-bearing, has milk in its breasts, and raises its own nestlings (...)
If these birds nest in the house, it means that the house will be deserted.[217]

There are several unidentified bird species among the night birds, including
the 'firebird' whose appearance merited a purification.

> There is also a bird of ill-omen called the firebird, on account of which
> we find in the annals that the city has often had a ritual purification,
> for instance in the consulship of Lucius Cassius and Gaius Marius
> (107 BCE), in which year the appearance of an eagle-owl also
> occasioned a purification. What this bird was I cannot discover, and
> it is not recorded. Some persons give this interpretation, that the firebird
> was any bird that was seen carrying a coal from an altar or altar-table;
> others call it a 'spinturnix,' but I have not found anybody who professes
> to know what particular species of bird that is. I also notice that the bird
> named by the ancients 'clivia' is unidentified—some call it 'screecher.'
> Labeo calls it 'prohibiting bird'; and moreover a bird is cited in Nigidius
> that breaks eagles' eggs. There are besides a number of kinds described
> in Tuscan lore that have not been seen for generations, though it is
> surprising that they should have now become extinct when even kinds
> that are ravaged by man's greed continue plentiful.[218]

Plautus (*Mil.* 989–90) uses the word *spinturnicium* – a diminutive meaning
little *spinturnix* – and describes it as a bird that hunts its prey. If the *spin-turnix*/firebird are the same creature, as Pliny suggests, it may be our old
friend the eagle-owl, for in his commentary on the *Aeneid*, Servius notes that
if an eagle-owl brings something from a tomb, perches on a house and
shrieks, it is a sign the house will catch fire (Serv. *Aen.* 4.462). The eagle-owl
also has huge orange eyes which, to the imaginative mind, might seem to
burn. Another theory is that the *spinturnix*/firebird is the Alpine chough
(*Pyrrhocorax graculus*), since this bird has been reported carrying flaming
objects, has orange legs, and choughs were called *pyrrhocorax* in Greek and
in Latin – fire raven.[219]

Another unidentified night bird is the *strix*. There are mixed descriptions
of the creature, and Pliny admits he does not quite know what it is (*HN*
11.232). Ovid gives us a haunting vision in the *Fasti*, describing hooked
claws, light grey feathers, a piercing shriek and a penchant for attacking
children (*Fast.* 6.131–40). Plautus claims it feeds on the intestines of living
people (*Pseud.* 820–1). Tibullus, Lucan, and Statius list it alongside the fu-nereal *bubo* when describing evil omens and supernatural stirrings.[220]
Isidorus links the word *strix* to *stridere,* explaining that it was named for its
shrill scream (*Etym.* 12.7.42). It is therefore likely that the *strix* is a barn owl
to match its screech and whitish feathers. But these descriptions of the *strix*
make it a monster fit to haunt children's stories, and should perhaps indicate
how an ordinary owl could take on nightmarish aspects in Roman minds.

Owls loomed large in the Roman imagination as harbingers of doom and detestable monsters of the night. They distinguished between them largely on the basis of their cries and dreaded the sounds of hooting and screeching in the night, believing that death and calamity were sure to follow. They exaggerated the fearful qualities of the owl to an extraordinary degree, speaking of them as monsters, purifying their city after unsolicited appearances, and killing them as a form of self-defence against the misfortune they carried on their swift, silent wings. Yet while the 'horned' varieties seem to have been shunned completely, those without horns – the barn owl, little owl, and tawny owl – occasionally appear in a positive light, dedicated to Minerva, adopted as patron by workers of the night, and in the case of the barn owl even delivering positive signs at auspices when seen on the traditionally unlucky right-hand side.

Woodpecker

The *picus* enjoyed great prestige as an augural bird in Rome, and there is strong evidence to suggest that the superstitions surrounding it were primarily indigenous Italic and not Hellenic in origin. The woodpecker was often hailed as a weather prophet, with the green woodpecker retaining its status as a rain bird even today.[221] It is the green woodpecker (*Picus viridis*) that the Greeks chiefly noted, and though their woodpecker lore is paltry when compared to Rome's, it is worth cataloguing briefly. Antoninus Liberalis (c. 19) preserves the legend of a man called Keleos (Κελεός) who entered the cave of Zeus to steal honey and was transformed into a green woodpecker – a *keleos*. Green woodpeckers do, in fact, pay unwelcome visits to beehives in winter, searching for larvae, and are occasionally confused with the bee-eater, which makes this a rather mundane tale.[222] But the particular connection with Zeus warrants further investigation. In Aristophanes' *The Birds,* the characters speak of a time when birds, not gods, ruled the world, and say that Zeus is not in a hurry to return his sceptre to a woodpecker tapping an oak (Ar. *Av.* 480–5). Jane Ellen Harrison suggests that this refers to Zeus eclipsing an old woodpecker god of some kind, naming the legendary king of Eleusis, Keleos, as a possible suspect.[223] This Keleos, distinct from the aforementioned honey-thief, is the father of Demophon and Triptolemos. In return for treating her hospitably, Demeter tried to bestow immortality on Keleos' son Demophon, but was interrupted and so gave Triptolemos the first wheat instead (*Homeric Hymn to Demeter* 96–479). He went on to become the Greek demi-god of sowing in the Eleusinian mysteries. In Ovid's Latin version of the tale, Demeter tries to give immortality to Triptolemos himself, and when interrupted she tells his mother, 'That boy of yours will indeed be mortal, but he will be the first to plough and sow and reap a guerdon from the turned-up soil'.[224] The first ploughman was the son of Keleos – 'green woodpecker' – on which point Edward Armstrong elaborates, pointing out that when searching for ants a green woodpecker thrusts its bill into the earth in a fashion that recalls early wooden ploughs.[225] This connects the woodpecker to farming and to the weather in Greece, but the paucity of other woodpecker stories tells us most of the Roman tales must have sprung up largely independent of Greek influence.[226] Plutarch remarks on the Romans' curious reverence for the woodpecker and seems to describe the black woodpecker rather than the green:

> Why do the Latins revere the woodpecker and all strictly abstain from [eating] it? Is it because, as they tell the tale, Picus, transformed by his wife's magic drugs, became a woodpecker and in that form gives oracles and prophecies to those who consult him? (...) Or is it rather because they regard this bird as sacred to Mars, even as other birds to other gods? For it is a courageous and spirited bird and has a beak so strong that it can overturn oaks by pecking them until it has reached the inmost part of the tree.[227]

With his impressive size, sleek black body and a bright crown of red plumage on his head, the black woodpecker was, to the Romans, the bird of Mars, and its scientific name today pays homage to that – *Dryocopus martius*. Exactly how the woodpecker became the familiar of the god of war makes for a detailed study, but first and foremost his prodigious strength must be considered. Capable of drilling into trees, the birds are hardy and strong, and they make a sound like thunder when they peck. Their lifestyles are difficult to ignore, and the black woodpecker is the largest and most striking of the European varieties.[228]

In mythology, the woodpecker figures are in the tale of Rome's founding. The twin sons of Mars, Romulus, and Remus, were famously suckled by a she-wolf after they were cast aside by their mother's pitiless uncle, but the boys had another foster parent – a woodpecker who brought them morsels of food as if they were her own chicks. Ovid asks: 'Who knows not that the infants throve on the milk of a wild beast, and that a woodpecker often brought food to the abandoned babes?'[229] According to Plutarch, this is why both wolves and woodpeckers were venerated by the Romans. Both were closely associated with dense woods, and both still inhabit the same wooded areas today (Plut. *Vit. Rom.* 4.2, 7.6). This connection to trees is echoed elsewhere in Ovid. When pregnant with Romulus and Remus, Rhea Silvia dreamed that her uncle was trying to cut down two magnificent palm trees, when *Martia picus avis* – Mars' bird, the woodpecker – and a she-wolf came to their defence and saved the trees.[230]

The bird's association with Mars goes beyond Rome's founding. In Italy, the Picentes allegedly settled in Picenum ('Woodpecker Town') because Mars' woodpecker led them there.

> Next after those cities of the Ombrici that are between Ariminum and Ancona comes the Picentine country. The Picentini are originally from the Sabine country, a woodpecker having led the way for their progenitors; and

hence their name, for they call this bird 'picus' and consider it sacred to Mars.[231]

The woodpecker as a guide or wayfinder is attested elsewhere in European folklore, leading A.H. Krappe to posit that people navigating the woods, particularly hunters, took note of where woodpeckers had scored trees to avoid getting lost.[232]

Roman mythology also alludes to a legendary king called Picus. In the *Aeneid*, King Latinus entertains the Trojans in the sacred temple of Laurentian Picus. This temple, which also doubles as a palace, is noted for its beautiful grove, as well as for a carving of Picus that depicts the king clutching a Quirinal staff in his hand – that is, an augur's *lituus*. Virgil tells us this king was changed into a bird by Circe, thus becoming his own namesake – *picus,* the augural woodpecker (*Aen.* 7.169–189). In a different version, Ovid relates in detail how Circe transfigured Picus into a woodpecker for spurning her advances (*Met.* 14.320ff). Dionysius of Halicarnassus states King Picus was transformed into a woodpecker and went on to give oracles (*Ant. Rom.* 1.31), while Plutarch adds the detail that Picus is the son of Mars and that Romans were forbidden to harm woodpeckers.[233] For the Romans, Picus was a king, an augur, and a bird.

If Virgil states that Picus held the augural staff before Romulus even became the first augur, and we compare this to other legends of Mars' woodpecker giving prophecies, we may infer that the woodpecker enjoyed great prestige as an oracular bird amongst the early Italic peoples, and became assimilated into Roman augural lore. Pliny tells us that 'Woodpeckers themselves have been of the first importance among auguries in Latium from the time of the king who gave his name to this bird'.[234] If woodpeckers were oracular birds as well as the birds of Mars, might we infer that Mars was once an oracular divinity to the Latins? There is evidence that this was so, as we see from the following passage:

> Again, as one goes from Reate by the road towards the Listine district, there is Batia, thirty stades distant; then Tiora, called Matiene, at a distance of three hundred stades. In this city, they say there was a very ancient oracle of Mars, the nature of which was similar to that of the oracle which legend says once existed at Dodona; only there a pigeon was said to prophesy, sitting on a sacred oak, whereas among the Aborigines a heaven-sent bird, which they call *picus* and the Greeks *dryocopus*, appearing on a pillar of wood, did the same.[235]

Unfortunately, though these prophetic pigeons of Dodona and their oaks were well-known in antiquity, we do not know exactly how the birds delivered oracles, and so cannot use their example to work out what the oracular woodpecker did.[236] Some pictorial representations of the woodpeckers at Tiora Matiene still exist, which will help our interpretation. Carved gems held in the British Museum depict a warrior consulting a bird perched atop a pillar.[237] A sacrificial ram lies at his feet and a snake coils upwards around the pillar.[238] Harrison suggests that the snake is meant to signify that the pillar, like a tree, springs from the earth – it is chthonic.[239] This connection of earth and heaven through bird and snake, mediated by a pillar rooted in the earth and stretching to the sky, makes for a powerful image. The fact that a warrior is shown consulting the war god's bird is noteworthy. One wonders exactly how the birds delivered their portents, and whether they were exclusively martial in nature, but without more evidence we can only speculate.

To return to Rome, in Plautus a woodpecker is noted on a character's left – a lucky sign (*Aul.* 624). We are then told that the bird is tapping on an elm tree, which tells us that a woodpecker's provenance as well as the tree it alighted upon were observed by an auspicant. In this case, an elm was positive, but it is very likely that a woodpecker on an oak was the best sign. Varro mentions that the original terrestrial *templa* were bordered with trees (*Ling.* 7.9). This might simply indicate that they observed groves through which birds could fly, perch, sing, and, in the case of woodpeckers, peck.[240] The *templum* at Bantia made do with good local limestone for their *cippi*, but it is entirely possible that different varieties of trees were once cultivated around the *fines* to encourage birds – especially woodpeckers – to roost and peck. Wood and trees are of immense importance to the woodpecker and can change the interpretation of an augural sign. They are unique among the augural birds for the sound of their activities – their drumming on trees – to count as an augural sign.

Pliny describes the birds thus:

> There are also small birds with hooked claws, for instance the variety of woodpeckers called Birds of Mars that are important in taking auguries. In this class are the tree-hollowing woodpeckers that climb nearly straight upright in the manner of cats, but also the others that cling upside down, which know by the sound of the bark when they strike it that there is fodder underneath it. They are the only birds that rear their chicks in holes. There is a common belief that when wedges are driven into their holes by a shepherd the birds by applying a kind of grass make them slip out again. Trebius states that if you drive a nail or wedge with as much force as you like into a tree in which a woodpecker has a nest, when the bird perches on it it at once springs out again with a creak of the tree.[241]

Owls also nest in tree hollows, but this is either unknown or omitted here to emphasise the woodpecker's special connection with wood. The Romans observed the way these birds navigated the forest, foraged for food, and nested in tree hollows, extrapolating from this that they had a magical affinity with the trees that protected their nests from man's meddling. Isidorus repeats the idea that the bird has a kind of supernatural quality, for a nail or anything else pounded into a tree that a woodpecker calls home will immediately fall out (*Etym.* 12.7.47). Pliny's tale continues:

> When Aelius Tubero, City Praetor, was giving judgements from the bench in the forum, a woodpecker perched on his head so fearlessly that he was able to catch it in his hand. In reply to enquiry the seers declared that disaster was portended to the empire if the bird were released, but to the praetor if it were killed. Tubero however at once tore the bird in pieces; and not long afterwards he fulfilled the portent.[242]

The portentous significance of Mars' bird perching on a man's head is not too far removed from the imagery of the oracular woodpecker perching on a pillar at Tiora Matiene. As for the nature of the omen, since the woodpecker is a martial bird, it suits an omen of violent destruction. The taboo about harming woodpeckers, and the fact that Tubero invited destruction on his own head by killing the bird, also fits. This myth serves to exemplify Roman ideals of valour and self-sacrifice in the service of one's country. The woodpecker's escape meant the ruin of the empire; his death – and the praetor's death – its salvation. In the same way, soldiers and martial men were required to offer up their lives for the greater good, in the service of their country.

The woodpecker is often cited as a weather prophet in general superstition, even in modern times, foretelling rain through his cries. Some suggest this is because rain brings out the insects on which it feeds, but it is more likely that the way his hammering on trees sounds like thunder is to blame.[243] Plutarch remarks on the bird's ability to destroy oak trees, while Aelian states that it nests in oaks.[244] This connection to a tree sacred to Jupiter – the sky god who is ultimately responsible for the weather – and moreover, the bird's ability to *destroy* those trees, may also explain his esteem. Lightning could obliterate an ancient oak. So too could a determined woodpecker. For the famous pigeons of Dodona, just living among Zeus' oaks was enough. Another possibility is that it is derived from his status as Mars' bird, since Mars was once more significant as an agricultural deity.[245] We see echoes of this in the way Cato the Elder instructs the farmer to secure Mars' protection and blessing for his crops through sacrifice (Cato, *Agr.* 141). Mars' connection with agriculture is further strengthened by the fact that the Romans began their year in the month of March, so that Mars' month marked the beginning of the season of war as well as the return of spring and vegetation.[246] If Mars was once more important for securing good weather for crops, his bird might well have been understood as the messenger of rain.

The woodpecker was a tremendously important bird to the early Italic peoples, serving as a wayfinder, an augur, and even a king. Though Romans observed all woodpeckers, the black woodpecker was the most revered, whereas the Greeks noted the green more, which supports the notion that the woodpecker's augural functions were Italic and not Hellenic in origin.

Though his sacred status had diminished by the advent of the Empire, the bird was still subject to protective taboo and closely observed when auspices were taken. They gave signs by pecking, and these signs changed depending on which tree they clung to. The distant sound of drumming woodpeckers may be heard in Rome even today, if one listens for them carefully.

Conclusion

In this chapter we have considered some of the practical questions surrounding the taking of auspices *ex avibus*. The choice of birds as divine messengers relates in part to their ability to fly, connecting them with the realm of the augural deity Jupiter, and in part to the way certain avian observations can reveal information about weather and the passing of time. The actual observation of birds took place in a *templum* that was aligned to cardinal and solstitial points. Birds gave signs by moving through, and singing in, different parts of the sky, with the relative strength and auspiciousness of such signs determined by their relationship to the movement of the sun. We have considered how birds could affect machinations of state and how magistrates and augurs relied upon them to exercise power in their official capacities. This in turn had consequences for cultural practices and beliefs, as birds were sought to deliver signs to ordinary people when they took private auspices, meaning birds could have far-reaching effects on the workings of state while also influencing ordinary people through the supposed omens they delivered. Finally, we catalogued the most important wild augural birds that were noted at auspices. Each bird carried diverse meanings, with some considered lucky on the left and others on the right, some thought to give omens by their flight, others through their cries. Picking apart the various rules applied to each bird allows us to see that a certain logic governs Roman auspices that we can relate to modern understandings of natural bird behaviour. Having considered the place of wild birds in the *auspicia publica,* we can now investigate the use of chickens in military auspices, and how they eventually came to supplant the importance of wild birds.

Notes

1 Torelli (1995) 107; Vaahtera (2001) 96; Mynott (2009) 265–82.
2 Ar. *Av.* 716–22. Hor. *Carm.* 1.15.5 is just one example of this usage in Latin. See also: Harrison (1912) 98–100; Mynott (2009) 268.
3 Origen, *C. Cels.* 4.88. This passage argues that the Christian god cannot exist because it cannot account for the prophetic powers of birds. See: Kleczkowska (2015) 104.
4 Aesch. *PV* 483–91. On divination among the Greeks, see Johnston (2008) 8–9 and Johnston (2015). For Greek ornithomancy, see Collins (2002) and Kindt (2021) 200–2.
5 Porph. *Abst.* 3.5.3; Xen. *Mem.* 1.3.

6 Cic. *Leg.* 2.45. Birds were also sacrificed to stars and heavenly bodies: Macrob. *Sat.* 3.8.4.

7 Ov. *Fast.* 1.441–56. Translated by Frazer (1931) 32 with amendments: *intactae fueratis aves, solacia ruris, adsuetum silvis innocuumque genus, quae facitis nidos et plumis ova fovetis, et facili dulces editis ore modos; sed nihil ista iuvant, quia linguae crimen habetis, dique putant mentes vos aperire suas. (nec tamen hoc falsum: nam, dis ut proxima quaeque, nunc pinna veras, nunc datis ore notas.) tuta diu volucrum proles tum denique caesa est, iuveruntque deos indicis exta sui.*

8 Hor. *Carm.* 4.12.1–6. For the swallow's departure, see Plin. *HN* 18.311.

9 Hes. *Op.* 448–51; Aratus, *Phaen.* 1075ff. Compare with a poetic account of this phenomenon: Eur. *Hel.* 1478–90.

10 Dembeck (1965) 200. See also Zeuner (1963) 449.

11 Ael. *NA* 3.14. See also: Theophr. *Hist. pl.* 6.3.39; Aratus, *Phaen.* 1010ff.

12 Elkins (1988) 57.

13 Elkins (1988) 80.

14 Elkins (1988) 81.

15 Plin. *HN* 18.361–4; Elkins (1988) 103.

16 Verg. *G.* 1.415–23. Translated by Fairclough (1916) 129 with amendments: *haud equidem credo, quia sit diuinitus illis ingenium aut rerum fato prudentia maior; uerum ubi tempestas et caeli mobilis umor mutauere uias et Iuppiter uuidus Austris denset erant quae rara modo, et quae densa relaxat, uertuntur species animorum, et pectora motus nunc alios, alios dum nubila uentus agebat, concipiunt: hinc ille auium concentus in agris et laetae pecudes et ouantes gutture corui.* See also Lucr. 5.1078–86.

17 Frontin. *Str.* 1.2.7. Translated by Bennett (1925) 21: *Aemilius Paulus consul, bello Etrusco apud oppidum Vetuloniam demissurus exercitum in planitiem, contemplatus procul avium multitudinem citatiore volatu ex silva consurrexisse, intellexit aliquid illic insidiarum latere, quod et turbatae aves et plures simul evolaverant. Praemissis igitur exploratoribus comperit, decem milia Boiorum excipiendo ibi Romanorum agmini imminere, eaque alio quam exspectabatur latere missis legionibus circumfudit.* It was actually Q. Aemilius Papus, consul in 282 and 278 BCE, who waged war on the Etruscans. See also Frontin. *Str.* 1.2.8 for another example, and Polyaenus, *Strat.* 2.37.

18 de Grummond (2013) 550.

19 Vervaet (2015) 201.

20 See Vervaet (2014) for a full appraisal of the complexities of the *imperium auspiciumque.*

21 Gell. *NA* 13.15.4. See also Vervaet (2015).

22 Vaahtera (2001) 96.

23 Festus ex Paulo 316–17 L: *Quinque genera signorum observant augures publici: ex caelo, ex avibus, ex tripudiis, ex quadripedibus, ex diris*; see also 262M and 316 L.

24 These signs trumped all others. See: Serv. *Aen.* 2.693; Dion. Hal. *Ant. Rom.* 2.5.5; Cass. Dio 38.13.3–4.

25 Isid. *Etym.* 12.7.75. Significance of flight and cries are also attested in Augustine's *Doct. christ.* 2.24.37. One wonders if the emphasis on both seeing and hearing bird omens parallels hearing thunder and seeing lightning in the observation of the *signa ex caelo.*

26 Cic. *Div.* 1.120. Translated by Falconer (1923) 355: *Eademque efficit in avibus divina mens, ut tum huc, tum illuc volent alites, tum in hac, tum in illa parte se occultent, tum a dextra, tum a sinistra parte canant oscines.* See also Varro, *Ling.* 6.7.76.

27 Cic. *Leg.* 2.21; Serv. *Aen.* 6.190.

28 Struck (2014) 313.

29 Hornblower and Spawforth (2014) 214.
30 Gordon (1990) 63; see also Scheid (2016) 5–6, who lays out the Roman mindset on the link between gods and men.
31 Ov. *Fast.* 4.813–14. Translated by Frazer (1931) 249 with amendments: *nil opus est dixit certamine Romulus ullo; magna fides avium est: experiamur aves.*
32 Aur. Vict. *Or.* 23; Cass. Dio 16.46; Dion. Hal. *Ant. Rom.* 1.86; Livy, 1.7; Luc. *Phars.* 7.337; Ov. *Fast.* 4.817ff; Plut. *Vit. Rom.* 9; Plut. *Quaest. Rom.* 93 286a; Suet. *Aug.* 95.
33 Enn. *Ann.* 72–91. Translated by Goldberg (2018) 153 with amendments: *interea sol albus recessit in infera noctis. exin candida se radiis dedit icta foras lux et simul ex alto longe pulcherrima praepes laeua uolauit auis. simul aureus exoritur sol, cedunt de caelo ter quattuor corpora sancta auium, praepetibus sese pulchrisque locis dant. conspicit inde sibi data Romulus esse priora, auspicio regni stabilita scamna solumque.* Skutsch (1985) 77–96, Vahlen.
34 Rüpke (2016) 101–2.
35 Emphasis by the author. Livy 1.36.3–8. Translated by Foster (1919) 131: *Id quia inaugurato Romulus fecerat, negare Attus Navius, inclitus ea tempestate augur, neque mutari neque novum constitui, nisi aves addixissent, posse. Ex eo ira regi mota, eludensque artem, ut ferunt, 'Age dum,' inquit, 'divine tu, inaugura fierine possit, quod nunc ego mente concipio.' Cum ille augurio rem expertus profecto futuram dixisset, 'Atqui hoc animo agitavi,' inquit, 'te novacula cotem discissurum; cape haec et perage quod aves tuae fieri posse portendunt.' Tum illum haud cunctanter discidisse cotem ferunt (…) Auguriis certe sacerdotioque augurum tantus honos accessit ut nihil belli domique postea nisi auspicato gereretur, concilia populi, exercitus vocati, summa rerum, ubi aves non admisissent, dirimerentur.*
36 Livy 10.6. For a reconciliation of the five vs. four augurs, see Catalano (1960) 55, n. 120, 562–3.
37 Forsythe (2005) 139.
38 Hornblower and Spawforth (2012) 214; Plut. *Quaest. Rom.* 99 287e.
39 Kvium (2011) 68.
40 Gulick (1896) 238.
41 Linderski (1990a) 34–48; Berthelet (2015) 49.
42 Cic. *Div.* 1.16.28; Juv. *Sat.* 10.336; Livy 6.41.4; Plaut. *Cas.* 86; Suet. *Claud.* 26; Val. Max. 2.1. See also Clay (1993) 172. On Juno as the patroness of nuptial auspices, see Ziolkowski (1993) 217. The fact that *auspicia privata* was in decline may be symptomatic of a competitive market. More people may have chosen to consult astrologers or *haruspices* for advice instead. See Bendlin (2000) 135.
43 Wardle (2006) 1.
44 Catalano (1960) 42–5.
45 Valeton (1890) 253 reliably asserts that *signa ex caelo* were observed at night, when lightning was easily visible.
46 Plut. *Quaest. Rom.* 38 273e; see Bouché-Leclerq (1879–82) 4.278 for an analysis of this passage. The founding myth of auspices, featuring Romulus' twelve vultures, records that the birds were seen at dawn, contributing to the sign's auspiciousness.
47 Elkins (1988) 81.
48 Paschall (1936) 222.
49 Gell. *NA* 14.7.8; Scullard (1981) 27.
50 Laurence (1994) 105.
51 Scheid (2003) 112.
52 Taylor (2000) 12.
53 Paschall (1936) 219–20; Linderski (1986a) 2159.
54 Wissowa (1896) 2313–44; Linderski (1986a) 2150–1.

55 Cic. *Leg.* 2.31; Cic. *Phil.* 2.79–84.

56 Linderski (1986a) 2229.

57 Cic. *Phil.* 2.4; Cic. *Brut.* 1.1; Plut. *Vit. Cic.* 36.1.

58 Rasmussen (2003) 199–219 considers divination as a science, taking the position that 'rationality' is culturally relative and that to dismiss divination as 'irrational' is a pointless exercise. On auspices, see 149–69.

59 Beard (1986) 33–5.

60 Tucker (1976) 171.

61 Polyb. 6.56.6–12; Linderski (1984) 482.

62 Giovannini (1983) 60.

63 Cic. *Div.* 2.75; Morrison (1981) 88.

64 Szemler (1971) 109.

65 Cic. *Fam.* 6.6.7. Translated by Shackleton Bailey (2001) 351: *Non igitur ex alitis involatu nec e cantu sinistro oscinis, ut in nostra disciplina est, nec ex tripudiis sollistimis aut soniviis tibi auguror, sed habeo alia signa quae observem: quae etsi non sunt certiora illis, minus tamen habent vel obscuritatis vel erroris. Notantur autem mihi ad divinandum signa duplici quadam via, quarum alteram duco e Caesare ipso, alteram e temporum civilium natura atque ratione.* See also Cic. *Tusc.* 1.33.

66 Cic. *Leg.* 2.31; Cic. *Phil.* 2.82.

67 Cic. *Phil.* 2.84. Translated by Shackleton Bailey (2010) 137: *Quam diu tu voles, vitiosus consul Dolabella; rursus, cum voles, salvis auspiciis creatus.*

68 Cic. *Sen.* 11. Translated by Falconer (1923) 21: *... augurque cum esset, dicere ausus est optimis auspiciis ea geri quae rei publicae salute gererentur; quae contra rem publicam ferrentur, contra auspicia ferri.*

69 Cic. *Div.* 2.76–7. Translated by Falconer (1923) 457: *Externa enim auguria, quae sunt non tam artificiosa quam superstitiosa, videamus. Omnibus fere avibus utuntur, nos admodum paucis; alia illis sinistra sunt, alia nostris. Solebat ex me Deiotarus percontari nostri auguri disciplinam, ego ex illo sui. Di immortales! quantum differebat! ut quaedam essent etiam contraria. Atque ille eis semper utebatur, nos, nisi dum a populo auspicia accepta habemus, quam multum eis utimur? Bellicam rem administrari maiores nostri nisi auspicato noluerunt; quam multi anni sunt, cum bella a proconsulibus et a propraetoribus administrantur, qui auspicia non habent! Itaque nec amnis transeunt auspicato nec tripudio auspicantur. ubi ergo avium divinatio? quae, quoniam ab eis, qui auspicia nulla habent, bella administrantur, ad urbanas res retenta videtur, a bellicis esse sublata.*

70 Seneca, *QNat.* 2.32.5. Translated by Corcoran (1971) 153: *cur ergo aquilae hic honor datus est ut magnarum rerum faceret auspicia, aut coruo et paucissimis auibus, ceterarum sine praesagio uox est?*

71 Pliny, *HN* 10.37; McDonough (2003) 252.

72 Linderski (1990b) 68–70.

73 Rawson (1985) 27

74 Spivey (1997) 106–7.

75 Spivey (1997) 110–11

76 de Grummond (2013) 550.

77 Compare with the painting of the Vel Saties from the François Tomb in Vulci that shows a magisterial figure consulting a book as a male figure holds a bird in front of him. Dated to 340–320 BCE, it is held in Rome, Villa Albani. See: Grummond (2006) 41–2. Masseti (2022) provides an overview of birds in Etruscan art.

78 Sen. *QNat.* 2.32.2–4. Translated by Thomas H. Corcoran: *Hoc inter nos et Tuscos, quibus summa est fulgurum persequendorum scientia, interest: nos putamus, quia nubes collisae sunt, fulmina emitti; ipsi existimant nubes collidi ut fulmina emittantur; nam, cum omnia ad deum referant, in ea opirione sunt tamquam. non, quia*

facta sunt, significent, sed quia significatura sunt, fiant (…) Quomodo ergo significant, nisi deo mittuntur? Quomodo aues non in hoc motae ut nobis occurrerent dextrum auspicium sinistrumque fecerunt. Et illas, inquit, deus mouit. Nimis illum otiosum. et pusillae rei ministrum, facis, si aliis somnia, aliis exta disponit. Ista nihilominus diuina ope geruntur, si non a deo pennae auium reguntur nec pecudum, uiscera sub ipsa securi formantur. Alia ratione fatorum series explicatur indicia uenturi ubique praemittens, ex quibus quaedam nobis familiaria, quaedam ignota sunt. Quicquid fit, alicuius rei futurae signum est. Fortuita et sine ratione vaga divinationem non recipiunt; cuius rei ordo est, etiam praedictio est.

79   Varro, *Ling.* 7.8. Rüpke (2007) 71.

80   Varro in Gell. *NA* 14.7.7; Varro, *Ling.* 6.91, 7.6–13.

81   de Grummond (2013) 458–9. See also Rose (1974) 71; Macmullen (2011) 44. For a discussion of boundaries in Etruscan beliefs, see Edlund-Berry (2006) 116–31.

82   Scheid (2003) 113.

83   Valeton (1890) 240–3; Wardle (2006) 194.

84   Gell. *NA* 13.14.1–2; Varro, *Ling.* 5.143.

85   See Kindt (2021) 200 and the sources therein.

86   Festus, 339 M, 454 L; Varro, *Ling.* 7.7; Plin. *HN* 2.143.

87   Dion. Hal. *Ant. Rom.* 2.5.2–3; Livy 1.18.6; Plut. *Quaest. Rom.* 78 282e; Serv. *Aen.* 2.693.

88   See Torelli (1966) for the original reconstruction, heavily revised in Torelli (1969) when additional excavations were completed. The original essay is reprinted in Torelli (1995). Linderski (1986a) 2258ff incorporates Torelli's work in his masterful account of augural law to reconstruct fully the significance of the *templum.*

89   A simplified description may be found in Linderski (1986b) 339; see also Gottarelli (2013) 21.

90   Linderski (1986b) 339; Torelli (1995) 97.

91   Kvium (2011) 75.

92   Linderski (1986a) 2284.

93   Festus, 454 L: *A deorum sede cum in meridiem spectes, ad sinistram sunt partes mundi exorientes, ad dexteram occidentes. factum arbitror, ut sinistra meliora auspicia quam dextra esse existimentur.* Here, Festus is quoting a passage of Varro that is otherwise lost to us.

94   Aldrete (2004) 150.

95   Paulus ex Festo 67 L.

96   Torelli's reconstruction taken from Linderski (1986b) 339.

97   Linderski (1986a) 2284–5.

98   Festus 345 L: *remores aves in auspicio dicuntur, quae acturum aliquid remorari conpellunt.*

99   Paulus ex Festo, 15 L: *arcula … quae in auspiciis vetabat aliquid fieri.*

100   Dion. Hal. *Ant. Rom.* 2.5.2–4; Plin. *HN* 2.142–43; Serv. *Aen.* 2.693; Torelli (1995) 108–9.

101   Weinstock (1946); Pallottino (1956); Jannot (2005) 12–13.

102   Lulof and Van Kampen (2011) 122–3, 129.

103   Cornell (1995) 166. Cic. *Div.* 1.3. See also Livy 1.18 and Linderski (1986a).

104   Cornell (1995) 166–7.

105   Warden (2016) 171.

106   Thulin (1912) 2465–6; Jannot (2005) 29; Magli 2015.

107   Plin. *HN* 18.331–7; Gottarelli (2013) 36.

108   Ruggles (2015) 465–6 provides a simple definition of these orientations in astronomical terms. See also Belmonte 2015 for more on solar alignments.

109   Pernigotti (2019) conducts a survey on the orientation of Etruscan temples and concludes that it was determined by the movement of the sun.

110 Festus, 476 L. See also Kvium (2011) 66.
111 Thomsen (1961) 143.
112 Mignone (2016) 391.
113 Skutsch (1968) 65.
114 See Mignone (2016) for the full argument.
115 Plaut. *Asin.* 258–62. Translated by de Melo (2011) 169: *Impetritum, inauguratum est: quouis admittuntaues. Picus et cornix ab laeua, coruos, parra ab dextera consuadent: certum herclest uostram consequi sententiam. Sed quid hoc, quod picus ulmum tundit? haud temerariumst.*
116 Cic. *Div.* 1.7.12; Hor. *Carm.* 3.27.15–16.
117 Plaut. *Aulularia,* 624–5. Translated by de Melo (2011) 325: *non temere est quod coruos cantat mihi nunc ab laeua manu. Semul radebat pedibus terram et uoce crocibat sua.*
118 Serv. *Aen.* 3.374: *notum est esse apud augures auspiciorum gradus plures.*
119 Dion. Hal. *Ant. Rom.* 2.5.5; Cass. Dio 38.13.3–4; Serv. *Aen.* 2.693.
120 Serv. *Aen.* 3.374. Translation by the author: *ut puta, si parra vel picus auspicium dederit, et deinde contrarium aquila dederit, auspicium aquilae praevalet.*
121 See Linderski (2006) for an in-depth explanation of the factors affecting a sign's significance.
122 This is certainly true of ravens and crows. In weather divination, the number of times a raven or a crow croaked gave different significance to their appearance. See Theophr. *Hist. pl.* 6.4.16, 39, 52.
123 Cic. *Rep.* 2.51; Plut. *Vit. Rom.* 9.
124 Hes. *Theog.* 523; Aesch. *Ag.* 138; Aesch. *PV,* 1022. Greeks also considered vultures sapient birds, but not to the same extent as Romans: Apollod. *Bibl.* 1.9.12.
125 Plut. *Quaest. Rom.* 93 286a. Translated by Babbitt (1936) 139: "Διὰ τί γυψὶ χρῶνται μάλιστα πρὸς τοὺς οἰωνισμούς;" Πότερον ὅτι καὶ Ῥωμύλῳ δώδεκα γῦπες ἐφάνησαν ἐπὶ τῇ κτίσει τῆς Ῥώμης; ἢ ὅτι τῶν ὀρνίθων ἥκιστα συνεχὴς καὶ συνήθης οὗτος; οὐδὲ γὰρ νεοττιᾷ γυπὸς ἐντυχεῖν ῥᾳδίως ἔστιν, ἀλλὰ πόρρωθέν Βποθεν ἐξαπίνης καταίρουσι· διὸ καὶ σημειώδης ἡ ὄψις αὐτῶν ἐστιν.
126 Groot et al. (2010) 241–50.
127 Ruxton and Houston (2004).
128 Graves (1948) 192.
129 Buechley and Sekercioglu (2016).
130 Artem. *On.* 1.8; Rose (1974) 207.
131 Andreoni (2016) 5; Markandya et al. (2008).
132 Julius Obsequens 175: *Gravi pestilentia hominum boumque cadavera non sufficiente Libitina cum iacerent, vulturius non apparuit.*
133 Ov. *Tr.* 1.6.11–12; Mart. 6.6.
134 Arist. *Hist. an.* 563a; Ael. *NA* 2.46.
135 Spivey (1997) 67, fig. 50.
136 Basil, *Hexaemeron,* Homily 8.7. Translation by the author: *Quis praenuntiat vulturibus hominum mortem tum, cum sibi invicem inferunt bellum? Videas enim innumeros greges vulturum exercitus sequentes, et ex armorum apparatu exitum coniectantes.* See also: Horapollo 11.
137 Ingersoll (1923) 159–61.
138 Plin. *HN* 29.112, 29.123, 30.27, 30.30, 30.50, 30.110, 30.141, 30.130. See MacKinney (1942) 1264.
139 Rask (2014) 290.
140 Baillieul-LeSuer (2012) 52–3, 57.
141 Horapollo 1.11; Ael. *NA* 2.46; Plut. *Quaest. Rom.* 93 286a.
142 Durham (2013) 94; Serjeantsen (2009) 376.
143 Horapollo, 2.56; Diod. Sic. 1.87.9; Aesch. *Ag.* 49ff.

144 Cass. Dio 56.42. Mattingly (1967) 171 discusses this motif in iconography.
145 Toynbee (1973) 240.
146 Horn (1972) 77.
147 For an old depiction on a coin: Sutherland (1974) 21: Republic. *Obv., eagle, wings spread, holding thunderbolt. Rev., Pegasus prancing, wings spread;* ROMANOM. C. 300–275 BCE Rome. Cast bronze bar, 1389.64 gm., 167 × 99 mm.
148 Durham (2013) 89.
149 Livy 1.34.8–9; see also Cic. *Leg.* 1.4, where Cicero disparages those credulous enough to believe this story.
150 Suet. *Vesp.* 5.6; Tac. *Hist.* 2.50.5.
151 Eidinow (1993) 414.
152 Julius Obsequens 46. Translation by the author: *Decem legionum aquilae Gnaeo, Cn. Pompeii filio, quae fulmina tenebant visae dimittere et in sublime avolare. Ipse adulescens Pompeius victus et fugiens occisus.*
153 Holmes (2018) 183.
154 Durham (2013) 95.
155 Holmes (2018) 185–7.
156 Parker (1988) 201.
157 Holmes (2018) 187.
158 From the first half of the first century CE, held in the Romano-Germanic Museum, Köln, inv. 1939,0008.
159 Serjeantsen (2009) 185.
160 Durham (2013) 96.
161 Krauss (1930) 100.
162 Mynott (2009) 273.
163 Plin. *HN* 10.33. Translated by Rackham (1940) 313: *corvi in auspiciis soli videntur intellectum habere significationum suarum.*
164 Hor. *Sat.* 1.8.37–8. Translation by the author: *mentior at siquid, merdis caput inquiner albis corvorum.*
165 Skutch (1996) 120–1.
166 Krauss (1930) 104.
167 Plut. *Ti. Gracch.* 17.1 See also Julius Obsequens 133, which records ravens dropping pieces of roof tile at his feet.
168 Hor. *Epist.* 1.16.48; Petr. *Sat.* 58.
169 Armstrong (1958) 73. The Norse view of ravens makes for a useful comparison here. To make war was to 'feed and please the raven' (*hrafna seðja, hrafna gleðja*); see Hjelmquist 142. Norse poetry identifies ravens with war, blood and corpses; see Hjelmquist 143. And they too spoke of the ravens' love for human flesh - *Hrafnar skulu þér á hám galga slíta sjónir ór* – 'the ravens shall tear out your eyes in the high gallows'. See Stanza 45 in Fjölsvinnsmál, cited in Hjelmquist 144. Yet for all that, they loved the raven, and treasured it as a mascot and a familiar.
170 Julius Obsequens, 99. Translated by Schlesinger (1959) 261 with amendments: *Sex. Titius tribunus plebis de agris dividendis populo cum repugnantibus collegis pertinaciter legem ferret, corvi duo numero in alto volantes ita pugnaverunt supra contionem ut rostris unguibusque lacerarentur. Aruspices sacra Apollini litanda et de lege, quae ferebatur, supersedendum pronuntiarunt.*
171 Julius Obsequens, 88. Translated by Schlesinger (1959) with amendments: *Mithridati adversus socios bellum paranti prodigia apparuerunt. Stratopedo, ubi senatus haberi solet, corvi vulturem tundendo rostris occiderunt.*
172 Livy 7.26.1–10; Dion. Hal. *Ant. Rom.* 15.1.1–4; Gell. *NA* 9.11.1–10.
173 Oakley (1985) 394.
174 Ingersoll (1923) 161.

175 Sax (2003) 55. See Armstrong (1958) 83 for more on the 'Raven of Battle' and the Celtic raven goddesses.
176 Ennius, in Cic. *Div.* 1.107–8. Cic. *Div.* 1.106.
177 Serjeantsen and Morris (2011) 98–9.
178 Serjeantsen and Morris (2011) 100.
179 Johnson (1968) 76.
180 Hor. *Carm.* 3.27. Translated by Rudd (2004) 205: *Ego cui timebo providus auspex antequam stantis repetat paludes imbrium divina avis inminentum oscinem coruum prece suscitabo solis ab ortu.*
181 Theophr. *Hist. pl.* 6.16; Aratus, *Phaen.* 963–9.
182 Ael. *NA* 1.47–48. For another version of this legend, see: Hyg. *Poet. astr.* 40.
183 Ael. *NA* 2.51. Translated by Scholfield (1958) 151: ἦν δὲ ἄρα ὀρνίθων πολυκλαγγότατός τε καὶ πολυφωνότατος· μαθὼν γὰρ καὶ ἀνθρωπίνην προΐησι φωνήν. φθέγμα δὲ αὐτοῦ παίζοντος μὲν ἄλλο, σπουδάζοντος δὲ ἕτερον· εἰ δὲ ὑποκρίνοιτο τὰ ἐκ τῶν θεῶν, ἱερὸν ἐνταῦθα καὶ μαντικὸν φθέγγεται.
184 Wheye (2008) 99.
185 Wheye (2008) 13.
186 Plut. *Vit. Alex.* 27, 73; Paus. 10.15.5. Aesch. *Ag.* 1473 describes the murderess Clytemnestra as a raven.
187 Hor. *Carm.* 3.27.11; Ov. *Met.* 5.329. See also: Ael. *NA* 1.48.
188 Pollard (1977) 25. The hooded crow was the native in Greece and Egypt too.
189 Isid. *Etym.* 12.7.43. Ravens and crows are often observed eating eyes. Their relatively weak beaks are incapable of tearing flesh or breaking bone, so if they alight on a fresh carcass they will feed on the soft, exposed parts; namely, the eyes, the tongue, and around the anus. Only once other predators have torn the carcass apart can they reach other tidbits. See Foufopoulos and Litinas (2005) 17.
190 Hor. *Carm.* 3.17.13; 4.13.25. According to Hesiod, the crow lived for nine generations of men; see fr. 304.
191 Verg. *Ecl.* 9.14–16. Translated by Fairclough (1916) 85 with amendments: *Quod nisi me quacumque nouas incidere litis ante sinistra caua monuisset ab ilice cornix, nec tuos hic Moeris nec uiueret ipse Menalcas.*
192 Klingender (1971) 92; Ael. *NA* 3.9.
193 Foufopoulos and Litinas (2005) 15.
194 Suet. *Dom.* 23.2. Translated by Rolfe (1914b) 369 with amendments: *Ante paucos quam occideretur menses cornix in Capitolio elocuta est:* ἔσται πάντα καλῶς, *nec defuit qui ostentum sic interpretaretur: Nuper Tarpeio quae sedit culmine cornix 'Est bene' non potuit dicere, dixit: 'Erit'.*
195 Aesop 125; Pollard (1977) 127.
196 Harting (1871) 83.
197 Thompson (1936) 46.
198 Arnott (2007) 14.
199 *CIL* IV 9131. Translation by the author.
200 Jashemski (1993) 135. In both the inscription and the painting, the tawny owl rather than the little owl seems to be meant.
201 Pompeii IX.13.5; *CIL* IV 7963.
202 *CIL* IV 4118. Translation by the author: *Cresce(n)s fullonibus et ululae suae sal (utem) (…) ulula est.*
203 Gem no. 2456 in Walters (1926). Held in the British Museum, no. 1814,0704.1424.
204 Hor. *Carm.* 3.27.1–2. Translated by Rudd (2004) 205 with amendments: *impios parrae recinentis omen ducat.*
205 Rowland (1978) 115.
206 Morris (2009) 166; Fischer (2013) 263.
207 Porstner (2020).

208 Plin. *HN* 10.34–5. Translated by Rackham (1940) 595 with amendments: *Uncos ungues et nocturnae aves habent, ut noctuae, bubo, ululae. omnium horum hebetes interdiu oculi. bubo funebris et maxime abominatus publicis praecipue auspiciis deserta incolit nec tantum desolata sed dira etiam et inaccessa, noctis monstrum, nec cantu aliquo vocalis sed gemitu. itaque in urbibus aut omnino in luce visus dirum ostentum est; privatorum domibus insidentem plurium scio non fuisse feralem. volat numquam quo libuit, sed traversus aufertur. Capitolii cellam ipsam intravit Sexto Palpellio Histro L. Pedanio coss., propter quod nonis Martiis urbs lustrata est eo anno.*

209 See MacBain (1982) and Rasmussen (2003) for more on prodigies, and for full prodigy lists.

210 Julius Obsequens, 135. Translation by the author: *Bubonis vox primum in Capitolio dein circa urbem audita. Quae avis praemio posito ab aucupe capta combustaque; cinis eius in Tiberim dispersus.*

211 Julius Obsequens, 134. Translation by the author: *In Capitolio nocte avis gemitus similes hominis dedit.*

212 Julius Obsequens, 125, 122, 108, 104, 99, 98, 96, 92. See also Cass. Dio. 40.47.1–2.

213 Beard et al. (1998) 178. For a description of the purification, see Luc. *Phars.* 1.584–604.

214 See also Columella, *Rust.* 10.348 and Palladius 1.35.1 who claim that hanging owls can divert storms and hail.

215 Macrob. *Sat.* 2.4.26. Translated by Kaster (2011) 357 with amendments: *etiam militis non libertatem tantum sed et temeritatem tulit. in quadam villa inquietas noctes agebat, rumpente somnum eius crebro noctuae cantu. prendendam curavit noctuam miles aucupii peritus et spe ingentis praemii pertulit. laudato imperator mille nummos dari iussit. ille ausus est dicere, 'malo vivat,' avemque dimisit. quis non miratus est non offenso Caesare abisse militem contumacem?*

216 Varro, *Ling.* 5.9.76; Plin. *HN* 10.39.

217 Artem. *On.* 3.65. Translation by White (1975).

218 Plin. *HN* 10.36–7. Translated by Rackham (1940) 315 with amendments: *Inauspicata est et incendiaria avis, quam propter saepenumero lustratam urbem in annalibus invenimus, sicut L. Cassio C. Mario coss., quo anno et bubone viso lustratam esse. quae sit avis ea non reperitur nec traditur. quidam ita interpretantur, incendiariam esse quaecumque apparuerit carbonem ferens ex aris vel altaribus: alii spinturnicem eam vocant, sed haec ipsa quae esset inter aves qui se scire diceret non inveni. cliviam quoque avem ab antiquis nominatam animadverto ignorari—quidam clamatoriam dicunt, Labeo prohibitoriam; et apud Nigidium insuper appellatur avis quae aquilarum ova frangat. sunt praeterea conplura genera depicta in Etrusca disciplina saeculis non visa, quae nunc defecisse mirum est cum abundent etiam quae gula humana populatur.*

219 Arnott (2007) 222.

220 Tib. 1.5.52; Luc. *Phars.* 6.688–9; Stat. *Theb.* 3.508–9; see also Ov. *Am.* 1.12.19–20.

221 Flegg (2001) 156.

222 Krappe (1941) 243.

223 Harrison (1912).

224 Ov. *Fast.* 4.559–60. Translated by Frazer (1931) 229: *iste quidem mortalis erit, sed primus arabit et seret et culta praemia tollet humo.*

225 Armstrong (1958) 104.

226 See Krappe (1941) 241–57; Halliday (1922) 110–12; and Harrison (1912) 101–10 for further discussions on the woodpecker's alleged significance in Greece.

227 Plut. *Quaest. Rom.* 21 268f. Translated by Babbitt (1936) 37: "Διὰ τί τὸν δρυοκολάπτην οἱ Λατῖνοι σέβονται καὶ ἀπέχονται πάντες ἰσχυρῶς τοῦ ὄρνιθος;" Πότερον ὅτι τὸν Πῖκον λέγουσιν ὑπὸ φαρμάκων τῆς γυναικὸς μεταβαλεῖν τὴν φύσιν

καὶ γενόμενον δρυοκολάπτην ἀποφθέγγεσθαι λόγια καὶ χρησμῳδεῖν τοῖς ἐρωτῶσιν (…) Ἢ μᾶλλον, ὡς ἄλλον ἄλλου θεοῦ, καὶ τοῦτον Ἄρεος ἱερὸν νομίζουσι τὸν ὄρνιν; καὶ γὰρ εὐθαρσὴς 269καὶ γαῦρός ἐστι καὶ τὸ ῥύγχος οὕτως ἔχει κραταιόν, ὥστε δρῦς ἀνατρέπειν, ὅταν κόπτων πρὸς τὴν ἐντεριώνην ἐξίκηται.

228 Attenborough (1998) 88; Gorman (2017) 29–30.

229 Ov. *Fast.* 3.53–4. Translated by Frazer (1931) 125: *lacte quis infantes nescit crevisse ferino, et picum expositis saepe tulisse cibos?*

230 Ov. *Fast.* 3.2–40. Palms are not trees by modern botanical definition, but this is not a distinction the Romans would have made, so I call them trees here.

231 Strabo, *Geographica*, 5.4.2. Translated by Jones (1923) 303. Ἔστι δ᾽ ἡ Πικεντίνη μετὰ τὰς τῶν Ὀμβρικῶν πόλεις τὰς μεταξὺ Ἀριμίνου καὶ Ἀγκῶνος. ὥρμηνται δ᾽ ἐκ τῆς Σαβίνης οἱ Πικεντῖνοι, δρυοκολάπτου τὴν ὁδὸν ἡγησαμένου τοῖς ἀρχηγέταις, ἀφ᾽ οὗ καὶ τοὔνομα· πῖκον γὰρ τὸν ὄρνιν τοῦτον ὀνομάζουσι, καὶ νομίζουσιν Ἄρεως ἱερόν.

232 Krappe (1941) 250.

233 Plut. *Quaest. Rom.* 21 268f; Rose (1974) 40.

234 Plin. *HN* 10.41. Translated by Rackham (1940) 319: *ipsi principales Latio sunt in auguriis a rege qui nomen huic avi dedit.*

235 Dion. Hal. *Ant. Rom.* 1.14. Translated by Cary (1937) 47–8: Ἀπὸ δὲ Ῥεάτου πάλιν τοῖςτὴν ἐπὶ Λιστίνην ὁδὸν ἰοῦσι Βατία μὲν ἀπὸ τριάκοντα σταδίων, Τιώρα δὲ ἀπὸ τριακοσίων, ἡ καλουμένη Ματιήνη. ἐν ταύτῃ λέγεται χρηστήριον Ἄρεος γενέσθαι πάνυ ἀρχαῖον. ὁ δὲ τρόπος αὐτοῦ παραπλήσιος ἦν ὥς φασι τῷ παρὰ Δωδωναίοις μυθολογουμένῳ ποτὲ γενέσθαι· πλὴν ὅσον ἐκεῖ μὲν ἐπὶ δρυὸς ἱερᾶς πέλεια καθεζομένη θεσπιῳδεῖν ἐλέγετο, παρὰ δὲ τοῖς Ἀβοριγῖσι θεόπεμπτος ὄρνις, ὃν αὐτοὶ μὲν πῖκον, Ἕλληνες δὲ δρυοκολάπτην καλοῦσιν, ἐπὶ κίονος ξυλίνου φαινόμενος τὸ αὐτὸ ἔδρα.

236 Prop. 2.21.3 shows that their wisdom was proverbial: *sed tibi iam videor Dodona verior augur* – 'But now you seem to be a truer augur than that of Dodona'.

237 Italian, dated to the third or second centuries BCE, British Museum no. 1867,0507.373. A drawing from 1794 depicts the scene more clearly; see British Museum no. 2010,5006.1142.

238 The same image appears on a gem held by Corpus Christi College, Cambridge, pictured in Armstrong (1958) 102.

239 Harrison (1912) 101.

240 Palmer (1970) 91.

241 Plin. *HN* 10.40. Rackham (1940) 317: *Sunt et parvae aves uncorum unguium, ut pici Martio cognomine insignes et in auspicatu magni. quo in genere arborum cavatores scandentes in subrectum felium modo, illi vero et supini, percussi corticis sono pabulum subesse intellegunt. pullos in cavis educant avium soli. adactos cavernis eorum a pastore cuneos admota quadam ab iis herba elabi creditur vulgo. Trebius auctor est clavum cuneumve adactum quanta libeat vi arbori in qua nidum habeat statim exilire cum crepitu arboris cum insederit.*

242 Plin. *HN* 10.41. Translated by Rackham (1940) 319: *in capite praetoris urbani Aelii Tuberonis in foro iura pro tribunali reddentis sedit ita placide ut manu prehenderetur. respondere vates exitium imperio portendi si dimitteretur, at si exanimaretur praetori. ille autem protinus concerpsit, nec multo post implevit prodigium.*

243 Halliday (1922) 111.

244 Plut. *Quaest. Rom.* 21 268f; Ael. *NA* 1.45.

245 Armstrong (1958) 102.

246 Forsythe (2005) 127–8.

2   The Augural Chickens

Introduction

Impressive as vultures and eagles might be, no bird was more heavily observed in Roman auspices than the humble chicken. Wild birds were chiefly
consulted in urban public auspices within the *pomerium*, but beyond this
sacred boundary chickens reigned as the only birds from which one could
take the impetrative military auspices that were required to sanction military
movements, including going into battle.[1] This chapter examines the rite of
taking auspices from chickens – *auspicia ex tripudiis* – and attempts to
discover how and why chickens came to hold such prestige, with caged fowl
eventually eclipsing wild birds as the preferred messengers of Jove, especially
in the late Republic and early Empire.

Many eminent scholars have written about the various rites and lore
surrounding *auspicium* and augury, but thus far none have focused solely
on the simple question: why did they use chickens? Neglecting this question causes us to overlook some of the most basic practical considerations
when it comes to the task of taking auspices. Chickens are living,
breathing creatures that must be managed, cared for, corralled, and con-
jured up at the magistrate's command. More remarkably, they are distinct
in the catalogue of augural birds. Fowl are not only domestic as opposed
to wild, they are also an introduced species and not native to the Italian
peninsula, making them interlopers in the very ancient art of augury. The
use of chickens clearly represents a significant development in augural
lore, and focusing on the birds themselves can help us to untangle obscure
passages about augural rituals that survive to us. By investigating key texts
and unpacking the technical terminology, this chapter tracks how the
practice of divining with chickens evolved from the earliest days of the
Republic to the reign of Augustus. It considers the practicalities, limita-
tions, and advantages of using chickens in the military sphere and thoroughly interrogates the notion that these birds were used simply because
they were considered 'sacred'.

DOI: 10.4324/9781003247906-3

Origins of *auspicia ex tripudiis*

We have shown that the practice of divining by birds was an ancient one, employed by the Etruscans and believed by the Romans to date back to their own mythic founding. The use of chickens for the purpose is, however, less so. Archaeological evidence shows that chickens did not exist on the Italian peninsula until around the first half of the ninth century BCE, and not in any significant abundance until the third century BCE.[2] Auspication using *pulli* – the name given to the augural hens, which is often translated as 'sacred chickens' – similarly dates to the third century BCE.[3] Yet by the late Republic, we see Cicero lamenting that the *disciplina et ars* of augury had faded by his time (*Leg.* 2.33). According to him, despite the large body of rules governing augury and auspices, in practice many rules no longer applied, and interpreting signs was a straightforward affair.[4] An over-reliance on *auspicia ex tripudiis* was partly blamed for this, as the supposedly simplistic use of chickens meant more complicated rituals fell out of favour. As a result, 'through the indifference of the College, as Cato the Wise laments, many auguries and auspices have been entirely abandoned and lost'.[5] Reliance on chickens represented both a simplification and a decay in Cicero's eyes. But with magistrates needing a favourable answer – and quickly – in order to proceed with matters of state, it is perhaps unsurprising that this occurred. *Auspicia ex tripudiis* did not require extensive knowledge of avian symbolism or elaborate interpretation. As we shall see, to a large extent it did not even depend on chance. Chickens represented a solution for impatient or calculating magistrates, a way around complicated rules.

The name given to the procedure of taking auspices from chickens is *tripudium,* and it presents something of a puzzle. In this ritual, food was scattered to chickens and their feeding patterns determined whether auspices were favourable or not. Cicero tells us that the name derives from *terram pavire* ('to strike the ground') because they must eat so greedily that food falls from their beaks and hits the ground. In the next passage, he laments that the chickens were shut up in cages and starved to force them to eat, stating that if the birds were free to roam they might truly be called 'intepreters and satellites of Jove', but at present the whole thing is a farce.[6] The ancient augurs never operated this way, which he proves by citing an ancient augural ruling that *any* bird can make a *tripudium.*[7] This represents an opportunity to discover how chickens were adopted into the augural canon; if auspices *ex tripudiis* did not always refer to auspices taken from chickens, to what did it originally reference? If we take *tripudium* to mean 'things dropped by birds', we might compare it to the standard *topos* in Greek literature where a bird will drop an object or a living creature in front of a chosen individual as a sign of divine favour or ill-will.[8] Famously, in the *Iliad* (12.175–250), a sign sent directly from Zeus involved an eagle dropping a snake in front of the Trojans, an omen that Hector ignored to his own detriment. A more pertinent Roman example allegedly occurred during Caesar's rise to power when a kite dropped a sprig of laurel upon one of his companions in the Forum (Cass. Dio 41.39.2). The rarity and perceived significance of such an event would explain why the original auspices *ex tripudiis* were considered so favourable: a bird was literally casting down a sign from heaven. This sign must be considered an example of *auspicia oblativa,* sent by the gods unasked, which then became a form of *auspicia impetrativa* when chickens were employed, since one could easily corral chickens to see if food dropped from their beaks.[9] An investigation of the terminology around the ritual reveals how the transference was effected within the bounds of augural law. When chickens were used and they ate hungrily, a *tripudium sollistimum* was announced. *Sollistimus* is an old superlative of *sollus,* meaning 'unbroken, whole, complete'.[10] It only appears in connection to the auspices *ex tripudiis* and is the best result an auspicant could hope for. Chickens dropping food from their mouths induced a *tripudium sollistimum* on a technicality, and turned a rare and awe-inspiring event where a sign fell from heaven into a crumb falling from a starving hen's beak – remarkably easy to achieve, but still in substance a 'most favourable omen'. The simplicity and auspiciousness of this ritual easily explains why feeding caged chickens became so popular that the original meaning was all but forgotten. Essentially, feeding domestic chickens allowed the auspicant to observe a sign being dropped by a bird, a most favourable omen, with predictable certainty.

Some of the other terminology surrounding the ritual bears investigation. *Sonivius* is an adjective that means 'noisy', or 'rattling'.[11] It too is only used in conjunction with *tripudium,* and it signifies the rattling of food as it falls from the chickens' beaks to the ground, an excellent sign (Cic. *Fam.* 6.6.7). But surprisingly, *puls* was the name of the food fed to the chickens (Festus, *Gloss. Lat.* 245M). This translates as a thick porridge made of meal or pulse, perhaps a mixture of chickpeas, lentils, beans, and ground grains all boiled together. Allegedly it was a meal fit for primitive Romans before bread became the preferred subsistence food. It was also used at sacrifices, and we should note the symbolic weight of chickens being given food that had been cultivated for human consumption.[12] Wet porridge can hardly rattle as it hits the ground, so presumably the mixture was pressed into cakes and dried before it was given to the hens. A passage from Cicero intimates this: 'For with us magistrates make use of auspices, but they are "forced auspices," since the sacred chickens in eating the dough pellets (*offa*) thrown must let some fall from their beaks'.[13] The word *offa,* which can mean cake or a lump of food, confirms this idea that the chickens were given special cakes designed to crumble when pecked at. We may infer that someone – very likely the chicken-keeper, or *pullarius* – was in charge of preparing *puls* that would disintegrate into crumbs when the birds ate, guaranteeing a pleasing rattle and a *tripudium sollistimum.*

From this investigation it becomes obvious that a chicken makes a far more reliable messenger of the gods than a wild bird. An auspicant has no need to wait, possibly in vain, for a bird to appear in the sky if he can bring forth a cage full of hens. This is especially important for military auspices. John Scheid puzzles over the wisdom of committing one's fortunes to the whims of hungry chickens, especially when deciding whether to go into battle.[14] It seems likely, however, that the need to leave as little to chance as possible is precisely what led to chickens being used in the first place. It was imperative that the Romans went into battle *auspicato,* that is, after the commanders had taken auspices and received positive signs.[15] They could not fight without fulfilling this legal and religious prerogative. For the general wishing to receive a speedy response from the gods, it was impossible to conjure a wild bird in a desired fragment of sky, but chickens, transported along with the army, could be relied upon to sanction combat at a moment's notice. While one could auspicate either with chickens or by watching the sky (Cic. *Div.* 2.33), the evidence suggests that the latter was used inside the *pomerium,* while those in the field would use chickens, regardless of whether they were magistrates or promagistrates.[16] Wild birds do not seem to have been used in field manoeuvres except when our historians record oblative omens. From the third century BCE, if not earlier, a general's need to leave nothing to chance and to act quickly and decisively meant that chickens alone were permitted to give impetative military auspices. Pliny praises chickens as 'the auspices of all our victories won all over the world', telling us unambiguously that this was the case.[17] The sole use of hens in a military context supports the idea that they were favoured because they were more likely to give a positive and immediate answer. Having the gods on your side was a sensible military tactic, as well as a requirement.[18] Chickens made that happen.

Pullarii

Having established that chickens were introduced into augural law on a technicality as an easy way to induce 'most favourable auspices', it remains to ask how they were kept, cared for, and consulted. There was a job specifically dedicated to the management of augural hens, occupied by a *pullarius* – a chicken-keeper. These *pullarii* cared for hens and consulted them when the (pro-)magistrate commanded. For this reason, they deserve close examination. Cicero speaks disparagingly of chicken-keepers, disgruntled by the fact that magistrates typically employed a *pullarius* as their assistant when taking *auspicia ex tripudiis*. He complains that nowadays any old Quintus Fabius can assist with the auspices, whereas in the good old days that privilege was granted to an experienced augur (Cic. *Div.* 2.71–2). It seems to indicate a loss of prestige and control for men of Cicero's standing, and it also suggests that a magistrate could take auspices and get his favourable answer from the gods without the intervention or assistance of the Augural College at all. Since we know very little about the Roman civil service until the last fifty years of the Republic, *pullarii* are shrouded in mystery.[19] However, we can discern that they belonged to the privileged body of magistrates' assistants known as *apparitores*, and were part of the social class just below that of equestrian.[20] They had to be free, but not necessarily freeborn, and such a position meant that they were part of the 'working mechanism' of the Republic.[21] Like augurs, *pullarii* assisted magistrates in the name of the state.[22] A chicken-keeper was quite an attractive position, all things considered. A tomb for a *pullarius* from c. 100 CE was decorated with carvings of military insignia, including the chickens pecking in their cage, and recorded the following epitaph:

> To Marcus Pompeius Asper, son of Marcus, of the Aniensian voting tribe, centurion of the Fifteenth Legion Apollinaris, centurion of the Third Praetorian Cohort, primuspilus of the Third Legion Cyrenaica, camp prefect of the Twentieth Legion Victrix, Atimetus, freedman, chicken-keeper, made this for himself and for Marcus Pompeius Asper, son of Marcus, of the Collina voting tribe, his son, and Marcus Pompeius Asper, son of Marcus, of the Collina voting tribe, his younger son and for his wife Cincia Saturnina.[23]

Figure 2.1 Reproduction of the chickens in their cage, copied from the funerary relief of Marcus Pompeius Asper, c. 100 CE.

Source: Photo by iStock.com/Nastasic.

The chickens were naturally open to manipulation by the *pullarius*.[24] Cicero describes them as *inclusa in cavea et fame enecta* – 'enclosed in a cage and wracked with hunger' (Cic. *Div.* 2.73). The *pullarius*, subordinate to whichever magistrate he attended, was likely instructed to keep the birds hungry before auspices were taken. But a *pullarius* could induce a negative result too. Cicero records that Gaius Flaminius neglected the auspices in 217 BCE during the Second Punic War. The chickens refused to eat, and Flaminius spoke scornfully to his *pullarius:* "'Fine auspices indeed! For they counsel action when chickens' crops are empty and inaction when chickens' crops are filled'".[25] Such a statement implies that the birds had been deliberately stuffed with food prior to the ritual to ruin their appetites. Dissatisfied with this result, Flaminius marched into battle contrary to auspices, only to be defeated and slain by Hannibal at Lake Trasimene with a loss of 15,000 men (Livy 21.57, 63). If a *pullarius* was reasonably expected to control the appetite of his birds to ensure his magistrate received a favourable result, why did the chickens refuse to eat in this instance? The passage suggests there was some tension between this magistrate and his *pullarius,* and since a chicken's bulging crop betrays when it has eaten its fill, it would be easy for Flaminius to detect foul play. Why, then, would the *pullarius* sabotage Flaminius' auspices and attempt to stall battle?

The answer will come if we examine Flaminius' rocky relationship with the Senate. A maverick *novus homo*, Flaminius incurred the wrath of the other senators for his role as a popular leader, his controversial attempts at land reform, his push to give greater voting rights to the lower classes, and for the fact that he alone of his peers supported the *lex Claudia* aimed at restricting senatorial involvement in maritime trade (Cic. *Brut.* 57, 77). As consul for the first time in 223 BCE, the Senate (through the Augural College no doubt) had tried to make him abdicate on grounds that unfavourable omens had been reported. Inauspicious omens were often used as weapons in domestic politics, so even though Flaminius was in the middle of campaigning against the Gauls he was ordered to return to Rome at once.[26] In turn, Flaminius ignored (or failed to see) their missive, and instead entered into battle with the Gauls, winning a great victory. As a result, he ended up celebrating a public triumph by a vote of the People and *against* the wishes of the Senate.[27] To say the least, this was a precarious position to be in.

Livy recounts that towards the end of the consular year of 218, Flaminius as consul-elect requested that the consul Ti. Sempronius Longus make his troops ready in the camp at Ariminium on the Ides of March. His plan was to assume his second consulship there, having neither forgotten nor forgiven his former quarrels with the Senate. This was an incredibly controversial decision:

> For these reasons Flaminius felt the senators would keep him in the city by a phony interpretation of the auspices, using the delay imposed by the Latin Festival and anything else that could detain a consul; and so,

pretending he had a journey to make, he slipped away furtively to his province as a private citizen. When this became public knowledge, it generated fresh anger in the already hostile senators: Gaius Flaminius was now at war not merely with the senate but with the immortal gods, they said. When he was earlier elected consul without the sanction of the auspices, and the gods and men tried to call him back from the actual battlefield, he had not listened, they said. Now, guiltily aware of the disrespect he had shown them, he had avoided the Capitol and the formal pronouncement of his vows in order not to come to the temple of Jupiter Optimus Maximus on the day of his entry into office and in order not to see and deliberate with the senate, by which he was detested and which he and he alone detested. He wished to avoid giving notice of the Latin Festival, offering the customary sacrifice to Jupiter Latiaris on the Alban Mount, proceeding to the Capitol to make his vows after taking the auspices, and then setting off for his province dressed in his military cloak and accompanied by his lictors. Like a camp follower, he had set off without his decorations of office and without lictors, secretly, furtively, and no differently than if he had emigrated to become an exile. Of course, it better suited the majesty of his command to enter office at Ariminum rather than Rome, and to put on the *praetexta* in an inn rather than before his household gods![28]

Flaminius' decision to assume his consulship in his province and his failure to complete these compulsory rituals, including the vote of a *lex curiata de imperio,* meant that he did not have *imperium iustum* and therefore lacked the auspices *optima lege.*[29] Livy recounts that the Senate complained bitterly of Flaminius' actions, lamenting: 'They had elected two consuls, they said, but had just one; for what legal or what religious sanction did Flaminius have for his authority?'[30] Placed into context, it cannot be mere coincidence that the chickens withheld their consent when Flaminius tried to engage Hannibal in battle in 217 BCE. Under augural law he had no lawful *auspicium*, which raises the question of where the dissenting *pullarius'* loyalties lay. Of course, this may simply be another example of auspices and omens being used against Flaminius to discredit him, regardless of whether the omens actually occurred or not, but for the sake of argument we will take it at face value that the chickens truly were reported to have balked before battle.

The role of *pullarius* seems to have been born out of necessity. While augurs could be called upon to assist when magistrates were taking auspices, Linderski points out that we do not have any examples of augurs intervening in military auspices.[31] Valeton observes that unless augurs were serving in the army, they could not assist in the field.[32] This is where the *pullarius* comes in, taking the place of the augur and acting as assistant when the magistrate was in the field while also overseeing the care, transport, and feeding of the fowl. Access to the augural flocks placed a *pullarius* in a unique position of power, and it is not a stretch of the imagination to wonder if a *pullarius* could act as a mole for the Senate while a magistrate was in the field and far from their control. After Flaminius' wilful neglect of their rituals, the Senate could hardly suffer to see him march back to Rome victorious, celebrating another triumph against their will, so it may well be that his *pullarius* was following the directive of the Senate when his chickens fatefully refused their food (Cic. *Div.* 1.77). Yann Berthelet, after carefully investigating a number of cases, including that of Flaminius, shows that it is entirely plausible that *pullarii* manipulated the auspices according to the will of the Senate.[33] Similarly, Adalberto Giovannini found in his study that it was more important for a general to have the consent of the Senate than the consent of the gods when going into battle. He argues that favourable auspices were cultivated by the wily *pullarius,* who had control over his chickens' appetites, making auspices a manifestation of the Senate's will rather than heaven's. Therefore, a military leader who lost under favourable auspices – such as Lucius Aemilius Paulus in 216 BCE – was remembered well, and kept his good reputation. But a general who defied auspices and lost, such as Flaminius – well, that was plain insubordination, and it would see his reputation blackened, regardless of victory or defeat.[34] Even if he had won, he had still gone against the gods, and would surely have been hounded by the Senate all the same.

To return to Cicero's complaint about the power of *pullarii* in his own day, it may be that his chief grievance was that *pullarii* were not only watching chickens in the field, but also rendering assistance to auspices taken within city limits when an augur was available to help. A *pullarius* was a useful alternative to an augur when a magistrate was far from Rome, but there was no need for them to assist at urban auspices. This phenomenon may also indicate that the Senate no longer wielded uncontested influence over *pullarii* by Cicero's time, and that *pullarii* worked according to the interests of the individual magistrate instead. There is evidence that *pullarii* went further than merely assisting within the city limits, too. Dionysius of Halicarnassus states that taking auspices when assuming a magistracy was merely done for form's sake, and that 'bird-watchers' (ὀρνιθοσκόπων) employed by the state would announce there had been a left-hand lightning flash even when nothing had been sighted (Dion. Hal. *Ant. Rom.* 2.6.2). On the basis that augurs were not, to our knowledge, paid by the state, Françoise Van Haeperen posits that ὀρνιθοσκόπων refers to the *pullarii* rather than augurs.[35] If this is true, Cicero may be right that the *pullarii* were getting too big for their boots. *Spectio* was the exclusive reserve of magistrates; chicken-keepers had no right to watch the skies!

This investigation of the *pullarii* shows that these magistrates' assistants wielded a significant amount of influence through the simple fact that they controlled the birds that manifested the will of Jupiter. The practicalities of managing the chickens and their appetites allow us to observe how political struggles expressed themselves through the auspices *ex tripudiis.*

The use of chickens within the city limits is attested in multiple sources, showing how the ease of use caused them to spread beyond the military sphere, although it is sometimes difficult to determine if the auspices are being taken in a public or private setting. For example, it is said that Tiberius Gracchus took auspices on the day he was murdered:

> At break of day there came to the house the man who brought the birds with which auspices are taken, and threw food before them. But the birds would not come out of the cage, with the exception of one, though the keeper shook the cage right hard; and even the one that came out would not touch the food, but raised its left wing, stretched out its leg, and then ran back into the cage.[36]

Magistrates of the plebs did not possess *auspicium publicum,* so the anecdote would indicate that this is a private consultation.[37] This notion is backed up by the fact that the auspices were taken in his home, meaning that he must have been taking auspices pertaining to himself and not on behalf of the state.[38] A similar tale is told about the Ides of March. Out of the many omens surrounding Caesar's death, one involves him taking auspices in his own house at dawn. The chickens refused to eat, thus counselling him not to leave the house (Cass. Dio, 44.17.3). As we know, their advice went unheeded and Gracchus and Caesar were murdered the same day they took unfavourable auspices. Though these anecdotes seem to infer the use of chickens in private auspices, a passage in Pliny soundly confirms the increasing use of chickens in public, urban auspices:

> These are the birds that give the Most Favourable Omens; these birds daily control our officers of state, and shut or open to them their own homes; these send forward or hold back the Roman rods of office, and order or forbid battle formation, being the auspices of all our victories won all over the world; these hold supreme empire over the empire of the world.[39]

This passage implies that by the first century CE chickens were not only used in military auspices, but also in urban auspices, daily holding sway over magistrates in a legally binding and prohibitive fashion. In this climate it is little wonder that Cicero was so concerned about the decay of the College's influence when so much depended on the *pullarius'* control of his flock.

Negative Auspices

With chickens holding such enormous sway through their use in auspices, it is worth investigating cases where negative results were received from chickens and scheming *pullarii* cannot readily be blamed. The practicalities of using fowl reveal themselves in various ways. One famous example

Figure 2.2 'If they won't eat, let them drink!' A nineteenth-century depiction of
Claudius disregarding the auspices. Yonge (1882).

Source: iStock.com/Nastasic.

occurred in 249 BCE, where the consul P. Claudius Pulcher is said to have
lost almost his entire fleet in a naval defeat at Drepanum because he dis-
regarded the auspices.[40] In this oft-cited example, the chickens refused to eat
when called upon, so Pulcher threw them overboard, declaring, 'if they
won't eat, let them drink!' (Val. Max. 1.4.3). Since chickens are easily affected by motion sickness, the reason for their refusal may be attributed to
the fact that they were suffering from seasickness and too queasy to eat.

Another example is presented in the figure of C. Hostilius Mancinus,
consul in 137 BCE, who was beset by ominous prodigies, including the
following incident: 'When he was minded to offer sacrifice at Lanuvium, the
chickens on being let out from their coop fled into a nearby wood and could
not be found though most diligently searched for'.[41] This was said to augur
a lost battle, but assuming the *pullarius* had no part in the daring escape, it
cannot really be blamed on anything but poor camp security and the
chickens' natural inclination to make a bid for freedom at the first opportunity. A third example occurred in 293 BCE during a war with the
Samnites. The consul Papirius, stirred by the zeal of his soldiers for battle,
rose *tertia vigilia noctis* – at the third watch of night, between midnight and

three AM – and told his *pullarius* to take the auspices. In the 24-hour auspicial cycle that runs from one midnight to the next, this was the earliest one could take auspices for the coming day (Macrob. *Sat.* 1.3.7). But the birds, unsurprisingly, refused to eat at this absurd hour (Livy 10.40.1–14). In Pliny's words, '[Chickens] go to bed with the sun, and at the fourth camp-watch recall us to our business and our labour'.[42] Chickens rise with the sun. If disturbed before the fourth quarter of night, the pre-dawn hours, they will be unresponsive, and they will certainly be unwilling to eat. The best time for observing *signa ex avibus* was at dawn, and our other examples suggest that this was the ideal time to consult chickens, too.[43] Anyone who keeps chickens will know how eagerly they leave their coops in the morning, and how greedily they eat after a night's fasting. The story continues that the *pullarii* falsified the auspices and declared that the chickens had eaten hungrily, in spite of the fact that fowl simply cannot be roused at night. The consul went into battle, but upon learning of the falsification he averted the wrath of the gods by sending the guilty *pullarius* to the front line, where the man was killed. Papirius announced that the sin had been expiated and the gods were now with his army. Supposedly, this was confirmed by a well-timed caw from a raven. In this case, the *vitium* lay with the *pullarius* who had falsified the report, and once the guilty party paid the penalty it ensured the army was safe from heaven's wrath.[44] Interestingly, this anecdote indicates that it was not necessary for magistrates to observe the chickens themselves, which provided another safeguard against failure, since the magistrate could trust his *pullarius'* announcement, even if it did not reflect the truth.[45] One wonders whether the consul, eager for battle and triumphal honour, really was ignorant of the falsification, or whether the hapless *pullarius* merely provided a handy scapegoat. In any case, in these examples it is easy to identify an oversight that led to a negative verdict from the chickens. We can conclude that typically chickens could be relied upon to deliver the desired auspices, as long as magistrate and *pullarius* were of the same mind, and care was taken to control any extraneous variables.

What Kind of Chicken?

Further to the point that auspices *ex tripudiis* were used because they allowed reasonable control over the ritual outcome, we must consider what type of bird was employed. *Pulli* is the term used to designate chickens used in auspices, as opposed to the barnyard hen, *gallina,* and her chicken-keeper the *gallinarius*.[46] The word *pulli* is often translated as 'sacred chickens'.[47] This translation is misleading, for it conjures images of animals raised in temples and pampered or specially bred and raised for the purpose. While this is a possibility, the glaring lack of any evidence suggests otherwise, especially if we contrast it against the wealth of information we have about Rome's sacred geese.[48] Cicero's description of hapless creatures stuffed into cages and starved does not suggest that the animals were revered either. And if we examine Claudius Pulcher's actions, we find that his *vitium* lay not in drowning the chickens, or killing sacred animals, but in going *contra auspicia* and ignoring the will of Jupiter. In support of this, we should consider how the birds were consulted. In the same way that a raven seen when taking auspices *ex avibus* was not considered a sacred animal, the chickens were not considered sacred when the auspices *ex tripudiis* were conducted. Birds became significant at the moment the ritual was performed because they were ostensibly under the control of a deity, but were still perfectly ordinary birds. It would be a mistake to consider the augural chickens sacred when their true function was simply to act as vehicles through which divine will could manifest itself.[49]

Rather than calling the chickens 'sacred' as a way of explaining why they were used, let us examine the context in which chickens were first used in auspices. We know that fowl remains are sporadic in Italy until the third century BCE.[50] The impetus for their spread across Europe appears to have been related to cockfighting and their usefulness in entertainment, ritual, and sacrifice rather than for their value as meat producers. Eggs were more commonly consumed than the birds themselves, but the high ratios of cockerels to hens seen in Iron Age sites in Central Europe suggest that egg production was secondary to other factors.[51] Originally they were not 'food birds' as we think of them today. Consistent with the zooarchaeological record is Varro's assertion they were first kept on villas for use in ritual: 'The rearing of the last named, chickens, was the first to be attempted within the villa; for not only did Roman augurs raise chickens first for their auspices, but also the heads of families in the country'.[52] If their origin is as semi-exotic ritual animals bred and raised on Roman villas, this sheds some light on how they came to be the chief augural birds. It also provides an origin for the *pullarius*. Presumably he was originally the servant on whom the breeding and management of chickens was conferred.[53] It is not until the Imperial period that we see intensive and large-scale chicken farming for food and profit; before this time, the cultural attitude towards chickens would have centred around their usefulness when alive rather than their value when dead. The Roman view of chickens as ritual animals aligns with the opinions of other ancient cultures, including the Etruscans, but the Roman preference for hens in auspicial rites is unusual. In the first millennium BCE, whether in Iron Age Britain, Egypt, or the Levant, chickens appear usually or exclusively in the context of cockfighting.[54] The trend across the ancient world was to value the male bird for sacrifice and entertainment. Even in the Roman period the rooster was used in backyard divination, and admired for his pugnacity, sexual prowess, and prescience.[55] Roosters were popular victims of sacrifice, being especially fit for Aesculapius and the Bona Dea.[56] They were potent symbols in warfare and combat. Famously, the Gauls were fond of comparing themselves to victorious, strutting roosters.[57] Yet the rooster was specifically excluded from Roman auspices. Hens alone were used in this ritual. A simple explanation might be that it was to avoid any fighting or bloodshed between male birds, since auspices were bloodless rituals firmly distinguished from ritual sacrifice. Roosters together would fight one another and upset the proceedings, while a single rooster lording it amongst hens would doubtless also disrupt the ritual. We must also remember that the Romans considered cock-crow ominous. Given that roosters crow at all hours of the day and for many reasons, it would have been advisable for generals to avoid roosters so as not to encounter an oblative omen (Cic. *Div.* 2.56–7). With the evidence so far showing that chickens were valued for their ability to produce a predictable outcome, it is simplest to say that roosters and young cockerels could not be trusted to peck happily at grain when required. The high value placed on hens is a Roman peculiarity and likely results from utilitarian consideration. Pliny gives us a snapshot of how hens were viewed: 'Farmyard hens actually have a religious ritual: after laying an egg they begin to shiver and shake, and purify themselves by circling round, and make use of a straw as a ceremonial rod to cleanse themselves and the eggs'.[58] When we think of the augural chickens, we must lay aside our modern perception of chickens as stupid and useless except as a source of food. The Romans saw hens as clean animals that performed their own purification rituals. With their early status as exotic ritual birds and the way they could be easily manipulated, it is little wonder that the Romans preferred tame, clean, and reliable hens to act as the interpreters and satellites of Jove. In sum, when we translate the word *pulli,* we should avoid the temptation to say 'sacred chickens' and look at what the Romans are actually telling us. The word *pullus*, in most contexts, refers to the young of an animal, particularly the young of a bird, and may be translated as 'nestling' or 'chick'. More specifically, it refers to a young hen.[59] The *pulli* were just that – pullets, hens on the cusp of maturity. Older hens can become broody, even when isolated from roosters, and are more temperamental.[60] A broody hen, significantly, could refuse to leave her cage. Using young hens bypassed this problem. The sacred chickens were not sacred at all. They were simply young, eager hens that could be relied upon to leave the cage and eat. It is not until the Augustan period that we find any evidence of chickens specially bred for the purpose, and even they cannot be called sacred. We will consider these birds in the following sections.

From Republic to Empire

It is evident that by the late Republic, augural knowledge was in decline and many nobles had serious doubts about the validity of divination.[61] The taking of auspices had become farcical in many ways, yet *auspicium* was still a fundamental part of magisterial power and the structure of Republic, so the struggle for imperial power necessarily involved grappling over the right to watch birds. Cicero named auspices and the Senate as the foundations of the Republic (Cic. *Rep.* 2.1.17). He stressed that an augur's duty is to defend the Republic and said the sky itself is so divided so we can call on divine assistance for the sake of the Republic (Cic. *Leg.* 3.43). Therefore, the ascendant Augustus made it his business to take control of augury and auspices. In this way he could, under the guise of restoration, devise a new augural structure that would no longer benefit the Republic, but ensure its slow asphyxiation.[62] Birds, augury, and auspices allegedly founded the city of Rome. Under Augustus, they would found an Empire.

In an event already mentioned, the young Octavian is said to have observed twelve vultures when he took the auspices for his first consulship in 43 BCE.[63] This tall tale was spread as part of his propaganda, stressing the link between himself and Romulus, signalling he would found the City anew (Julius Obsequens 43). Augustus certainly made the most of this rehash of Romulus' auspices.[64] Famously, he restored the temple of Quirinus on the Quirinal Hill in his lifetime (Suet. *Aug.* 30.2). Quirinus had been identified with the deified Romulus since the late Republic. While the original decoration of the temple has not survived, a portion of a relief from the late first century CE depicts the temple pediment. This pediment shows two augurs watching the skies, overseen by gods, undoubtedly a representation of the augury of Romulus and Remus. Kenneth Scott describes the scene, making particular note of the great flight of birds directed towards the figure seated on the extreme left, whom he identifies as Romulus.[65] At the centre of the scene is a lattice door that probably alludes to an *auguraculum* entrance, the space in which augury was conducted.[66] Note that Romulus is on the extreme left – the west – looking east, with birds coming down from the east and the auspicant's left. In restoring this temple and placing this scene on the pediments, Augustus ensured visitors would be reminded of how the City was founded, and of the vultures that also appeared to himself, thus stressing that Romulus' rule and his own were sanctioned by birds. A year after his miracle with the vultures, like his adoptive father Julius Caesar before him, Octavian was appointed augur, and many coins depict Octavian with the *lituus* of the augural trade. The *lituus,* sometimes paired with a libation jug to symbolise auspices and sacrifice (the prerequisites for every political act), first appeared on coins under Sulla in 83 or 84 BCE, who was himself made an augur in 82 BCE.[67] The mint was under Octavian's influence from the late 40s onwards, but the *lituus* did not appear with his image until 27 BCE.[68] One suspects that the augural symbol was used to legitimise his office. The strong connection of the *lituus* to Romulus and the founding of the city suited him best at this time, once he had become sole triumvir.[69] He proudly lists his position as augur among his various other priesthoods in the *Res Gestae*.[70] He also used his position to revive an old augural tradition called the *augurium Salutis* – Augury of Safety. This required consuls coming into office to take the auspices before praying to Salus, and what is so deviously clever about this move is that the Augury of Safety could only be taken in times of peace.[71] This ancient augural ceremony was essentially revived to advertise the *pax Augusta.* And, of course, there is the most obvious exploitation of all – the name Octavian chose in 27 BCE, the name by which he is now known: Augustus.

For when some expressed the opinion that he ought to be called Romulus as a second founder of the city, Plancus carried the proposal that he should rather be named Augustus, on the ground that this was not merely a new title but a more honourable one, inasmuch as sacred places too, and those in which anything is consecrated by augural rites are called 'august' (*augusta*), from the increase (*auctus*) in dignity, or from the movements or feeding of the birds (*avium gestus gustusve*), as Ennius also shows when he writes: "After by augury august illustrious Rome had been founded."[72]

Augustus implied augury, august, and august augury.[73] It was a perfect name, and it reminds us that he owed a considerable part of his success to the divine approval of birds and the augural discipline.[74]

Part of Augustus' monopoly included making it so that battles were increasingly fought and won under his own auspices. No matter what his real contribution was, Augustus always claimed the kudos. In his own words: 'For successful operations on land and sea, conducted either by myself or by my lieutenants **under my auspices**, the senate on fifty-five occasions decreed that thanks should be rendered to the immortal gods'.[75] Never mind who the commanders were – all due credit went to the man who held the supreme auspices. Again, 'On my order and **under my auspices** two armies were led, at almost the same time, into Ethiopia and into Arabia which is called the "Happy", and very large forces of the enemy of both races were cut to pieces in battle and many towns were captured'.[76] Augustus could not be in two places at once, but his all-embracing auspices certainly could, as when, 'An army of Dacians which crossed to the south of that river was, **under my auspices**, defeated and crushed, and afterwards my own army was led across the Danube and compelled the tribes of the Dacians to submit to the orders of the Roman people'.[77] Over and over, we see this theme of battles being won and armies vanquished under Augustus' auspices, ensuring that the people knew that it was the divine favour bestowed upon *him* that vouchsafed these victories. It is an exceedingly clever tactic, and it changed the nature of *auspicium* forever. As Scheid lays out, Augustus gradually transformed the system of auspices following his victory at Actium, taking *de facto* possession of urban auspices, and finally coming to wield sole *imperium* and the *auspicia militaria*.[78] Possessing *auspicium* meant possessing the right to triumph, for victorious commanders only had the right to triumphal celebrations if they had their own *auspicium*.[79] As *summus imperator,* the highest authority in the land, all victories were won under Augustus' auspices whether he actually led the army into battle or not. Now wars were fought under the leadership of a general and the *auspicium* of the emperor.[80] M. Licinius Crassus, proconsul of Macedonia, famously demanded the honour of *spolia opima* that had been awarded to only two Romans since Romulus had killed an enemy chief with his own hand in single combat. Augustus rejected the claim on the grounds that Crassus was a proconsul, and therefore had not fought under his own auspices, and miraculously happened upon evidence to show that the last man to win the *spolia opima,* Cornelius Cossus, was a consul, and therefore fighting under his own auspices (Livy 4.20). This precedent thus barred Crassus from the honour he had won. As an old man, Augustus bestowed this privilege of universal supreme command and overarching auspices upon his successor Tiberius Caesar, thus securing the line of Julio-Claudian emperors.[81] All campaigns were conducted under imperial auspices. All military glory belonged to the Emperor now.[82] Tiberius wisely kept up the exploitation of *lituus* and augur symbolism too.[83]

The importance of auspices to securing power can be seen in what Augustus omits from the *Res Gestae.* The military losses and revolts that occurred throughout his reign are simply absent, since this would have called into question the legitimacy of his auspices. Nathan Rosenstein makes the observation that in the Late Republic, military losses rarely damaged one's political status or career.[84] Losses were simply diminished and excuses were found, but to ignore them completely as Augustus did is unusual. For example, Caesar records his loss at Gergovia and blames it on the conduct of his soldiers (Caes. *BGall.* 7.52). He writes of the defeat at Dyrrachium and manages to spin the story so that it shows him in a heroic light (Caes. *BCiv.* 3.69ff). One might expect Augustus to do the same, especially when many defeats can be blamed on others, such as on Varus at Teutoburg Forest. As for revolts, the best we get are oblique references to 'settling affairs', a mighty gloss over the serious revolts in Spain, Gaul, and Pannonia (Aug. *RG.* 30). Augustus' sole custodianship of auspices was a double-edged sword. It won him accolades for victories, but it also meant he was responsible for losses and revolts in which he had no active hand.[85]

When a general suffered backlash for a loss, it was attributed to a lack of piety or ritual fault in the taking of auspices that caused the gods to withdraw divine favour.[86] We need only think back to Claudius Pulcher drowning the augural hens, and how his defeat was blamed on this act of impiety.[87] Flaminius' absolute contempt of augural rituals meant that he did not wield the *imperium auspiciumque.*[88] It is suggested that Crassus lost against the Parthians because the commander had set himself against the divine (Dion. Hal. 2.6.4). Ovid warns Augustus to heed the auspices, advising him not to move his standards if the auspices forbid it, no matter how great his desire for a speedy victory (Ov. *Fast.* 6.763–64). Ovid later has Jupiter explain that Augustus will have the gods with him in his battles, and that all the people of the earth will be his to rule (Ov. *Met.* 15.821, 830–31). Only if the gods were on Rome's side could they be victorious.[89] To acknowledge revolts against his supposedly divinely sanctioned rule, or worse, to acknowledge military losses, was to admit that the gods were in some way displeased with him or that impiety or ritual fault threatened the validity of his auspices. In earlier times, the loss at Teutoburg might have been mentioned, excused, and blamed on Varus, but under the principate this would have called into question Augustus' divine favour and his all-encompassing *auspicium.*

The Empress' Hens

Having considered Augustus' meticulous exploitation of augury and auspices, we may now place his special use of chickens into context. While the
'sacred chickens' cannot truly be called sacred, towards the Empire there is
evidence that special augural chickens did exist. A key event in Augustan
history involves Empress Livia, an eagle, a white hen, and a sprig of laurel.
Let us compare two different accounts of this omen.

> Years before, as Livia was returning to her estate near Veii, immediately
> after her marriage with Augustus, an eagle which flew by dropped into her
> lap a white hen, holding in its beak a sprig of laurel, just as the eagle had
> carried it off. Livia resolved to rear the fowl and plant the sprig, whereupon
> such a great brood of chickens was hatched that to this day the villa is called
> The Henhouse, and such a grove of laurel sprang up that the Caesars
> gathered their laurels from it when they were going to celebrate triumphs.
> Moreover it was the habit of those who triumphed to plant other branches
> at once in that same place, and it was observed that just before the death of
> each of them the tree which he had planted withered. Now in Nero's last
> year the whole grove died from the root up, as well as all the hens.[90]

We might call this a *tripudium* according to the old definition, for it involves
a bird dropping something from the sky. The *villa ad gallinas,* which we shall
hereafter render as The Henhouse, is the subject of many archaeological
surveys, and is in fact where our most famous statue of Augustus comes
from, the Augustus of Prima Porta. Unfortunately, direct evidence of
chicken habitation has not been recovered, possibly due to the fact that
bombing in World War II destroyed a part of the site that had yet to be
excavated.[91] To return to our written sources:

> When Livia Drusilla, who afterwards received the name of Augusta on
> her marriage, had been betrothed to Caesar, while she was seated an eagle
> dropped into her lap from the sky a hen of remarkable whiteness, without
> hurting it; she regarded it with wonder, but undismayed, and there was a
> further miracle: it was holding in its beak a laurel branch bearing its
> berries. So the *haruspices* ordered that the bird and any chickens it
> produced should be preserved, and that the branch should be planted in
> the ground and guarded with religious care. This was done at the country
> mansion of the Caesars standing on the banks of the River Tiber about
> nine miles out on the Flaminian road; the house is consequently called
> The Henhouse, and the laurel grove so begun has thriven in a marvellous
> way. Afterwards the Emperor when going in a triumph held a laurel
> branch from the original tree in his hand and wore a wreath of its foliage
> on his head, and subsequently every one of the ruling Caesars did the
> same; and the custom was established of planting the branches which they

had held, and groves of laurels distinguished by their names still survive; and it was perhaps in consequence of this that the change was made in the laurels worn in triumphs.[92]

Juvenal also tells this story, as does Dio.[93] Like Suetonius, Dio adds that the deaths of these white chickens and the withering of the laurel grove in Nero's time heralded the downfall of the Julio-Claudian line (Cass. Dio 63.29.3). Since the laurel represented victory and chickens were used in the auspices of all military victories, this omen has a strong whiff of martial glory and triumphal celebration to it. But why was such an omen bestowed upon Livia and not Augustus himself? At this early stage, M.B. Flory argues, it must have been to gain support for their controversial marriage.[94] Livia and the young Octavian both divorced spouses in order to marry, and Livia was, at the time, pregnant with her former husband's child, her second son Drusus. On this point we may consider another story about Livia and chickens relating to her first son, the future emperor Tiberius:

> Moreover eggs can be hatched even by a human being. Julia Augusta in her early womanhood was with child with Tiberius Caesar by Nero, and being specially eager to a bear a baby of the male sex she employed the following method of prognostication used by girls—she cherished an egg in her bosom and when she had to lay it aside passed it to a nurse under the folds of their dresses, so that the warmth might not be interrupted; and it is said that her prognostication came true.[95]

By this, Pliny means she hatched out a rooster. Suetonius also tells this story, remarking that she hatched out a male chick with a splendid comb (Suet. *Tib.* 14). If we conflate the two omens, we see that in the early days Livia desired to be associated with the hen's fertility. The omen of the white hen appearing to her allows it to function as a positive marriage portent, indicating the favour of the gods and the hope that, like the fertile hen, she would bear a great brood of children to Augustus. This, of course, did not eventuate.

Livia aside, the whiteness of the hen demands further explanation. The gods below received dark red or black victims, while the gods above were given white sacrificial animals. Aesculapius traditionally received white cockerels.[96] Were white chickens perhaps special in some way? Our agricultural authors did not think so. According to Columella, there were two major kinds of farmyard hens, a red variety and a white variety. Red chickens, a hardy Italian breed, were prolific layers and excellent mothers. White chickens, likely a predecessor of the Leghorn breed, were apparently not as fertile, and their conspicuous colour made them easy prey for raptors. Due to this, they were not as popular among farmers (Columella, *Rust.* 8.2.7). Yet much is made of this bird's remarkable whiteness. It is tempting to attribute its colour to some ritual significance, but hens (unlike roosters) were generally not associated with particular gods, regardless of their colour. Because this omen is attached to triumph, it is more probable that the white colour served to recall the gaudy white horses pulling Julius Caesar's chariot in his triumph, and the white horses Augustus subsequently used at his triumphs.[97] We are told that at his spectacular triumphs in August of 29 BCE, which advertised him as the master of the Roman world, he carried a laurel branch plucked from a tree that was bestowed upon his family by heaven. It is not a stretch of the imagination to wonder if Livia's brood of conspicuous white hens was also used in the auspices that sanctioned these victorious battles. Though our written sources are silent on this point, if we examine the evidence we can make some tenuous conclusions.

Iconographic depictions of auspices *ex tripudiis* are rare. The earliest comes from the Republican *aes signatum,* c. 260 BCE, which we have already explored. It is not until Augustus' time that we begin to see more depictions. The most famous comes from the altar to the *Lares Augusti*, now in the Galleria degli Uffizi in Florence. The inscription states it is from the Vicus Sandalarius in Rome, 2 BCE. This altar features four characters: two men, one woman, and one hungry hen. The figure in the middle is undoubtedly Augustus, veiled and holding a *lituus* in the role of augur. The hen pecks at his feet. On his left is the second man, probably Gaius Caesar, and on his right the woman, who is

Figure 2.3 Altar dedicated to the Lares Augusti by the Vicomagistri of the Vicus Sandalarius. 2 BCE. Replica, c. 1900, of the original held in Florence, Uffizi Museum, inv. 972.

Source: Photo by DEA/A. DAGLI ORTI/De Agostini via Getty Images.

sometimes identified as Livia in the role of priestess.[98] This possible family involvement with taking auspices from hens is striking when we consider that heaven blessed the *gens Iulia* with the gift of a white hen.

The most persuasive interpretation is that this depicts Gaius Caesar taking auspices before his departure on a military campaign to the East.[99] Since the scene is inconsistent with what we know of how the ritual of *tripudium* was performed, however, it is best to view it as a symbolic pastiche. Augury, represented by Augustus, and sacrifice, represented by the female figure, were the two pillars upon which Gaius' success rested. Livia may not be present in this piece after all, but rather a priestess of the Magna Mater, a goddess to whom it would be most appropriate to pray for success in the East.[100] Even if Livia is not present, this does not take away from the notion that Augustus would want to be seen with white chickens to make his control over auspices more meaningful. Juvenal gives us a clue in one of his satires, demanding to know why someone believes they deserve special treatment: 'What? Are you the son of a white hen, and we the common pullets hatched from cursed eggs?'.[101] If the white hen was not favoured as a barnyard breed, then its greater felicitousness must surely come from its status as a bird favoured in auspices. Another depiction of the Augustan chickens comes to us in a small gemstone. Now held at Cologne University, it is dated to between 37 and 31 BCE, which makes it especially significant as it closely coincides with the advent of the omen. Flory posits that it was a prototype from which copies were made and distributed to others in Octavian's circle. It shows a tripod around which a snake rises, while two hens peck at the base. A *lituus* and *simpuvium* fill out the space.[102] In a study on the gem, Erika Zwierlein-Diehl interprets the hens as symbolic of Octavian's military success in the battle of Actium, making a dating of 31 BCE most likely.[103] It celebrates victories won under his auspices – and possibly, taken from his chickens. The Henhouse was nine miles distant from Rome, but according to Sextus Aurelius Victor there was a place in the City where white birds were kept for religious purposes (Aur. Vict. *Caes.* 5.17). On the western portion of the Viminal Hill there also existed a street or district called *gallinae albae*.[104] This link is made more remarkable by an inscription discovered in 1909 which tells us the villa *ad gallinas* was *also* referred to as *gallinae albae*.[105] On the basis of this evidence, Flory speculates that these special white birds were brought from The Henhouse and kept in The District of White Chickens on the Viminal Hill so they could be used easily in augural and auspicial rites.[106] Using white chickens in urban and military auspices that were ostensibly bred by the Empress from a hen dropped into her lap by an eagle would have been the perfect way for Augustus to clinch ideological control over this ancient art. Despite the dwindling of lore, augury and auspices continued to be of great importance well into the Empire and were fundamental to Imperial control. Their importance may be seen in the fact that a list of auguries from the years 1 and 17 CE survives on stone.[107] Augurs, responsible for maintaining the *pomerium* and overseeing the auspices, continued to be appointed until the end of the fourth century CE.[108] Since we have already established the use of chickens in public auspices, the breeding of special white hens with a link to the Imperial family for this very purpose makes sense.

When considering the Roman use of chickens, it is worth comparing their system to other forms of divination. Roman divination, like Mesopotamian and Egyptian, is noted as being particularly systematised. This quality is particularly valued in structured, hierarchical societies where divination can have a significant political impact. In such cases, Lindsay Driediger-Murphy argues, divination cannot be left to arbitrary or mystic interpretation, but must be controlled through consistent and logical rules with fairly pre-dictable outcomes.[109] The augural hens represent the most Roman and most utilitarian contribution to the field of divination, hijacking rules and tech-nicalities surrounding avian auspices to create a ritual that could reliably produce divine sanction.

Conclusion

This chapter has examined the ritual of *auspicia ex tripudiis* from a practical point of view, interrogating all the vagaries that come from utilising live chickens. An investigation of the chicken's introduction and spread in Italy allows us to conclude that these birds were originally ritual animals, and that the Romans' curious preference for hens over roosters may be attributed to their wishing to control variables that might lead to undesirable outcomes for the auspicant, with young tame hens serving as the most pliable, and therefore reliable, messengers of Jupiter. Their early use in military auspices demon-strates a desire to achieve divine sanction for battle or movement in the field without having to wait for a sign from a wild bird, which might not come, or which might produce a negative sign, thus foiling a general's well-laid plans. The sign given by the hens involved food dropping from their beaks, which induced a *tripudium* on a technicality, since any bird could make a sign by dropping something in front of an auspicant, allowing chickens to join the small and exclusive club of augural birds listed in Chapter 1. Generally, hens could be relied upon to eat the crumbly cakes offered to them, except in some recorded instances where they were hampered by extraneous factors. For example, they enter a sort of hypnosis at night and will not eat, and at sea may lose their appetites from motion sickness. While at first glance it might seem bizarre that Roman generals consulted chickens in the field, a quirk to be blamed on the quaint belief that these animals were sacred in some way, in actuality this was the most expedient way of securing a favourable answer that satisfied all the legal and religious prerogatives.

The need to transport live fowl with the army raises the question of who was responsible for caring for the birds, and the shadowy figure of the *pullarius* rises to provide answers. Their ability to manipulate the animals in their care has the potential to shed light on political struggles between the

Senate and individual magistrates, or between magistrates. The power of these *pullarii* appears to have increased with the use of chickens in urban auspices as well as military, with the ease of consultation and simplicity of ritual causing the meteoric rise of chickens to supreme augural birds, satellites of Jupiter himself. Their pre-eminence is further attested by their use in Augustan propaganda, as it seems likely that Augustus not only used augural hens as symbols to assert his claim to over-arching auspices, but even cultivated a distinctive flock of white chickens that could be sent from the Villa of Livia into the City. In light of this, Pliny's praise of chickens as ruling over the Empire itself (*imperio imperant*) scarcely seems overblown. From small beginnings, the augural hens became fundamental to the social, political, and religious life of Rome, ruling the roost in the field and in the City as magistrates conducted their daily business.

Notes

1 Brennan (2014) 25.
2 Corbino et al. (2022); de Grossi Mazzorin (2005) 352.
3 Foti (2011).
4 Rüpke (2014) 215.
5 Cic. *Div.* 1.28. Translated by Falconer (1923) 255: *Itaque multa auguria, multa auspicia, quod Cato ille sapiens queritur, neglegentia collegi amissa plane et deserta sunt.*
6 *Div.* 2.73: *interpres et satelles Iovis.*
7 *Div.* 2.73. See: Valeton (1890) 211–15; Wissowa (1912) 532; Foti (2011) 90–1.
8 Reeder (1997) 97.
9 Linderski (1986a) 2156.
10 P.G.W. Glare (ed), *OLD²* (2012), 'sollus'.
11 P.G.W. Glare (ed), *OLD²* (2012), 'soniuius'.
12 Varro, *Ling.* 5.105; Val. Max. 2.5.5; Macrob. *Sat.* 1.12.33.
13 Cic. *Div.* 1.27. Translated by Falconer (1923) 255. *Nam nostri quidem magistratus auspiciis utuntur coactis; necesse est enim offa obiecta cadere frustum ex pulli ore cum pascitur.*
14 Scheid (2012) 15. For an appraisal of how the use of divination in the military sphere can be considered 'practical' or even 'rational', see Anderson (2018) and (2022).
15 Vaahtera (2001) 27.
16 Vervaet (2014) 283.
17 Plin. *HN* 10.49. Translated by Rackham (1940) 323: *victoriarum omnium toto orbe partarum auspices.*
18 Holladay and Goodman (1986) 152.
19 Jones (1949) 38.
20 Kunkel (1995) 127.
21 Purcell (1983) 127.
22 Van Haeperen (2012) 88.
23 *CIL* XIV 2523. The original is housed in Rome, Palazzo Albani del Drago. *M (arco) Pompeio M(arci) f(ilio) Ani(ensi) Aspro | (centurioni) leg(ionis) XV Apollinar(is) (centurioni) coh(ortis) III Pr(aetoriae) | primop(ilo) leg(ionis) III Cyren(aicae) praef(ecto) castr(orum) | leg(ionis) XX Victr(icis) | Atimetus lib (ertus) pullarius | fecit et sibi et | M(arco) Pompeio M(arci) f(ilio) | Col(lina)*

Aspro | filio suo et | M(arco) Pompeio M(arci) f(ilio) Col(lina) | Aspro filio minori | et Cinciae | Saturninae | uxori suae. See Koortbojian (2013) 74–6.

24 Rüpke (2014) 215.
25 Cic. *Div.* 1.77. Translated by Falconer (1923) 309: *Praeclara vero auspicia, si esurientibus pullis res geri poterit, saturis nihil geretur.*
26 Vishnia (2012) 35.
27 Polyb. 2.22–23; Plut. *Vit. Marc.* 4; Zonar. 8.20. See also: Petrucci (1996) 88; Pittenger (2008) 40.
28 Livy 21.63. Translated by Yardley (2019) 187: *Ob haec ratus auspiciis emen-tiendis Latinarumque feriarum mora et consularibus aliis impedimentis retenturos se in urbe, simulato itinere privatus clam in provinciam abiit. Ea res ubi palam facta est, novam insuper iram infestis iam ante patribus movit: non cum senatu modo sed iam cum dis immortalibus C. Flaminium bellum gerere. Consulem ante inauspicato factum revocantibus ex ipsa acie dis atque hominibus non paruisse; nunc conscientia spretorum et Capitolium et sollemnem votorum nuncupationem fugisse, ne die initi magistratus Iovis optimi maximi templum adiret, ne senatum invisus ipse et sibi uni invisum videret consuleretque, ne Latinas indiceret Iovique Latiari sollemne sacrum in monte faceret, ne auspicato profectus in Capitolium ad vota nuncupanda, paludatus inde cum lictoribus in provinciam iret. Lixae modo sine insignibus, sine lictoribus profectum clam, furtim, haud aliter quam si exsilii causa solum vertisset. Magis pro maiestate videlicet imperii Arimini quam Romae magistratum initurum et in deversorio hospitali quam apud penates suos prae-textam sumpturum.*
29 Vervaet (2014) 320. See Rafferty (2019) for more on these rituals.
30 Livy, 22.1. Translated by Yardley (2019) 193–5: *duos se consules creasse, unum habere; quod enim illi iustum imperium, quod auspicium esse?*
31 Linderski (1986a) 2198.
32 Valeton (1890) 452–5. In the early days, however, an augur may have joined a consul or a praetor.
33 Berthelet (2015) 232.
34 Giovannini (1998) 109.1921
35 Van Haeperen (2012) 88.
36 Plut. *Vit. Ti. Gracch,* 17.1. Translated by Perrin (1921) 185: Ἅμα δ' ἡμέρα παρῆν ὁ τὰς ὄρνιθας αἷς διαμαντεύονται κομίζων, καὶ προέβαλλε τροφὴν αὐταῖς. αἱ δ' οὐ προῆλθον, εἰ μὴ μία μόνη, διασείσαντος εὖ μάλα τοῦ ἀνθρώπου τὸ ἀγγεῖον· οὐδὲ αὕτη δὲ τῆς τροφῆς ἔθιγεν, ἀλλ' ἐπάρασα τὴν ἀριστερὰν πτέρυγα καὶ παρατείνασα τὸ σκέλος πάλιν εἰς τὸ ἀγγεῖον κατέφυγε.
37 This fact is disputed, but see: Rawson (1974) 196; Linderski (1990) 34–48; Lanfranchi (2015) 215.
38 This is in spite of the fact that a tribune's home had to be open to the public at all times.
39 Plin. *HN* 10.49. Translated by Rackham (1940) 323: *Horum sunt tripudia sol-listima, hi magistratus nostros cotidie regunt domusque ipsis suas claudunt aut reserant, hi fasces Romanos inpellunt aut retinent, iubent acies aut prohibent, victoriarum omnium toto orbe partarum auspices; hi maxime terrarum imperio imperant.*
40 Cic. *Nat. D.* 2.7; Cic. *Div.* 1.29, 2.20; Livy, *Per.* 19.4; Val. Max. 1.4.3; Suet. *Tib.* 2.2.
41 Val. Max. 1.6.7. Translated by Shackleton Bailey (2000) 71: *cum Lavinii sacri-ficium facere vellet, pulli cavea emissi in proximam silvam fugerunt summaque diligentia quaesiti reperiri nequiverunt.* See also Julius Obsequens 137.
42 Pliny, *HN* 10.24. Translated by Rackham (1940) 321: *Cum sole eunt cubitum, quartaque castrensi vigilia ad curas laboremque revocant.*

43 Enn. apud. Cic. *Div.* 1.108; Plut. *Quaest. Rom.* 38 273e.
44 There is a comparable case in (176 BCE) where the Romans won a battle in spite of vitiated auspices. The victory was explained because the guilty general, Quintus Petilius had died in the fighting; since the fault lay with him, the gods punished him alone and spared the army. See Livy 41.18 and Val. Max. 1.5.9.
45 Kunkel (1985) 31.
46 We will discuss the *gallinarius* and barnyard fowl management in Chapter Three.
47 Almost invariably. For only a few examples, see: Scott (1925) 103; Lattimore (1934) 442; Dembeck (1965) 199; Tucker (1976) 174; Purcell (1983) 129; Linderski (1986a); Aldrete (2004) 144; Hornblower and Spawforth (2012) 223; de Grummond (2013) 550; Berthelet (2015) 49; Vervaet (2015) 211.
48 Petron. *Sat.* 136; Plin. *HN* 10.51; Plut. *Quaest. Rom.* 98 287c; Plut. *De fort. Rom.* 12.325C.
49 Greek divination regarded animals and birds in the same way: see Kindt (2021) 197.
50 de Grossi Mazzorin (2005) 352.
51 Sykes (2012) 162.
52 Varro, *Rust.* 3.3.5. Translated by Boyd Ash (1934) 441: *Earum rerum cultura instituta prima ea quae in villa habetur; non enim solum augures Romani ad auspicia primum pararunt pullos, sed etiam patres familiae rure.*
53 Kunkel (1985) 31.
54 Sykes (2012) 162.
55 Sheasley (2008) 45.
56 Zeuner (1963) 448; Ov. *Fast.* 1.455–6; Plin. *HN.* 10.156; Artem. *On.* 5.9. Chickens were also sacrificed to gods of magic (Tibullus 1.2.61–2; Martial 7.54.7) and made inexpensive offerings to the Lares (Juv. *Sat.* 13.233). Pliny *NH* 10.49 tells us that they were as pleasing to the gods as the costliest of victims.
57 Dembeck (1965) 201–2.
58 Plin. *HN* 10.51. Translated by Rackham (1940) 367: *Villaribus gallinis et religio inest: inhorrescunt edito ovo excutiuntque sese et circumactae purificant ac festuca aliqua sese et ova lustrant.*
59 P.G.W. Glare (ed), *OLD²* (2012), 'pullus'.
60 Columella, *Rust.* 8.5.13 is especially proud of the Roman hen's reputation as a broody and attentive nurse, mother and incubator.
61 Rüpke (2011) 29.
62 Small (1982) 97; see also Green (2009) 148.
63 Suet. *Aug.* 95, Cass. Dio 46.46.2.
64 Scheid (2005).
65 Scott (1925) 92–3.
66 Beard et al. (1998) 182–3.
67 Stewart (1997) 170.
68 Sutherland (1974) 102.
69 Vaahtera (2001) 127; Vervaet (2010).
70 Aug. *RG.* 7.
71 Suet. *Aug.* 31; see also Cass. Dio 37.24.
72 Suet. *Aug.* 7. Translated by Rolfe (1914) 159: *Cum, quibusdam censentibus Romulum appellari oportere quasi et ipsum conditorem urbis, praevaluisset, ut Augustus potius vocaretur, non tantum novo sed etiam ampliore cognomine, quod loca quoque religiosa et in quibus augurato quid consecratur augusta dicantur, ab auctu vel ab avium gestu gustuve, sicut etiam Ennius docet scribens: Augusto augurio postquam incluta condita Roma est.*
73 Scott (1925) 85; Momigliano (1984) 162. Ov. *Fast.* 1.593–616 shows the connection with *augurium.*

74 Dalla Rosa (2011) 244.

75 Aug. *RG.* 4. Translated by Shipley (1924) 351: *Ob res a me aut per legatos meos auspicis meis terra marique prospere gestas quinquagiens et quinquiens decrevit senatus supplicandum esse dis immortalibus.*

76 Aug. *RG.* 26. Translated by Shipley (1924) 389. *Meo iussu et auspicio ducti sunt duo exercitus eodem fere tempore in Aethiopiam et in Arabiam quae appellatur Eudaemon, magnaeque hostium gentis utriusque copiae caesae sunt in acie et complura oppida capta.*

77 Aug. *RG.* 30. Translated by Shipley (1924) 395: *Citra quod Dacorum transgressus exercitus meis auspicis victus profilgatusque est, et postea trans Danuvium ductus exercitus meus Dacorum gentes imperia populi Romani perferre coegit.*

78 Scheid (2003) 119.

79 Vervaet (2014) 120.

80 Popkin (2016) 94.

81 Vell. Pat. 2.121.1; Vervaet (2014) 273.

82 Campbell (1994) 68.

83 Scott (1925) 104.

84 Rosenstein (1990) 13–27, 41. In this analysis, Rosenstein finds that there is little correlation between military loss and political progression in the late Republic.

85 Zhao (2018).

86 Rosenstein (1990) 55; Ando (2000) 284; Woolf (2012) 114–16.

87 Cic. *Nat. D.* 2.7; Suet. *Tib.* 2. See also Rosenstein (1990) 79.

88 Liv. 21.63.6. C.f. Cic *Nat. D.* 2.8. Rosentein (1990) 78; Gottlieb (1998) 22.

89 Rosenstein (1990) 56; Ando (2000) 285; Woolf (2012) 17.

90 Suet. *Galb.* 1. Translated by Rolfe (1914) 183 with amendments. *Liviae, olim post Augusti statim nuptias Veientanum suum revisenti, praetervolans aquila gallinam albam ramulum lauri rostro tenentem, ita ut rapuerat, demisit in gremium; cumque nutriri alitem, pangi ramulum placuisset, tanta pullorum suboles provenit, ut hodieque ea uilla ad Gallinas vocetur, tale vero lauretum, ut triumphaturi Caesares inde laureas decerperent; fuitque mos triumphantibus, illas confestim eodem loco pangere; et observatum est, sub cuiusque obitum arborem ab ipso institutam elanguisse. Ergo novissimo Neronis anno et silva omnis exaruit radicitus, et quidquid ibi gallinarum erat interiit.* For eastern origins of the suppliant bird motif, see Gaál (2017) 8.

91 Reeder (2001) 14.

92 Plin. *HN.* 15.136–7. Translated by Rackham (1945) 381 with amendments: *namque Liviae Drusillae, quae postea Augustam matrimonii nomen accepit, cum pacta esset illa Caesari, gallinam conspicui candoris sedenti aquila ex alto abiecit in gremium inlaesam, intrepideque miranti accessit miraculum, quoniam teneret in rostro laureum ramum onustum suis bacis; conservari alitem et subolem iussere haruspices ramumque eum seri ac rite custodiri: quod factum est in villa Caesarum fluvio Tiberi inposita iuxta nonum lapidem Flaminiae viae, quae ob id vocatur Ad gallinas; mireque silva ea provenit: ex ea triumphans postea Caesar laurum in manu tenuit coronamque capite gessit, ac deinde imperatores Caesares cuncti; traditusque mos est ramos quos tenuerant serendi, et durant silvae nominibus suis discretae, fortassis ideo mutatis triumphalibus.*

93 Juv. *Sat.* 13.140–2; Cass. Dio 48.52.3–4.

94 Flory (1989) 353.

95 Pliny, *HN* 10.154. Translated by Rackham (1940) 391. *Quin et ab homine perficiuntur. Iulia Augusta prima sua iuventa Ti. Caesare ex Nerone gravida, cum parere virilem sexum admodum cuperet, hoc usa est puellari augurio, ovum in sinu fovendo atque, cum deponendum haberet, nutrici per sinum tradendo ne intermitteretur tepor; nec falso augurata proditur.*

96 Scheid (2007) 264.
97 Cass. Dio 43.14.3; Beard (2007) 234–5. White horses were associated with Jupiter and the Divine Sun. The use of such horses in triumphs was rare, but not unprecedented, as it was frowned upon as an attempt to claim divine status for oneself. However, after Ceasar and Augustus, the Romans seem to have envisioned white horses as a natural part of the triumph. For example, Statius in *Thebaid* 12.532–3 imagines a Roman-style triumph for Theseus in which he is drawn by snowy horses.
98 Zanker (1990) 129; Reeder (2001) 101.
99 Pollini (1987) 34.
100 Koortbojian (2013) 76–7.
101 Juv. *Sat.* 13.141–2. Translated by Braund (2004) 445: *quia tu gallinae filius albae, nos uiles pulli nati infelicibus ouis.*
102 Flory (1989) 350.
103 Zwierlein-Diehl (1980) 405–22.
104 Platner and Ashby (1929) 246.
105 Ashby and Fell (1921) 145.
106 Flory (1989) 352.
107 *CIL VI* 36841. See Braund (1985) no. 774.
108 Beard et al. (1998) 179.
109 Driediger-Murphy (2018) 15–16.

3 Farming and Aviculture

Introduction

Having considered the place of birds in the augural lore of Rome, we now turn to more practical matters: namely, the farming and consumption of birds. Roman society was inherently unequal, and inequality was expressed in various ways; between free people and slaves, rich and poor, citizen and non-citizen.[1] Animals as property can yield information about this social and economic inequality.[2] So too can the consumption of animals, through patterns of butchery, choice of animal, choice of cuts, choice of young as opposed to old, and so on.[3] In Rome and Italy during the Empire, meat-eating was a standard display among the rich, as landowners could more readily afford to dedicate arable land to the raising of livestock for consumption, or pay for meat to be imported.[4] There was a marked difference between the cuisines of the wealthy few and the more modest diets of both the rural and urban masses. As Peter Garnsey tells us, rich men use food as a key way to advertise wealth and win prestige in hierarchical or status-conscious societies.[5] 'Gastro-politics', or the use of food to reinforce social status, allow us to view birds as commodities that the Romans manipulated to generate wealth and prestige.[6] In this chapter we will investigate how the farming of birds for consumption communicated information about wealth and inequality in the Roman world, with a particular focus on the transitional period from the late Republic to the early Empire.[7]

Jack Goody defines the five distinct phases of food. The first is food production, the province of the farm and the natural world. The second is food distribution, the province of trade, markets, and storage. The third is food preparation, the realm of the kitchen. The fourth is consumption, which takes us to the table and the meal. Finally, there is food disposal, where scraps and refuse are discarded.[8] The final phase is naturally where the majority of archaeological evidence about diet is recovered and interpreted.[9] On an archaeological site, for example, taxonomic richness is often a key component in distinguishing elite and non-elite diets.[10] Sites can be characterised as 'high-status' or 'low-status', depending on the absence or presence of certain animal species, body parts, or age groups in food dumps.[11] However, as Naomi Sykes

DOI: 10.4324/9781003247906-4

demonstrates, deducing the presence of inequality in such assemblages can be complex. Perception and recognition of inequality are temporal and situational. Inequality is subject to great shifts over time, and what marks a site as elite in one era may be totally outmoded in another.[12] In this chapter and the next, zooarchaeology is used alongside art and literature to focus on the first four 'phases of food' listed here to examine how birds were hunted and farmed, traded and distributed, cooked and eaten, and what implications these had for the status of the consumer.[13] Birds are an especially rich foodstuff to examine; not only were they used as powerful symbols of wealth and luxury, they were also the most commonly available sources of meat for poorer citizens, who could raise barnyard poultry or catch smaller birds in the wild.[14]

The transitional period under investigation saw the establishment of new transport and communication networks, an increase in military and state demands, and a burgeoning urban population that triggered specialised and more intensive farming in the interests of sale and profit. Alan Bowman and Andrew Wilson outline the main changes in agriculture that occurred with the establishment of the Empire, including:

- Greater quantities of land, including marginal lands, brought under cultivation
- More efficient cultivation and crop rotation; increasing cultivation of fodder crops
- Increased output
- Increased specialisation and commercialisation
- The rise of larger and more efficient estates[15]

There were, of course, many regional differences. Across the Empire a general trend shows that urban sites, villas, and military sites demonstrate a greater degree of change as opposed to rural sites where food production remained similar to the Iron Age.[16] In Italy and the west the two predominant types of unit management were the villa estate and large estates that consisted of agglomerations of individual farms let out to tenants or exploited through tenancy and slave labour. Nevertheless, mobility in general surged during the Roman period, with the creation of roads and expansion of maritime trade making travel easier and safer, and facilitating greater movements of people and their animals. Commerce allowed farmers to grow crops and raise animals for profit, and profit could be invested into technical improvement. These general trends are abundantly evident in the way birds were farmed and how they reached the table for consumption.

What is striking to the modern reader is the sheer variety of birds that Romans farmed. A poulterer today will generally specialise in one kind of bird, but even a middling Roman farmer in the early Empire would have kept chickens, geese, ducks, pigeons, and thrushes. The income brought by these birds could then be supplemented by more exotic breeds such as peacocks, guineafowl, pheasants, storks, partridges, cranes, and swans. Not all birds were bred on the farm. It was common practice to catch wild birds and fatten them in captivity before selling or slaughtering them. When examining archaeological evidence, the presence of abundant wild game and farmed game in the diets of many elite and sub-elite Romans betrays that these seem to be prestige foods, primarily eaten (along with pork, lamb, and kid) by the affluent. Speciality meats were in so much demand that they began to be consumed by people of more modest means too. In the first century BCE, feasts of *collegia* held by craftsmen included cuts of venison, boar, goose, duck, peacock, and eventually pheasant.[17] Studies from a range of sites, from cities, villages, legionary camps, *villae* and farms show wild game representing a significant portion of the meat consumed – in a few cases 20 per cent or more. Deposits from less affluent communities show lower proportions of game, typically ranging from 1 to 3 per cent, but as Kron points out, these so-called game-poor sites are still impressive when compared to the 0.3 per cent of game meat consumed in Western Europe and North America in the early 1970s.[18]

Rare and imported animals and plants have always been markers of status among the elite.[19] A villa with a diverse and well-stocked game preserve was a symbol of wealth and power.[20] Through the power to control surplus, the owner shored himself up against hard times and could maximise profit by waiting until market demand tipped in his favour. Importantly, the production of luxury foods for the urban market was considered a legitimate and respectable part of agriculture.[21] That is, it was an acceptable way for the aristocracy to accumulate wealth. Land, animals, and agriculture were the means by which proper men could possess and generate wealth, while trading and manufacturing were seen as inferior and low-class (though of course, despite the rhetoric, elites were often involved in these money-making pursuits too).[22] Catering to the luxury food market was a way for elites to generate great profit without inviting too much disapproval, for it still fell within acceptable bounds of economic activity. Elites claimed an ideological connection with agricultural activity that led some Romans to compose agricultural manuals. The works of Cato (c. 160 BCE), Varro (37 BCE), and Columella (c. 60 CE) provide a great deal of information on traditional farming practices and approaches to land management. This chapter draws heavily on these works, as well as on the compendium of Pliny the Elder (79 CE), but readily acknowledges that they represent the elite perspective only. Yet as we are interested in how birds indicate status and inequality, the elite view offered in these sources remains an excellent starting point.[23] In contrast to the world presented to us by these authors, most farmers would have engaged in small-scale farming rather than in capital-intensive estates.[24] Zooarchaeological evidence provides the best means to interrogate the picture of agriculture left to us by written sources and can reveal the side not presented in these manuals.[25]

Varro and Columella testify to the fortunes that enterprising farmers made from expanding into the exotic game market. Their recommendations for game farming to maximise profit are detailed and correspond closely to best practices of game farmers today.[26] In Varro's writing, the character Axius is advised to look at college dinners and public and triumphal banquets as potential sources of profit (Varro, *Rust.* 3.2.16). Suetonius gives an example of one such banquet that called for 2,000 fish and 7,000 birds, thrown by Vitellius' brother when the emperor arrived in Rome (Suet. *Vit.* 13.2). Varro records that it was at the banquet that marked his entry into the Augural College that Q. Hortensius first served peacock in 70 BCE, a move that was met with disapproval by upright and traditional men (Varro, *Rust.* 3.6.6). We can discern evidence for demand for great quantities of fowl, and for strange and exotic birds that can impress rivals and bring prestige for the organiser at banquets. We note that examples of these banquets are given in a moralising tone, and *luxuria* is held responsible for the fact that lavish feasts are now held almost every day in the City (Varro, *Rust.* 3.12.16). Changes in the raising of birds, as well as of fish, hares, and bees, are indicted as part of the history and rise of luxury in Rome; as demand increased, farmers maximised production methods to meet it (Varro, *Rust.* 3.3.5–10). The most interesting part of Varro's dialogue is perhaps that the interlocutors show a general disapproval of luxury in keeping with traditional values, but the promise of great profit nevertheless overcomes any qualms they have. A thrush selling at three *denarii* per bird and a peacock fetching fifty is enough to tempt even the strongest traditionalist. Varro goes on to describe the efforts of Fircellia on the Via Salaria near Rome, who brought in 60,000 sesterces a year from selling thrushes. If these birds were not enough, a new fad for guineafowl was proving profitable (Varro, *Rust.* 3.9.18–19). The canny villa owner could capitalise enormously on the latest dining fads if he had a mind. Varro's characters stress that the greatest profits can be made at moments when the price of luxury foodstuffs suddenly escalated, so it is a wise idea to hold on to flocks until the market is ripe. The idea of making a fortune on little birds, as when the triumphal banquet of Metellus Scipio in c. 54 BCE called for 5,000 birds, is enough to make Varro's characters practically salivate (Varro, *Rust.* 3.3.10, 3.2.16). This urban and elite demand had a direct bearing on how agriculture changed and developed, with farmers adapting to catch, breed, and fatten birds in purpose-built enclosures.[27] These changes can be tracked, with the most remarkable transformation occurring around the transition of Republic to Empire. We will treat the rise of keeping aviaries for profit, then examine some of the most common farmed table birds in individual detail.

Rise of the Aviary

The drive to generate profit using birds can be seen escalating in the written records. Cato the Elder's *On Agriculture* gives a snapshot view of rural life in the Republic. It reads like a farmer's notebook, resounding with good, sensible advice for the contemporaneous agriculturalist, even if modern readers find parts difficult to stomach. What is particularly notable for us, however, is that advice relating to birds is patchy. Cato recommends pigeon dung as a fertiliser, which tells us that dovecotes – *columbaria* – were in common use at this time (Cato, *Agr.* 36). He also advises the farmer to fatten wild-caught wood pigeons for the market by force-feeding them a mixture of beans and barley, again affirming that the Romans had an appetite for pigeon meat. He then says every good female housekeeper must have 'many hens and eggs'.[28] Elsewhere, eggs are used in medicine and everyday tasks (Cato, *Agr.* 71, 106). We may infer that Cato took it for granted that every farm would have a number of chickens and fresh eggs available. He instructs the farmer how to fatten young hens, geese, and pigeons for the table with barley and wheat flour, again implying he assumed the reader would have these birds on hand (Cato, *Agr.* 89–90). But the variety ends there. Chickens, geese, and pigeons appear to be the only birds commonly farmed and sold for profit at this stage, and the methods are not particularly sophisticated; for example, there is no mention of fattening capons (castrated cocks) for the table, and he has no advice for how to manage and house large flocks. Fowl, it seems, was an essential part of the *villa rustica*, but the science of aviculture was yet to emerge.

It is around the first century BCE that we see Romans developing a taste for exotic birds, discerning between different cuts of meat, and eating only certain parts of certain birds.[29] Sumptuary laws, beginning with the Lex Fannia of 161 BCE, attempted to curb such extravagance, but the rich easily ignored or circumvented them.[30] The more outlandish birds one could serve at a feast, the better. In 115 BCE, the consul M. Aemilius Scaurus banned imported birds from being served at public baquets, indicating a healthy trade existed for the importation of rare and costly poultry (Plin. *HN* 8.223). Varro gives us a view of a fine villa around the advent of the Empire. He dedicates an entire book in his farming treatise to the management of fowl. The great villas were now keeping a variety of birds in huge numbers, and the wealthy were taking pride in consuming rarer breeds at lavish banquets as a display of their wealth and productivity, as we saw above. The scientific and intensive management of poultry was new at this time; Varro remarks that previous authors had left only brief and unsystematic remarks on the subject (Varro, *Rust.* 3.2.13). He names two kinds of aviary, one for pleasure and one for commercial use that functioned as a large poultry farm (Varro, *Rust.* 3.4.2). In this second type, he included a town aviary, which was like a shop adapted to the keeping and selling of live birds. The pleasure aviary was known by its Greek name, *ornithon.* This is not because it was a Greek invention. Its name merely provided a means of distinguishing it from the common Roman aviary, since the Latin *aviarium* could also mean henhouse or dovecote. *Ornithon* suggested something more refined.[31] Birds were therefore kept for their ability to indicate status through display as well as through farming and consumption. Columella's farming treatise, written under the Julio-Claudians, expands on this picture and shows that Roman aviculture was only becoming more sophisticated, and that demand for fowl was also increasing.

M. Laenius Strabo of Brundisium in the first century BCE is credited as being the first Roman to establish a diverse aviary.[32] Whether this was private or commercial is a matter of conjecture – Strabo was of the equestrian class and a businessman, which supports the latter, but Johnson points out that the structure was set into the peristyle of his house like the private aviaries that flourished in later years. It is entirely possible that Strabo intended the aviary to be both. Even emperors used their private, pleasure aviaries to turn a profit.[33] Varro distinguishes between birds kept for pleasure and birds kept for profit, but many birds could serve both functions. That aviaries could be turned to both pleasing and profitable ends while remaining socially acceptable likely added to their popularity. It was not long before every fashionable villa had an aviary attached to it, usually called an *ornithon,* and usually large in size. Cicero writes to Quintus about the construction of an aviary (Cic. *QFr.* 3.1.1). Augustus and Livia had an entire villa dedicated to the raising of chickens. Tiberius raised peacocks.[34] The extent to which bird fever gripped the Romans during the Empire is perhaps best illustrated by Emperor Severus Alexander, who loved breeding tame birds and kept aviaries of peacocks, pheasants, chickens, ducks, and partridges, as well as 20,000 turtle doves. To ensure the people did not feel the burden of his beloved birds' upkeep, he made these aviaries self-sufficient and paid for their food by selling eggs, chickens, and squabs (SHA, *Alex. Sev.* 41). That this is added as an afterthought suggests that Severus Alexander's primary motive was pleasure rather than profit.

The relative peace and prosperity of the Empire created the perfect environment for large commercial aviaries to flourish. These aviaries provided a steady supply of cheap poultry to the urban market while also providing luxury goods in the form of rare birds.[35] Aviaries were made even more profitable by the valuable dung they provided, which could be sold or spread directly onto the owner's fields to increase the bounty of his land.[36] Such use of nitrogen-rich fertiliser would help to mitigate the very real threat of soil depletion on Roman farms.[37] The largest of the aviaries required teams of slaves to run them, and descriptions indicate that their existence was in a large part facilitated by the Romans' advanced aquaculture and their ready access to fresh water.[38]

Under the Empire, we can also see that infrastructure was in place to deliver farmed birds to the urban markets. A town aviary, wherein one would sell live birds, has survived at Pompeii and is situated at Regio VII, Insula vii, No.16, behind the Forum and the Temple of Apollo in the garden of the House of the Veteran Julianus.[39] This town aviary doubtless supplied the residents of Pompeii with pet birds as well as poultry for the table.[40] The southern half of the house consisted of a garden seven metres square, in which the circular aviary six metres in diameter was situated. Poles were set into the walls, supporting a cone-shaped roof of lath, and netting covered the entire structure.

Vases were found within the aviary, which perhaps contained food and water for the birds. It is speculated that wooden perches were attached to the poles, but of course no wood has survived. An aviary was found to be depicted in a painting from another Pompeian house (Regio 1, Insula iv, No. 25). A passage from Cicero gives us a clue as to how the urban poulterer ran his business. The *De Officiis* (1.150) declares all crafts unworthy of the freeborn citizen, especially those that catered to *voluptates* – pleasures – in some way. Bird-stuffers were included in the list, along with fishermen, cooks, and butchers for their role in catering to gustatory delight. A specialist in fattening poultry was a *fartor.* This is an uncommon word, but Sarah Bond points to a small number of inscriptions that attest these individuals existed, and seem to have been especially clustered within Rome.[41] It was not the fact that they sold poultry that made Cicero look down on them; it was the fact that they fed and fattened the birds to *excess* before selling them. This association with softness and excess lasted for a long time. In the *De re militari* of the late Empire, Vegetius proposes to strengthen the army by banning fowlers, fishermen, confectioners, and weavers from encampments. The proposal was linked to the wish to improve the moral and physical character of the soldiers, as if eating foods that provided pleasure damaged them somehow.[42] In Rome, we have records of *aviarii*, one of them an *aviarius altillarius,* who bought directly from farms and fattened birds before selling them.[43] Diocletian's *Edict of Maximum Prices* distinguishes between fattened and unfattened birds, with fattened stock being twice as valuable in the case of the goose. Fattening in town and close to the marketplace ensured that the birds would not lose weight during transportation. The presence of these sellers in the City, and of the aviary in Pompeii, shed light on how birds made their way from farms and fowlers to the dinner tables or birdcages of citizens. They also indicate the symbolic power of a fat, delicious table bird. The act of eating a fattened bird bought from the urban poulterer had moral and cultural implications. It indicates demand for luxury foodstuffs and shows that an entire network of infrastructure supported the sale of exotic and fattened birds. A description of a rich man's aviary comes to us from Martial:

> All the crew of the dirty poultry yard wander around, the cackling goose and the spangled peacocks, the bird that owes its name to its ruddy plumage [flamingos], the painted partridge, the speckled guineafowl, and the pheasant of the wicked Colchians. Proud cockerels press their Rhodian wives and the cotes are loud with the flappings of doves. Here moans the wood pigeon, there the waxen-hued turtle-dove.[44]

This menagerie inevitably made its way onto the feast tables of the rich, who sought to impress through sheer extravagant variety. Demand was so strong that Seneca even mentions that there was a slave whose sole purpose was to carve expensive game birds (Sen. *Ep.* 47.6). The raising of game birds like the flocks in Martial's poem became as routine as the raising of ducks, chickens, and geese in the Empire, a far cry from Cato's comparatively humble flocks. When certain displays become fashionable among elites, sub-elites inevitably seek to imitate them, and so demand for game birds swelled among the lower classes as well. Geoffrey Kron details how ancient game farming increased the supply of game and reduced its cost, allowing the *plebs media*, and eventually many ordinary citizens, to enjoy a wide array of meats.[45]

A Roman villa discovered at the site of Kom al-Dikka in Alexandria that dates to the second century CE reveals more about bird-raising practices among the elite. Christened the Villa of the Birds, the most remarkable find in the excavation was mosaic α-5, a square divided into nine panels. Seven of the panels survive, and each shows a different bird. Birds are incredibly common motifs in Roman mosaics, but the Villa of the Birds stands out because it displays in one image the variety of birds one could expect to find being raised in rich men's villas. There are pigeons, a purple swamphen, a quail, a teal duck, a parrot, and a peacock.[46] Though at first glance it seems as though two squares depict ordinary pigeons – a strangely redundant choice – the Romans would have distinguished between the *columbae,* or domestic pigeons drinking from a bowl in the central panel, and the *palumba,* or wood pigeon, a larger bird with different plumage in the panel above. All of these birds had the potential to generate profit and prestige for the person who raised them. Using their images as decoration invited association with the wealth and esteem of aviculture.

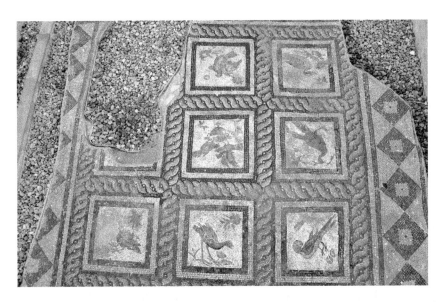

Figure 3.1 Mosaic from the Villa of the Birds, Kom al-Dikka, Alexandria. Second century CE.

Source: Photo by the author.

We have shown how the production and consumption of birds increased from the time of Cato to the early Empire. Elite demand saw aviaries diversify, with a focus on producing bigger, fattened, and more exotic birds. Infrastructure on farms catered to intensive and profit-driven husbandry, and an urban network of poulterers acted as middlemen to get birds from farm to table. Elites despaired of how fattened, exotic birds heralded the decadence of their fellow Romans, even as they provided both the supply and the demand. Increased production also saw swelling demand among sub-elites, who sought to imitate the banquets of their social superiors. Birds communicated status in a powerful way, but to appreciate fully what they can tell us about Roman society we must consider some of the most commonly raised birds in individual detail and look for the perspective of poor or subsistence farmers amidst elite consumption.

Chickens

Chickens provide a fascinating window into the agricultural activities of the Romans. These birds were kept and eaten by all, from the poorest to the wealthiest. While we think of chickens almost exclusively as food-producing animals, this was not always so, and in fact the Romans were somewhat peculiar for valuing chickens as table birds. To illustrate the Romans' unique relationship with these birds, we should contextualise their place in the wider Mediterranean world. We have already touched on the fact that chickens were originally considered semi-exotic and that their status as food producers was initially far less important than their status as ritual animals.[47] The earliest faunal evidence for the chicken in Italy is dated to the ninth (or possibly tenth) century BCE.[48] The contexts in which bones were found indicate that they were raised primarily for symbolic rather than food value.[49] Naomi Sykes convincingly lays out the evidence to prove that the spread of chickens across Europe was driven not by their value as food producers, but due to cockfighting.[50] Historical and iconographic records indicate that chickens were known from the mid-second millennium BCE in the Levant, Egypt, and Mesopotamia, although finds are very sparse at this time and not associated with the domestic context.[51] These sources refer almost exclusively to roosters and indicate they were seen as exotic fighting birds. Finds become more common in the first millennium BCE. Seventh-century BCE seals and ceramics from Egypt and the Levant region depict cocks and cockfights; all evidence points to their being used as fighting birds rather than as a source of food.[52] The early Greeks mainly bred chickens for use in cockfighting and medicine, and only later focused on the production of meat and eggs.[53]

Their introduction to Europe was traditionally credited to the Phoenicians, who brought their chickens with them when they colonised the west. This theory is based on the fact that some of the earliest chicken remains in Europe were retrieved from Phoenician sites, mainly in Iberia, though recent research has shown that they were present in at least some numbers before this time.[54]

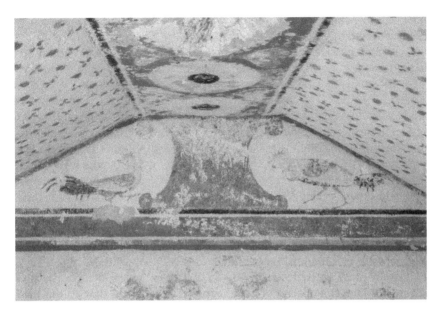

Figure 3.2 Detail from the Etruscan Tomb of the Flowers, 475–450 BCE. Images of cocks squaring off like this are common across the ancient Mediterranean.

Source: Photo by Edward Blume-Poulton.

In northern Italy, by the second half of the eighth century BCE chickens can be found as ritual offerings in human graves. It is possible that cockfighting and their innate connection to bloodshed made them popular victims of sacrifice. In the Etruscan context, fighting cocks may be seen in art and fowl remains have been recovered from cultic, funerary, and elite sites.[55] Hens' eggs were deposited in Etruscan tombs, and egg imagery in art also indicates their use in funerary ritual.[56] Fowl remains continue to be sporadic until the fourth century BCE, when they gradually increase in abundance and may be discovered more often in domestic as well as ritual contexts.[57] A gradual increase in archaeological representation continues from the fourth century BCE to the sixth century CE.[58] The evidence suggests that chickens only became widespread in the domestic context in the Roman period, at which point attitudes similar to our own began to emerge – that is, that they are valuable producers of meat and eggs rather than exotic curiosities. While cockfighting was certainly practised and enjoyed in the Republic and throughout the Imperial period, they did not show an obsession with the sport on the same level that the Greeks did. In Roman art, proud cocks are shown fighting, or with trophies and betting paraphernalia in tow, symbols of masculine strength.[59] Written sources, however, betray that pride in their broody, fertile hens outweighed their regard for pugnacious roosters. The works of Varro and Columella provide detailed information about chicken breeds and their management. In the Italian Middle Ages, the chicken may have been a food source, but there are no written sources that detail husbandry practices such as the efficient and intensive ones transmitted by the Romans.[60]

The Roman passion for raising hens places them in stark contrast to other Mediterranean cultures. Our ancient authors would even have us believe that the Romans first raised hens – not roosters – so they could be used in auspices.[61] Roosters were fine sacrificial animals, but when it came to bloodless rituals such as the taking of auspices, a lively flock of pullets was considered most suitable for the task. It is a small step from valuing hens as ritual animals to making the most of their ability to produce meat and eggs. Romans selectively bred for size and productivity of the females rather than the aggressiveness of the males. For a people who adored beast hunts so much, it is almost jarring to hear the way they disparage the Greeks for their devotion to cockfights and the savageness of their chicken breeds.

Chickens can even be used to assess Romanisation under the Empire.[62] Among the Britons in the first century BCE, geese and cocks were bred, but they could not be eaten owing to a religious taboo (Caes. *BGall.* 5.12). They were chiefly used for entertainment.[63] Zooarchaeological evidence shows that, in Britain, the majority of ritual deposits of chickens date to the Iron Age and Romano-British period, with only a few Romano-British and early Medieval deposits being interpreted as food waste, in contrast to later Medieval deposits where domestic fowl are interpreted as commonly consumed domestic animals.[64] Chicken was not regularly eaten on all types of

Figure 3.3 Hen and cockerel, first century CE. Naples Archaeological Museum, inv. 9714.

Source: Photo by the author.

Figure 3.4 Hens pecking at wheat. This domestic, non-aggressive imagery stands in contrast to pre-Roman depictions of fighting roosters. Fresco from the *columbarium* of villa Doria Pamphili, Palazzo Massimo alle Terme.

Source: Photo by the author.

sites.[65] Finds are also skewed towards male birds, in particular towards mature roosters, suggesting that productivity and breeding for meat and eggs were less important than the male bird's use in ritual and cock-fighting.[66] In one study, M. Maltby looked at proportions of domestic fowl, sheep, and goats among the faunal assemblages of different sites to assess the contribution that poultry made to the diet. Results indicated a significant urban-rural divide, as large towns contained the highest proportions of chickens. A moderate representation was found among military and villa sites, while rural sites revealed no chickens, or only a few. Though urban chicken-keeping might be attributed to the ability to keep the birds on small plots, it may also be an indication of how Romanisation affected some sites, but not others.[67] H.E.M. Cool points out that rural sites often showed a high proportion of chicken bones recovered from grave sites, pointing to their consumption in funeral ritual, but not in everyday life.[68] These 'native' practices stand in contrast to the urban and military populations.

The Romans recognised several different breeds of chickens, although the term 'breed' is somewhat problematic. As Michael MacKinnon points out, the Roman view of what constituted a 'breed' is different to the modern definition, which employs an understanding of genetic principles and how they factor into the manipulation of physical and behavioural traits in animals to create new breeds. Ancient cultures were capable of breeding to promote certain traits in animals, but tended to distinguish the same species according to geographic location rather than the genetic and reproductive features we use today.[69] Poulterers generally disliked Greek birds because they were bred for cockfighting; one could not turn a profit with these aggressive animals.[70] Discussing Greek and Roman chicken breeds, Columella tells us that the scientific method of raising fowls for profit was begun by the Greeks, particularly by the people of Delos, and that they favoured 'long' bodies and spirited fighting natures in their birds. The most famous breeds were the Tanagran of Boeotia, the Chalcidian from Euboea, and the Median – that is, Persian. Tanagra was an especially famous site for breeding fighting cocks. For the enterprising farmer, native Italian breeds were typically recommended, a red variety that probably resembled the Rhode Island Red, and a white variety, probably the ancestors of the Leghorn breed.[71] The red hen, even despite the white flock kept by Augustus and Livia, remained the preferred barnyard breed for its hardiness, fertility, and for the fact it was less visible to predators like hawks.[72] Like the Greeks, the Romans employed selective breeding, but they chose different traits. Looking down on Greek birds, they raised their birds with the aim of increasing meat and egg production, selecting not for the males' fighting spirit but for docility and fecundity of the females (Columella, Rust. 8.2.4). Columella later specifies that although Italian breeding cocks should be spirited and muscular, these birds were *not* used for cockfights. They were bred to protect their flock of wives from snakes and vermin. If a man wanted a good fighting cock, he would choose a Greek bird (*Rust.* 8.2.11). Aristotle mentions Adrian, or Adrianic fowl, that come from Adria in the Veneto region of north-east Italy.[73] These were said to be small, prolific, and very bad-tempered, most likely a bantam breed.[74] Columella was dismissive of bantams, saying that despite their fecundity they were bad-natured, and should only be kept if one took pleasure in their dwarf appearance.[75] Pliny repeats that they are especially prolific egg-layers (Plin. *HN* 146). We can see Roman values emerging: Roman chickens were for eating, laying eggs, and being good mothers. If you wanted a fighting bird, you would invest in a foreign breed. Romanisation facilitated size improvement in many animal breeds, particularly in domestic cattle, ovicaprids, and pigs.[76] The same pattern is apparent in Roman chickens, which were as big as some modern breeds.[77] Large animals are typically indicative of profit-driven agriculture; smaller chickens suit subsistence farmers, as they consume less food and can forage with less need to have their diets supplemented with grain or fodder crops. A farmer producing birds for the market desires larger animals to net a larger profit. Zooarchaeology has confirmed the presence of at least three distinct breeds of chickens at the Roman and early Byzantine site of Sagalassos.[78]

Chickens were present on almost every Roman farm (Columella, *Rust.* 8.1.4). They were the most acceptable of sacrificial animals, possibly because it was an animal that most people had ready access to, and could offer up

Figure 3.5 Though faded, we can distinguish red, white, and black fowl in this painting. House of the Vettii, Pompeii.

Source: Photo by the author.

without much inconvenience (Plin. *HN* 10.24.49). On large farms, a professional *gallinarius* would tend to hens. Graffiti in Pompeii indicate that there were enough *gallinarii* to give group support for a political candidate (*CIL* IV 241, 373). A single *gallinarius* could look after about 200 chickens, provided he had the assistance of a boy or a crafty old woman to ensure the animals did not stray or get picked off by men or hawks (Columella, *Rust.* 8.2.7). By contrast, on the average farm, hens were the responsibility of the farmer's wife and an important renewable source of protein (Palladius, 1.27). Country-dwellers would keep their own flocks, while city-dwellers could procure meat and eggs from markets supplied by larger farms. The middleman in this transaction was a poultry merchant, called a *negotians pullarius* (*CIL* VI 9674). In Cato's time, he expected farmers to have a few chickens, but by the Empire, if it fell within your means, you could easily establish large flocks of a few hundred and make a handsome profit by supplying the urban market.

When it came to housing chickens in large or small numbers, light and ventilation were key components in the design of coops. This helped to ward off rot and dampness.[79] The coops were kept scrupulously clean of dung (which could be composted and used as fertiliser). They were regularly cleansed and fumigated (Columella, *Rust.* 8.5.20). Nesting boxes were lined with chaff, and these would be cleaned and purified with sulphur and bitumen before the hens were allowed to nest in them (*Rust.* 8.5.11). This helped prevent lice infestations. Romans also knew to provide dust and ashes with which chickens could have dustbaths, another safeguard against lice (*Rust.* 8.4.4). Presumably the ashes were taken from the hearthfire, so even household soot did not go to waste. At night they slept on square-hewn wooden perches. These were at the same height to prevent bickering over who would sleep on the highest (and therefore, best) perch. This measure kept their feet free from dung as they slept, preventing infection. The poultry yard allowed ample space for exercise. To protect them from predators they were often kept enclosed in the outdoor space, but were free to peck, scratch, preen, squabble, and roam about. Netting would prevent hawks from picking them off. It does not take a flock of chickens long to pick an enclosure bare. The decision to keep them penned meant they could not effectively forage for themselves and were reliant on a supplemented diet.

Most importantly, fresh, clean water was in abundance, and accessed through lead troughs with small holes on the side to stop the chickens from fouling their water supply with food or faeces (*Rust.* 8.3.8–9). Columella stresses the importance of good, nutritious food for hens, recommending a diet of grape husks, chickpeas, and half-cooked barley mixed with greens (*Rust.* 8.4.1–2). The practice of half-cooking the barley made it easier to digest, and the addition of greens is equally sound, since hens require fresh pasture to keep them in prime condition.[80] A third of their food was distributed in the morning and two-thirds towards the evening. This helped ensure they would return compliantly to the henhouse, and made it easier to count them and herd them into their sleeping quarters at dusk. On this point, Columella advises us to beware, 'for winged creatures easily delude the watchfulness of the man who looks after them'.[81] Anyone who has tried to herd chickens into their coop can relate to this. The high standard of care and attention to disease prevention shines through in the sources. Goebel and Peters comment on the effectiveness of the Romans' hygienic principles and their various remedies for diseases and ailments.[82] For intensive poultry farming to flourish, such hygienic practices are essential. Though the production of poultry became highly commercialised, it seems chickens spent most of their lives in healthy, free-range conditions. Those that were destined for the market, however, underwent an intensive fattening process during their final three weeks of life. Romans constructed enclosures where birds gorged themselves in dark, cramped conditions with barely enough room to turn around.[83] Their diet consisted of barley mashed up with honey water, or wheat bread soaked in wine. The addition of sugar to their diets would have the effect of fattening them more quickly and giving the meat a sweeter flavour. The methods employed by the bird-stuffers were akin to modern battery farming. In Martial's words: 'The accommodating hen is fed on sweetened meal and on darkness. Ingenious is the palate!'[84] To improve taste further, young male birds were gelded (Mart. 13.63, 64). This was

allegedly done by burning their spurs off. While this does not sound particularly effective, our sources seem convinced that this method of castration
worked.[85] We should perhaps interpret this to mean the animals were seared
at the height of the loin – that is, on the copulation organ on the ventral side
of the cloaca. A passage in Pliny confirms this interpretation.[86] It is unlikely
that burning spurs would have any real effect, though perhaps crippling the
young birds would reduce activity and help them fatten more quickly. It is
also unlikely the Romans could remove the internal testes without seriously
injuring the young cockerels, but cauterising the papilla, in which the *ductus
deferens* opens into the cloaca, would have an effect similar to real castration. It causes the bird to stop crowing, become disinterested in hens, and
fatten more quickly.[87] Martial jokingly compares capons to the eunuch
priests of Cybele, saying, 'In vain the hen succumbs to her sterile husband.
He should have been Mother Cybele's bird'.[88] And again: 'Lest the cockerel
grow thin by over-draining his loins, he has lost his testicles. Now I shall
consider him a priest of Cybele'.[89] Capons were considered delicious, with
juicy and tender flesh. A guest from the countryside could impress his host
by bringing capons to dinner (Mart. 3.58.37). Fat capons were a luxury dish
at banquets (Petr. *Sat.* 65). By contrast, unfattened birds were the poor
man's fare.[90] Sumptuary laws prescribed chickens for banquets, and in the
Empire one could make a show of frugality by eating chicken instead of
peacock (SHA, *Alex. Sev.* 37.5) But while Diocletian's *Edict of Maximum
Prices* (4.23) shows that chickens were much cheaper than other birds, they
were still expensive enough that the poorest could not eat them. For those
living a hand-to-mouth existence, egg-laying hens would have been too
valuable to eat. They would have enjoyed chicken only occasionally, in the
form of surplus unfattened cockerels and hens past laying age.

Eggs formed an important part of the Roman diet, with chickens providing the bulk of those consumed. They were commonly served in egg cups
and eaten with a spoon. Hard-boiled eggs were called *ova elixa* (Apicius
7.19.2). Soft-boiled were *ova hapala* (Apicius 7.19.3). Commenting on the
properties of eggs laid by various different birds, Galen adds that there are
also 'sucking eggs', which are boiled only until they are warm (Galen, *Alim.
Fac.* 3.20–2). Apicius also records a milky omelette (*ova spongia ex lacte*)
that was cooked only on one side (Apicius 7.13.8). Aside from these examples, around half of Apicius' recipes contain eggs, suggesting they were a
staple in many recipes. Banquets traditionally began with an egg course,
hence the expression *ab ovo usque ad mala* – literally, 'from the egg to the
apple', from appetisers to dessert (Hor. *Sat.* 1.2.115–16). Eggs were used as
funeral offerings (Juv. *Sat.* 5.84–5). Because chickens are cheap and easy to
rear, eggs would have provided a valuable source of protein to the poor.
According to Aristophanes, every Athenian had his hen, even the poorest, so
we can assume that the same was true of the Romans.[91] Roman hens were
not as prolific as modern breeds, which can lay an egg a day, but it seems they
could produce one every second or third day and only ceased laying for two

months in winter (Plin. *HN* 10.53). For this reason, there was a great deal of advice on how to store eggs for later consumption. Eggs may be eaten up to four months after laying if stored at room temperature; the most important thing is to keep the temperature consistent as fluctuations in temperature allow bacteria to penetrate the shell due to pores expanding and contracting.[92] Ancient advice on egg storage reads as fairly sound.[93] Columella says eggs may be kept over the winter buried in chaff, or buried in bran in the summer, after they have first been covered with salt for six hours. The salt would have had the effect of killing any moulds or spoilage organisms on the shell. Thus treated and stored in a desiccant, the eggs could have been kept for up to a year. Other methods listed are to bury the eggs in fresh beans or bean flour, or to pickle them in brine.[94] In Pompeii, we can see records of egg-laying inscribed onto the walls of villas (*CIL* IV 3890, 6873).

The detail that a coop should be built to face the rising sun had the effect of helping to keep the coop warm in the cold months, and also probably assisted with prolonging the laying season.[95] Egg-laying in hens is governed by light levels. Researchers have discovered a pigment called pineal opsin in the pineal gland, located on the top of the brain in chickens. This pigment predates the development of eyesight in animals, and seems to respond to sunlight filtering through the chicken's thin skull. It is thought this is linked to the bird's biological clock and the way light exposure governs when it sleeps, when it rises, when it lays, and when it stops laying.[96] In the absence of artificial light sources that modern poultry farmers employ, maximising exposure to the sun in winter was the best the Romans could do to keep the non-productive winter season as short as possible. That the ancients were well aware of how sensitive chickens were to sunlight is also evident in the way the rooster was always considered a solar animal – though cock-crow explains that just as well.

Young hens were the most prolific layers, but when it came to hatching eggs, large, older hens with good dispositions were preferred as incubators and nurses. Calling chickens companions in the homes of men, Oppian describes the quality of their alarm calls upon seeing a hawk, and the way a mother hen will shelter and defend her chicks from attack (Oppian, *The Chase*, 120–30). Such maternal behaviour invited a feeling of respect.[97] Any hen that broke or ate eggs was immediately culled (Columella, *Rust.* 8.5.6–7). The eggs were marked so they could be regularly checked and turned if the hens had missed any.[98] Damaged eggs were removed. Food was placed near brooding birds to discourage them from leaving the nest.[99] There were reliable methods for testing the fertility of eggs; namely, holding them up to the sun and testing their specific gravity against that of salt water. Romans also knew that eggs need not be incubated until up to ten days after being laid.[100] Though Romans knew of artificial egg incubation techniques thanks to the Egyptians, the practice never really caught on. They always preferred to trust their broody red hens as incubators.[101] Myriad other birds would also be hatched under the broody hens, who made excellent foster mothers. Taking eggs from the more valuable or rare birds, like peafowl, caused them to lay again, thus maximising the number of chicks one could hatch. We should note that modern egg producers cull laying hens at around two years of age once peak productivity has passed. The Romans instead found use for their older, less productive hens by having them incubate and raise the next generation. In addition, the fact that their red hens are dual-purpose birds allowed them to avoid the practice of culling male chicks, as occurs today. Male chicks hatched from egg-producing hens were simply raised as table birds, avoiding waste.

The Romans caused something of a revolution when they got their hands on chickens. In contrast to the ritual and entertainment exploitation of roosters typical of the wider Mediterranean world, Romans were deeply invested in the economic potential of hens.[102] They were the first to unlock chickens' true potential as a food source, engaging in selective breeding and intensive farming. The success of Roman poultry farming should not be underestimated. Roman chickens were as large as many modern breeds, and the hens were hardy, good layers, and excellent mothers.[103] Large-scale and intensive poultry farming for food collapsed with the decline of the Empire, and their scale would not be matched again in Europe until the nineteenth century.[104] Studying the production and consumption of chickens reveals much about how the Romans conceived of themselves in contrast to other cultures such as the Britons and the Greeks, and it also reveals divisions within their own culture. The difference between eating a purchased fat capon, an unfattened hen from one's own flock, or not being able to eat a chicken at all, reflects the inequality inherent in Roman society.

Geese

Geese have been among the birds raised by Romans since the earliest times. Unlike chickens, geese are native to Europe, and so appear even in Homer as domestic companions. We shall look at the diverse ways Romans kept and related to geese to discover how their changing management reflects social values. Traditionally, geese were sacred to Juno and kept at her shrine on the Capitol from the early days of the Republic.[105] If Petronius is to be believed, geese were kept at other temples too. In a typically ludicrous scene, the character Encolpius finds himself attacked by three geese sacred to the phallic deity Priapus. He beats one to death with a table leg, and for this crime he must undergo penance (Petr. Sat. 136). Humorous though the scene is, temple geese attacking strange visitors probably was not all that un-common, and it must have been taboo for visitors to do them harm, though the creatures usually ended up being sacrificed and ritually eaten.[106] The goose was also an appropriate sacrifice for Isis since she was identified with Io, daughter of the river god Inachus.[107] According to the famous legend, Juno's geese saved the Capitol in 390 BCE. When Rome was taken by Gauls, the marauders tried to invade the Capitol in the night, but although the watchdogs were silent, the geese woke with a fury. The ensuing clamour and cackle woke the Romans and allowed them to defend themselves in time. In gratitude to the vigilant geese, securing food for the temple flock was one of the first contracts a censor would arrange upon assuming the role. Thereafter, the goose was honoured, but dogs annually paid the price for their treachery (Ael. *NA* 12.33). Geese are loud, aggressive, and territorial, and they do make excellent watchdogs. They respond quickly to anything that sounds suspicious, and if kept with other barnyard poultry they will protect the more vulnerable birds from small predators. An ominous line in Lucretius betrays the dangers of a trespassing upon a goose's territory: 'and from afar the scent of man is caught by the white goose, preserver of the citadel of the Roman race'.[108] The goose's sacred status diminished as years went by, and by the Augustan Age the peacock had definitively replaced the goose as Juno's familiar.[109] Perhaps the goose could not compete with this beautiful, foreign interloper; perhaps the increased presence of peacocks on farms and villas allowed for a more natural association of the birds with home, hearth and the goddess of marriage, or perhaps it was a matter of Greek influence. Athenaeus records that Hera of Samos had peacocks dedicated to her, and suggests that it is from Samos that the peacocks spread (Ath. 14 655b). Varro and Aulus Gellius also link peafowl to Samos, and given Samos' proximity to the Persian Empire and associated luxury trade, it is highly likely that this was indeed a breeding ground for the exotic birds.[110] It is not until Ovid's time that we find a Roman myth that attempts to explain why the peacock became Juno's familiar, linking it to the death of Argus, the hundred-eyed giant, whose eyes came to bejewel the peacock's tail (Ov. *Met.* 1.621–8, 633–722). The goose's loss of prestige might be related to changing farming practices, which saw them raised more intensively with an eye for profit, rather than as faithful watchdogs and household companions.

Geese were well-established as farmyard birds from early on. Cato gives advice on how to cram geese, which shows that the average farmyard was expected to have geese, and that geese were eaten regularly (Cato, *Agr.* 89). By Varro's time, landowners were keeping large flocks of the birds, reared in special pens that were called *chenoboscion*. Varro's use of this Greek term suggests Romans modelled their goose farming on Greek practices (*Rust.* 3.10.1). We know that the Greeks had a very long tradition of raising the birds. In the *Odyssey*, Penelope has twenty geese, and says it cheers her sad soul to look at them (Hom. *Od.* 19.535–40). Aristotle distinguishes between a large variety, a small variety, and the imported Egyptian goose, which they called *chenalopex* – 'fox-goose' – presumably the reddish *Alopochen aegyptiaca*.[111] In Thessaly, geese were farmed conjointly with cranes (Pl. *Plt.* 264c). For the Romans, the undisputed goose of choice was the white breed:

> You must take care that the male and female birds which you choose are
> of the largest possible size and of a white colour; for there is another

Figure 3.6 Byzantine depiction of a child herding a grey goose and a white goose. Tending geese was often entrusted to children. C. sixth century CE. Great Palace Mosaic Museum, Istanbul.

Source: Photo by iStock.com/burcintuncer.

kind which is of various colours and, originally wild, has been tamed and become a domestic bird, but it is not so prolific and commands a lower price, and so should certainly not be reared.[112]

Varro gives the same advice (*Rust.* 3.10.2). These white geese are the domestic breed we are familiar with today, descended from the wild European greylag (*Anser anser*), while the parti-coloured geese mentioned by the writers are most likely the greylag itself. These must have been caught wild on a fairly regular basis, but obviously were not as pliable as their domesticated cousins.

A description of the goose pen runs thus. Columella advises keeping geese in a courtyard with walls nine feet high. The wall should be surrounded by porticoes, and the goose-keeper's hut was situated amongst them. Under the porticoes were pens three feet square in which the birds were enclosed when laying or sitting. If there was no pool or river nearby, an artificial pond should be constructed; for geese cannot live without water just as they cannot live without earth. They should be allowed to forage in marshy ground in which greens like endive and vetch are sown, and this should be supplemented with barley (Columella, *Rust.* 14.1–2). No netting was required for their enclosure, since few raptors will attack a goose; indeed, the goose is useful for discouraging birds of prey. Such an arrangement was feasible only for large landowners, but on smaller farms it was good practice to keep at least a few geese mixed in with the chickens, provided the land was suitable. In such situations, they were largely self-sufficient, and excellent watchdogs (Columella, *Rust.* 13.1–3). We are told that cranes and swans were fattened on Roman farms, and it is likely that these birds were shunted into goose pens such as the one Columella describes (Plut. *De esu carnium*, 997a).

Geese bond readily with humans, and humans in turn, like Penelope, grow to love their savage yet devoted gaggle:

> The goose also keeps a careful watch, as is evidenced by its defence of the Capitol during the time when our fortunes were being betrayed by the silence of the dogs; for which reason food for the geese is one of the first contracts arranged by the censors. Moreover there is the story of the goose at Aegium that fell in love with the supremely beautiful boy Amphilochus of Olenus, and also the goose that loved Glauce, the girl that played the harp for King Ptolemy, whom at the same time also a ram is said to have fallen in love with. These birds may possibly be thought also to possess the power of understanding wisdom: thus there is a story that a goose attached itself continually as a companion to the philosopher Lacydes, never leaving his side by night or day, either in public or at the baths.[113]

Tim Birkhead studies these odd incidents of amorous geese stalking humans and suggests that these are ancient examples of imprinting behaviour. Imprinting is a learning process in young birds involving a rapid attachment during a 'sensitive period' to a parental figure or future mate.[114] Poultry farmers would have been aware of such behaviour, but it was not studied experimentally and explained until the 1870s, so until that time people made their own reasons. For the Romans, that reason was love and a sensitivity to wisdom, when really the goose was just following the human who had raised it, and whom it saw as a mother figure, mate, or both. The animal behaviourist Konrad Lorenz conducted the most famous studies on imprinting and could often be seen with an imprinted brood of goslings or geese devotedly following him. Birds raised by humans, though affectionate, are sexually stunted, for they become fixated on humans rather than their own kind. It is little wonder that the ancients blamed such behaviour in birds on love. One even wonders if the ability of the goose to 'love' is partly responsible for its association with Eros and Aphrodite. Greek and Roman art often depicts the love deities riding geese or in the company of geese.

In contrast to these sentimental stories, Pliny says: 'Our countrymen are wiser [than the Greeks], who know the goose by the excellence of its liver. Stuffing the bird with food makes the liver grow to a great size, and also when it has been removed it is made larger by being soaked in milk sweetened with honey'.[115] Goose liver is widely attested as a favourite delicacy among the Romans and was also offered as a sacrifice and used to foretell the future.[116] As a foodstuff, it was all the rage from the late Republic onward. During the Empire, Romans became particularly adept at force-feeding geese to swell the

Figure 3.7 Cupid and a goose. Villa Oplontis, first century CE.
Source: Photo by the author.

liver to outrageous proportions. Martial says, 'See how the liver swells larger than the big goose. You will say in astonishment: "Where, pray, did this grow?"'[117] The cramming was commonly done by enclosing the choicest and fattest goslings in a small pen and feeding them barley meal and flour soaked in water. Varro stresses the importance of cleaning out the enclosure after every feeding, adding wryly that although geese love a clean place, wherever they go they leave nothing clean. After two months, they were ready for slaughter. On average, they were about six months old, and very tender, when butchered.[118] Geese could also be crammed with figs, and were sometimes made to drink mead directly before being slaughtered, ostensibly to give the flesh a sweeter flavour.[119] To maximise production, goose eggs were sometimes hatched under hens (Columella, *Rust.* 8.14.6). Pliny records that geese were bred en masse in Gaul and marched on foot to Rome each year, where they were presumably fattened before being slaughtered (Plin. *HN* 10.27). One imagines this was done during their annual moult in summer, when geese lose their flight feathers and are grounded until new ones grow in.

Apart from its liver, the goose was not especially beloved by epicures, though Pliny records a recipe of geese feet grilled with cocks' combs that was in vogue (*HN* 10.27). Apicius lists a few recipes, most importantly for a special astringent sauce that would make the greasy flesh more palatable (Apicius 6.5, 6.8). Yet although it was common, the goose was expensive. In Diocletian's *Edict of Maximum Prices* (4.21, 22) they are worth 200 *denarii* fattened and 100 *denarii* unfattened.

In contrast to elites breeding intensively and eating the choicest and fattest livers, the impoverished kept their geese alive, as they did with chickens, in order to eat their eggs (Petr. *Sat.* 65). Ovid gives us a touching scene of generosity and compassion in his tale of Philemon and Baucis, where an elderly couple offers shelter to gods in disguise. Their extreme poverty is indicated by the fact they can offer nothing but vegetarian fare and a few pieces of stringy dried meat.[120] Determined to show hospitality, they offer to kill their goose, the guard of their humble cottage. At this show of selflessness, the gods reveal their identities and the goose is spared (Ov. *Met.* 8.647–50). For the poor, the goose was an essential and precious animal. Aside from eggs and meat, the goose produced other valuable products, namely feathers and grease. Farmyard geese could be plucked twice yearly in spring and autumn, a process which Columella compares to the shearing of sheep (Columella, *Rust.* 8.13.3). The best feathers came from wild-caught geese in Germany. This goosedown was so valuable that Pliny claims commanders of auxiliary cohorts on the frontiers were often reprimanded for sending men to go fowling for the birds.[121] The down was used for bedding, particularly pillows, and he complains that even the male neck cannot do without goosedown bedding these days (Plin. *HN* 10.27). As for goose fat, it was fine enough to be used as an ingredient in medicine or as an aphrodisiac (Plin. *HN* 10.28; 28.261. 30.131). Goose grease was often mixed with fragrant herbs to create a soothing salve that could treat minor afflictions such as sprains, aches, or nipples chafed from breastfeeding. This mixture was prepared at the beginning of winter and stayed hard in the cold months for easy storage and use (Plin. *HN* 29.55; 30.131). All in all, the goose was a versatile animal. It had value alive, as a watchdog and producer of eggs and feathers, and dead, for its flesh and its fat. Elite consumption points to a predilection for young, fattened animals and foie gras, while on a subsistence farm geese functioned as loyal companions that formed strong bonds with their owners.

Ducks

Ducks represent an interesting case study, since the poor could procure them from the wild quite easily. The raising and fattening of ducks was generally attempted on larger farms. Columella informs us that duck enclosures required a similar amount of attention as goose pens, but they were more expensive.[122] The enclosure had to be surrounded by walls fifteen feet high and a net or lattice frame was fastened over the top to prevent the ducks from flying out and raptors from flying in. The wall was plastered over inside and outside to deter vermin and predators, and in the middle of the yard a pond two feet deep was dug. This was to be as large as the dimensions of the enclosure would allow, while still retaining room for a grassy lawn and nesting boxes. The edges of the pond were plastered over and sloped gradually downwards to allow a graceful descent into the water. Stones were rammed into the plaster to stop vegetation from growing, but the middle of the pond was left unplastered so vegetation could be grown from the soil. The pond, therefore, was cleared for swimming around the outside, but the centre was cultivated as a sort of shady marsh. The plants grown here were not for eating, but for providing a pleasant habitat that would suit the birds. Columella's charming description of the scene is worth quoting here: 'Nevertheless the whole space should not, for this reason, be occupied by little plantations, but, as I have said, should be left free all round the circumference, so that, as they are cheered by a day of sunshine, the water fowl may vie with one another to see which swims the fastest'.[123] The Romans plainly understood what many factory farms today do not: that ducks need water to grow and thrive. This description shows that real effort was made to recreate the ducks' natural habitat, and they allowed them to swim and dabble among thickets as they pleased. As a result, the farmer raised happy, healthy ducks. Varro even tells us that several species of waterfowl kept in such duck ponds did not need to be crammed – providing a fine enclosure and a steady diet caused them to become deliciously fat on their own (Varro, *Rust.* 3.11.1–4). The landowner who possessed a natural pond was considered fortunate, for he could provide for his ducks without going to much trouble, and in Roman art there are plenty of mosaics that show ducks splashing happily in the water.[124] Part of the joy of raising ducks plainly came from watching them paddle in ponds, natural or otherwise. Their low price in Diocletian's *Edict of Maximum Prices* confirms that the Romans produced a steady supply, but this may also be due to wildfowlers catching the birds in large numbers.[125] The average Roman could enjoy duck for dinner, while the gourmet could say: 'Let a duck be served whole, but it is tasty only in the breast and neck. Return the rest to the cook'.[126] As for duck eggs, there does not seem to have been much enthusiasm for their consumption.[127]

The banks of the duck ponds were cultivated with grass, and the nesting boxes were placed against the high walls. These were a foot square and made of stone covered with smooth plaster. Box trees and myrtle were planted next to them to provide shelter and security. In the month of March, when the nesting season began, the farmer took care to scatter stalks and twigs in the pen so they could build their nests. Interestingly, Columella qualifies that anyone wishing to set up a duck pen for the first time should collect wild ducks' eggs and hatch them under barnyard chickens. This would produce a docile flock accustomed to farm life that would breed more willingly than wild-caught adult birds. Pliny records how the surrogate mothers felt about the situation:

> Above all things is the behaviour of a hen when ducks' eggs have been put under her and have hatched out—first her surprise when she does not quite recognise her brood, then her puzzled sobs as she anxiously calls them to her, and finally her lamentations round the margin of the pond when the chicks under the guidance of instinct take to the water.[128]

Chicks, unlike ducklings, can easily drown. One feels a pang of sympathy for the mother hen running rings around the duck pond, fretting for her delinquent water-loving children. It is also difficult for mother hens to communicate with ducklings, as they do not understand the hen's calls to food or shelter, which explains why Pliny remarks on the unusual quality of the mother's unheeded clucks. Roman aquaculture allowed them to provide artificial duck ponds with a constant stream of fresh, flowing water through a single channel. Into this channel the ducks' food was dumped once a day, and the water carried it into the pond so they could forage and dive as they would in the wild. Millet, pulse, and barley formed the bulk of their diet, but this could be supplemented with any food that was in local or seasonal abundance such as grape husks and acorns. Small freshwater fish and crabs could also be added, but this was expensive if one could not take them from a nearby river.

Mallards, teals, pochards, shelducks, wigeons, coots, purple swamphens, and even partridges could be kept in these enclosures. Other species of waterfowl may have been kept at one time or another, but since the mallard is depicted most frequently in Roman art it was probably the mallard that was most favoured by Roman farmers. This preference would have been subject to regional variations across the Empire, especially where eggs were taken from wild ducks, as the farmer could only take eggs from the species that bred naturally in his area. If one did not already have access to naturally swampy ground or a river, constructing a duck enclosure as these writers describe would not have been a feasible option except for the very wealthy landowner. The average farmer may have kept a small flock to his liking, but we should not confuse large commercial practices with common practices. Overall, ducks were less common as barnyard animals than geese and chickens. For many, it would have been easier to hunt them according to seasonal availabilities than raise them. But as we see from the examples of Strabo and Varro, waterfowl were valued as handsome additions to the ornamental aviary. The ability to keep and fatten ducks in a custom-built pond advertised wealth, but duck consumption was seldom viewed as a luxurious act because it was so easy for the poor to hunt these birds in the wild.[129]

Figure 3.8 Nile scene. Such variety would not be out of place in a Roman duck pond. From the House of the Faun, Pompeii. Naples Archaeological Museum, inv. 9990.

Source: Photo by the author.

Pigeons

Pigeons have been kept for a very long time in Italy and, like chickens, were assumed to be present on the average farm in Cato's time. They were prolific and easy to rear for profit, and they were also well-loved for their sweet natures, which made them popular as pets. Their small size and ability to forage for themselves, breed all year round, and live on roofs made it easy for farmers of all means to keep them; even city-dwellers could do so if they had a mind. Yet pigeon-raising was subject to the same pressures as other forms of animal husbandry, and we see elites farming intensively for eggs and squabs from the late Republic onward.

General Roman attitudes to pigeons were overwhelmingly positive. Primarily because they formed lasting, monogamous relationships, they were dedicated to Venus, with Martial advising that those initiated in the goddess' mysteries should not eat them (Mart. 13.66). We should note that there is no real zoological distinction between doves and pigeons. 'Pigeon' is generally applied to the larger species and 'dove' to the smaller, but they are all part of the same family, Columbidae.[130] The Romans did not distinguish by name between doves and pigeons, but called both *columba,* while the wood pigeon, the largest bird in the family, was known as *palumba,* and the pretty, distinct turtle-dove was the *turtur.* For all our hatred of pigeons as feathered rats, Romans showed a keen appreciation for their beauty and sweet temperaments. One of the few surviving snatches of Emperor Nero's poetry even mentions pigeons. Seneca quotes: 'Besides, as Nero Caesar says so elegantly: "The neck of the dove of Venus glistens in movement." And the neck of the peacock gleams with many colours whenever it moves one way or another'.[131] Large town houses had dovecotes to provide squabs and eggs for the table. There is one in the garden of the House of the Faun at Pompeii, and Martial wrote of a dovecote in his own garden.[132] Rural villas might have a freestanding dovecote, or they might incorporate one into the villa's tower.[133] Such dovecotes were a source of pride for the Roman estate owner.[134] The towers and turrets built for the birds were circular, with conical roofs, and rows of nesting holes. Pigeons were believed to like the colour white, so the cotes were painted white and kept scrupulously clean.[135] It was also believed one had to keep it clean and airy or the birds would abscond and never return, given the opportunity (Columella, *Rust.* 8.8.6). Columella, following Democritus' advice, describes a rather morbid method of ensuring a pigeon would remain in its dovecote. Kestrels, he says, commonly nest on buildings. If you take chicks from the nest and enclose them alive in pots covered in plaster, then hang them on the corners of the pigeon houses, it will cause the pigeons to love the dovecote and never leave it (Columella, *Rust.* 8.8.7). Pliny repeats the recipe, and cites that the reason is because the presence of kestrels discourages hawks from visiting dovecotes. The way he describes it suggests that kestrels were encouraged to live and nest near the dovecotes to keep the pigeons safe. Kestrels can kill pigeons, but more typically fly against mice, voles, and small passerines, so do not pose a huge threat to them. Whether they would actually frighten much larger hawks away is unclear, though protective nesting parents might make a hawk think twice (Plin. *HN* 10.109). The value of pigeon dung was another reason to keep the cotes clean. It was considered the best fertiliser and could be sold or spread generously on the fields.[136] Pigeon guano was so valuable the Romans even placed a tax on pigeon houses.[137]

Three types of pigeons appeared to fall under the name *columba*. There were the wild rock doves (*Columba livia*), almost identical to modern feral pigeons which settled on the turrets and gable-ends of farmhouses, flying from the fields and back to their towers as the fancy took them. Then there were domesticated white doves, gentler and more at home with people, content to scrounge about on the doorstep. A third hybrid species was produced by breeding the two. These were kept for profit and housed in what Varro calls a *peristeron*. This he describes as a large building with a vaulted roof, one narrow door and windows with double lattice that filled the structure with light. The interior and exterior were covered in smooth plaster to keep out pests. Round nests were made for each breeding pair, side by side and in rows that climbed to the height of the building. The nests had little walkways leading to them and one small entrance and exit. Fresh flowing water was provided so they could drink and bathe. They ate from troughs filled with barley, wheat, peas, beans, millet, and vetch. On average, once a month the droppings were cleaned out. Any injured birds received treatment. Any dead birds were removed. Brooding birds were removed to a separate area partitioned by a net. These birds were granted the liberty to fly in and out as they chose. This assisted their health, and because they had young it ensured they would return (Varro, *Rust.* 3.7.1–11).

When the squabs were covered with down, it was time to fatten them. They were stuffed with chewed bread. When they fledged, their legs were broken and they were left in the nest so their parents could continue to feed them. Pigeons breed multiple times a year, making this industry a profitable one. A fattened squab can be as large as a bantam chicken, with meat accumulating particularly around the pectoralis and flight muscles. Despite the economical ways one could raise these largely self-sufficient creatures, it is worth noting that Apicius only records two pigeon recipes versus eighteen chicken recipes, an indication of the latter bird's pre-eminence as a table bird. Such methods, with intense management, a freestanding cote, and attention to breeding the most profitable birds were generally employed near urban areas. Those who lived near cities could not let their flocks forage for themselves or they would lose their stock to the traps of the bird-catchers, so they were shut up in the manner Varro describes (Columella, *Rust.* 8.8.1–3).[138] A single dovecote could house as many as 5,000 birds.

Turtle-doves do not breed in captivity, so the Romans caught them wild and fattened them. They bulked up quickly in summer but languished in winter and had to be placed on a richer diet. Their enclosures were built to prevent them from flying, as this would make them thin. Hempen mats allowed them to waddle about their enclosure. They were only given the purest water as a means of disease prevention. Their dung was valuable and collected often (Columella, *Rust.* 8.9.1–3). Plump turtles were eaten with relish. Martial says, 'When I have a plump turtledove, good-bye, lettuce. And you may keep the snails. I don't want to waste my appetite'.[139] A special prestige is attached to turtle-doves, perhaps due to their taste, or perhaps to their scarcity in comparison with ordinary pigeons. Turtle-doves migrate away from Italy in the winter. The enterprising farmer who caught them and fattened them until winter, when they could no longer be caught wild, stood to make a handsome profit.[140]

Wood pigeons (*Columba palumbus*) were caught wild and fattened, though the bird is common enough that even the poorest could catch one for dinner. They made a fine meal, but Martial turns his nose up at them: 'Wood pigeons retard and dull the loins. Let him who would be salacious not eat this bird'.[141] Leaving aside the luxury market, it is likely that most *columbaria* were in rural areas, housing free-flying pigeons that could forage for themselves in the fields. Given that wild pigeons will nest in dovecotes without prompting, it is no wonder that the practice of constructing towers was so widespread. The addition of a small cote on a pre-existing structure is enough to tempt birds, which could then be managed with relatively little effort. On small holdings, pigeons were likely left to their own devices and the squabs eaten by the household. The intensive breeding and feeding we see described by our agricultural writers are directed towards those running enterprises with access to urban markets, where fattened birds could net a profit. Although *columbaria* were quite common on farms and townhouses, the habit of building them in towers or atop upper storeys has resulted in few examples surviving. The Roman period town of Karanis in the Egyptian Fayoum contains some well-preserved examples of *columbaria*. As described by Varro and Columella, these towers had pottery jars built into the walls of the columbaria to provide nesting niches for the birds, with larger niches intended for raising squabs. Many of the towers at Karanis are quite large, easily capable of housing birds in the thousands, again in line with the commercial production espoused by our authors.[142] In Juvenal (3.201–2), we also have mention of doves nesting under the eaves of houses, though it is not clear whether these birds are wild or part of an owned flock. As birds kept by rich and poor alike, we see prestige attached to the consumption only of fattened squabs and rare, difficult to keep turtle-doves as opposed to ordinary pigeons and the easily-caught *palumba*.

Peafowl

The peacock is a richly symbolic bird. Consumption and ownership were monopolised by elites, and their proliferation occurred at the same time that aviary-keeping was evolving as a whole to cater to the luxury markets.

Originally from India, peacocks were beloved by the Romans for their pride and beauty (Ov. *Ars am.* 1.627). They were extremely rare in the early and middle Republic, but in the imperial period it was exceptional *not* to see a tame peacock strutting about a rich man's house (Ath. 14.654d-e). The 'extravagant beauty' of the peacock was often reproduced in Roman paintings, and common reproduction on villa walls probably indicates that real peacocks once roamed there.[143] Oppian sang that the gods had made nothing more beautiful on earth for man to look at (*The Chase,* 2.590–8). There are stories of these fowl falling in love with humans and choosing to display their beautiful feathers for their darlings alone (Ath. 8.606c). And while the soul of a dead emperor was conceived as being borne by an eagle, from the Flavian period onwards a deified empress was associated with Juno's bird, the peacock.[144] Forty-two coins altogether use the peacock as a symbol of the Roman Empress. It is curious that despite the extreme sexual dimorphism of the species and the male bird's predominance in art and iconography, it was consistently associated with powerful females – with Juno, Hera, and the Empresses – rather than powerful males.[145]

It was in Varro's lifetime that peacock farming became popular. He distinguishes between those who keep peacocks for pleasure (who acquire far more male birds), and those who keep for profit (who acquire females) (Varro, *Rust.* 3.6). The fad of eating peacocks was begun by Cicero's rival Hortensius, who served them at a feast in 70 BCE.[146] The trend caught on like wildfire, to the point that it was a bold man who would throw a banquet without a peacock as the centrepiece (Cic. *Fam.* 9.20.2). Once the fashion for eating peacocks caught on, aviarists began to raise them commercially in huge numbers. The operation was a profitable one; the peacock was always one of the most expensive birds on the market. Varro tells us raising peafowl was far more profitable than raising chickens (Varro, *Rust.* 3.4.1).

According to Diocletian's *Edict of Maximum Prices* (4.39), one bird could fetch 300 *denarii*. Pound for pound, they were marginally more expensive than wild boar, 50 per cent more expensive than geese, and half as expensive as thrushes, turtle-doves, and partridges, though peafowl bones have been identified at fewer sites than many other game birds.[147] Gilbert calculates, however, that the cost of peacocks had risen exponentially by Diocletian's time. A single bird cost 6 per cent of a legionary soldier's annual salary in the Augustan period. This rose to between 15 and 33 per cent of a legionary soldier's annual salary by the time the price edict was written. The steady rise in price was probably driven by elite demand for peafowl at luxury banquets.[148] Peacock eggs were equally valuable and also eaten.[149]

Peacock flesh is not especially palatable, and its place on royal tables was probably assured by the decorative value of its feathers. Peacocks were served feathers and all, which is probably why a male bird cost a third more than a female bird in the Edict. Pageantry was part of the feasting process. Cooks dressed up the meat for display before carving.[150] The bird's beauty when alive made some cringe when they saw it dead: 'Do you admire him whenever he spreads his jewelled wings, and can you hand him over, callous man, to the cruel cook?'[151] Others raged against the senseless opulence:

> Yet, if a peacock be served, I shall hardly root out your longing to tickle your palate with it rather than with a hen. You are led astray by the vain appearance, because the rare bird costs gold and makes a brave show with the picture of its outspread tail – as though that had anything to do with the case! Do you eat the feathers you so admire? Does the bird look as fine when cooked? Yet, though in their meat they are on a par, to think that you crave the one rather than the other, duped by the difference in appearance![152]

Alive, the peacock was cherished. Dead, he became a symbol of Roman decadence and slothfulness. Snapshots of this come to us through satirical works. Horace asks, 'When hungry, do you disdain everything save peacock and turbot?'[153] Juvenal mocks, 'The punishment is instant, though, when you take off your cloak and, completely bloated, carry an undigested peacock to the baths'.[154] So it is that when someone inevitably yearns for the good old days, they say that people used to derive pleasure from live peacocks instead of dead ones (Ov. *Fast.* 6.175–7). The notoriously extravagant Emperor Vitellius served up the novel dish of peacock brains (Suet. *Vit.* 13.2). To top it off, the feathers were turned into fashionable fly-flaps (Mart. 14.67). Single feathers fetched a fine price, perhaps for this purpose, or perhaps for personal

Figure 3.9 Peacock from a wall painting. Villa Oplontis, first century CE.
Source: Photo by the author.

adornment. Peacocks moult their feathers yearly, and happily they do so before the feathers become too ragged. Thus, an intrepid landowner with a single ornamental bird could still make a smart profit by collecting fallen feathers. Peacocks are quite long-lived, with males surviving in good condition for twenty years or more.[155] A single breeding pair could be a fine investment.

Peafowl were often raised by those who lived close to the city, but one who lived in the countryside might keep a small flock to cheer his garden and delight visitors. Those who had villas on small, wooded islands off the coast of Italy were able inexpensively to raise great flocks of peafowl. Left to run wild and protected from predators – including human thieves – by the sea, they foraged for themselves, raised large broods, and their human carers only had to summon them once a day to count them and give them supplementary feed.

Those without a private island for protection had to construct a domed building made in proportion to the number of peafowl that would inhabit it. Each bird had its own private sleeping box, and the middle was kept clear so they could emerge to eat and stretch. Their attendant kept the place clean by regularly removing droppings, which were used as fertiliser. Smooth plaster prevented pests and snakes from entering (Varro, *Rust.* 3.6.4–6). It is later advised to place removable perches in the enclosure so that the birds do not step in their own dung, and so the perches can be taken out, the floor cleaned, and the dung collected.

It was common practice to place a clutch of peafowl eggs under chickens, which encouraged the peahens to lay again. Peahens could be trusted to incubate about three eggs themselves, and foster mothers took the rest. Every egg was precious. At laying times they were watched to ensure they laid only in their nesting boxes. They allowed only the most trustworthy chickens to hatch the eggs, and it seems the chickens did a fine job of caring for their foster children. It was said that one should not allow hens raising chicks to look upon another hen with a brood of peachicks, for they would become so envious of the peachicks' size and beauty that they would hate their own brood (Columella, *Rust.* 8.11.1–17). In Varro's time, no other breed of fowl brought in so great a profit: one could amass a small fortune with one hundred birds (Varro, *Rust.* 3.6.6).

Despite the abundance of peacocks that are found in art and literature, the picture is complicated by a dearth of peacock bones found at Roman archaeological sites. Thus far, no peafowl bones have ever been found for the Roman period in Italy; they have only been recovered from the north and west of the Empire. Such evidence may be the result of unequal archaeological investigation, but it may also indicate that certain areas predominated in peacock breeding or consumed more peacocks. But, as Gilbert points out, peacock imagery spread uniformly across the Empire. Their ubiquity in art represents an obsession with their beauty, but does not necessarily confirm a common presence. Like the lion, the peacock took on a number of symbolic meanings that made it important even to people who were completely unfamiliar with the living bird. The peacock as a symbol or simply a decorative motif was far more widespread than the bird itself, which remained rare and expensive from the beginning to the end of the Empire.[156] That peafowl were still being consumed in late antiquity is attested by breeding advice in the *Geoponica* (14.18.1) and by St Augustine, who wrote that he was served roast peacock. He then claims that he experimented with the meat and put it away for over a month and was amazed when it showed no sign of putrefaction.[157] Later Christian art and symbolism commonly used the peacock to express the idea of resurrection and immortality due to the belief that peacock meat did not spoil. The bird was also associated with the Virgin Mary.[158] This was, perhaps, a continuation of its traditional association with the Queen of Heaven. In all, the peacock was a powerful symbol of wealth and luxury that graced only the tables and gardens of the most privileged members of Roman society.

Pheasants and Guineafowl

Having treated peacocks, we come now to pheasants and guineafowl, similarly rare and prestigious table birds. Pheasants were originally imported from Colchis, land of the River Phasis at the south-east corner of the Black Sea. They were rarities in Greece from the fifth century BCE, and also in Ptolemaic Egypt, where they were bred as table and ornamental birds.[159] When exactly the Romans got hold of them is unknown. Neither Varro nor Columella allude to the intensive breeding of pheasants, but Columella does speak of extravagantly priced game birds from Phasis (Columella, *Rust.* 8.8). They were among the catalogue of birds thought fit to be sacrificed to Caligula's godhood (Suet. *Calig.* 22.3). Vitellius ate their brains alongside those of peacocks (Suet. *Vit.* 13.2). Pliny tells us that along with the guineafowl, the pheasant is 'now' found in Italy (Plin. *HN* 10.132). Martial catalogues them among the rare birds kept by his friend, so we may assume that by the late first century CE, they were being bred on farms (Mart. 3.58.16). A satirical diatribe against gluttony and luxury includes a vision of over-hunted pheasants (Petr. *Sat.* 118.36–8). Later, pheasant breeding seems to be more widely spread. The profligate Elagabalus was said, on some days, to dine on nothing but pheasant (SHA, *Heliogab.* 32.4). The pheasant is priced a little higher than the goose in Diocletian's Edict, and in the fourth century Palladius gives us a detailed description of how to care for them. That he includes cramming methods tells us this was a table bird (Palladius 1.29). It has often been suggested that the bird displayed as a fabled phoenix under Claudius in 47 or 48 CE was a golden pheasant brought to Rome from the Far East.[160] It would appear that the expanding luxury market of Rome encouraged farmers to try their hand at raising this strange, foreign bird, and they made quite an impression when served at banquets.

Guineafowl are in similar straits, and are widely attested as gracing the tables of the wealthy.[161] According to Pliny, *Meleagrides* were the last birds

Figure 3.10 Male and female pheasant. Detail, Four Seasons Mosaic from Rome, end of the fourth century CE. Palazzo Massimo alle Terme.

Source: Photo by the author.

to be enclosed by the Roman palate (Plin. *HN* 10.74). This name derives from their supposed connection with Meleager. As birds from North Africa, they were commonly referred to as *Numidica gallina* – 'Numidian fowl', or more simply as African fowl.[162] They were newly popular in the late Republic, with Varro advocating for breeding to be taken up to capitalise on the sudden fad for the speckled birds (Varro, *Rust.* 3.9.18–19). Despite initial demand coming from the luxury market (Juv. *Sat.* 11.142–3), there are indications that the guineafowl had a more widespread appeal and trickled onto smaller-scale farms. Guineafowl are temperamentally flighty and difficult to contain – if care is not taken they will wander away to fend for themselves. This independence means, however, that they are excellent foragers and very self-sufficient.[163] The thrifty farmer could pen them with his chickens at night and let them forage in the fields during the day. They are also excellent at eradicating weeds, seeds, small rodents, snakes, and other undesirable pests.[164] Pausanias described a spring and autumn festival to Isis at Tithorea in Phokis. When time came for sacrifices to be made, the wealthy sacrificed oxen and deer, while the poor sacrificed geese and

Figure 3.11 Guineafowl (top right) presented alongside fruit, a rooster, and partridges. End of the second century CE. Palazzo Massimo alle Terme.

Source: Photo by the author.

guineafowl (Paus. 10.32.15–16). This would indicate that they were valuable to the poor, but not so valuable as to be beyond their means to possess. Guineafowl bones have been found as far afield as a Roman *limes* camp called Saarburg in the Taunus mountains of West Germany.[165] Guineafowl died out as table birds in Europe following the decline of Rome. Several African communities domesticated them, and Europeans reintroduced them from West Africa at the same time the turkey was brought back from America. In Tudor England, the two birds were even initially confused.[166]

Conclusion

The transition from Republic to Principate was a period characterised by high levels of trade and production, with many farmers seeking profit rather than subsistence. Birds play an important part in this story; as farming methods became more intensive and sophisticated, this allowed poultry to be raised en masse to service urban markets. Greater demand for luxury goods saw a spike in the raising of exotic and fattened birds as elites sought to impress at lavish banquets. Peacocks, pheasants, and guineafowl are all examples of foreign birds that were enclosed in the Roman palate as part of these extravagant displays. Elites attempted to outdo each other by serving stranger and more expensive dishes, and the competitive nature of such banquets meant that serving an unfattened hen as opposed to the expected peacock dressed in its feathers – even if the chicken was more palatable – was unthinkable, unless one was trying to make a grand show of austerity. Birds communicated a great deal about status and wealth, and although the skewed evidence has forced us to concentrate on elite behaviour, we can still see snatches of how the poorer citizens related to their birds. Small flocks of chickens and geese provided eggs. Ducks and wood pigeons could be caught wild and eaten, leading to elites turning up their noses at these birds. Their pigeons were free-flying and foraged for themselves, whereas birds meant for market were enclosed in massive cotes and crammed. Poorer citizens might not have been able to engage in the intensive farming practices of the larger farms, but the existence of urban markets and the demand for fowl in general saw them have access to a greater variety of birds than had been around in Cato's time, and selective breeding saw animals become bigger and more productive. If they could not breed birds for profit, the poor had the opportunity to catch wild birds and sell them – a matter we shall treat in the next chapter.

Notes

1 Potter (2004).
2 Barth (1969); Dahl and Hjort (1976); Mullin (1999); Bussata (2007).
3 Hoffman (2014) 117l; van der Veen (2018) 68.
4 Garnsey (1999) 123
5 Garnsey (1999) 113. See also Morley (2007) 47 and André (1998).
6 Appadurai (1981).
7 Erdkamp and Holleran (2019) provide an excellent introduction to the study of food in the Roman world. In the same volume, Halstead (2019) looks at the contribution of zooarchaeology.
8 Goody (1982).
9 MacKinnon (2018) 100.
10 Arbuckle and McCarty (2014) 6.
11 Ashby (2002); Crabtree (1990).
12 Sykes (2014b) 353.
13 Hoffman (2014) 117–8; van der Veen (2018) 68.
14 Wilkins and Hill (2006) 150.
15 Bowman and Wilson (2013) 5–6. See also Kron (2012) for an outline of the sophisticated and productive nature of Roman farming, as well as its intensification and commercialisation to meet the needs of trade and urban markets. De Grossi Mazzorin (2001) looks specifically at faunal remains in Central Italy and how they show a move away from subsistence. For a general overview of Roman farming, see White (1970).
16 Valenzuela-Lamas and Albarella (2017) 408–9.
17 Kron (2015) 165. Donahue (2019) 97–8 discusses *collegia* feasts and available evidence.
18 Kron (2015) 165.
19 Bergmann (2002) 89.

20 Green (1997) 440.
21 Marzano (2013) 86.
22 Howe (2014) 138–40; see Cato, *Agr.* 1.
23 Hoffman (2014) 38.
24 Garnsey (1988) 44; van der Veen (2018) 54.
25 Peters (1998) demonstrates this amply. The literature is vast and growing, but for some instructive examples centred on Roman Italy and Roman Britain see: Maltby (1984, 2010 and 2015), King (1988), MacKinnon (2001 and 2004). Doherty et al. (2021) provide an example of how studying chicken bones can completely overturn traditional assumptions about how and why poultry were raised in the past.
26 Kron (2015) 165.
27 Hoffman (2014) 118.
28 Cato, *Agr.* 143.3: *gallinas multas et ova uti habeat.*
29 Johnson (1968) 3.
30 For legislation, see: Gell. *NA* 2.24; Macrob. *Sat.* 3.17. For evasions of the laws, see Plin. *HN* 10.138–40.
31 Johnson (1968) 7.
32 Varro, *Rust.* 3.5.8; Plin. *HN* 10.141.
33 Johnson (1968) 6.
34 Suet. *Tib.* 60; cf *CIL* VI 8848 and 8849.
35 In Greece, the lavish market that exemplified times of peace was said to be filled with diverse and imported birds: Ar. *Pax* 1000–5.
36 Littlewood (1987) 14.
37 Hoffman (2014) 36.
38 Thomas and Wilson (1994) 168.
39 Jashemski (1993) 188.
40 Jashemski (1979) 108.
41 Bond (2016) 152; *CIL* VI, 6286, 8848, 8849, VIII 9432.
42 Veg. *De re mil.* 1.7; Bond (2016) 164–5.
43 *CIL* VI 9200, 9201.
44 Mart. 3.58.12–19. Translated by Shackleton Bailey (1993a) 227–9 with amendments: *vagatur omnis turba sordidae chortis, argutus anser gemmeique pavones nomenque debet quae rubentibus pinnis et picta perdix Numidicaeque guttatae et impiorum phasiana Colchorum; Rhodias superbi feminas premunt galli; sonantque turres plausibus columbarum, gemit hinc palumbus, inde cereus turtur.*
45 Kron (2017) 129.
46 Kolataj et al. (2007) 35–8.
47 Poole (2010) 156; Serjeantsen (2009) 268.
48 Corbino et al. (2022).
49 Corbino et al. (2022).
50 Sykes (2012).
51 Perry-Gal et al. (2015) 9852.
52 Taran (1975); MacDonald and Blend (2000) 497; Crawford (2003) 12; Sykes (2012) 161; Sykes (2014a) 85.
53 For some of the earliest Greek images of roosters, see Lamberton and Rotroff (1985) 6–7.
54 Perry-Gal et al. (2015) 9852; Corbino et al. (2022) 81.
55 Trentacoste (2014) 64–5. See Corbino et al. (2022) 82 for a catalogue of the earliest finds and their contexts.
56 de Grossi Mazzorin (2005) 352–3; see Pieraccini (2014) for images.
57 Trentacoste (2014) 65.
58 de Grossi Mazzorin (2005) 354.

59 Watson (2002) 380.
60 Corbino et al (2017) 50.
61 Varro, *Rust.* 3.3.5; Cic. *Div.* 1.28; 2.73.
62 Diet and animal use are effective tools for assessing Romanisation. See Meadows (1994) and King (2001).
63 Armstrong (1958) 32.
64 Morris (2011) 162–3.
65 Cool (2006) 99.
66 Doherty et al. (2021).
67 Maltby (1997).
68 Cool (2006) 101.
69 MacKinnon (2014) 323.
70 Columella, *Rust.* 8.2.4–5; Cato, *Agr.* 143.3
71 Columella, *Rust.* 8.2.4–5; Johnson (1968) 22–3.
72 Varro, *Rust.* 3.9.4; Collumella, *Rust.* 8.2.7; Palladius 1.27
73 Arist. *Hist. an.* 558b, 17; *Gen. an.* 749b 28.
74 Jennison (1937) 14.
75 Columella, *Rust.* 8.2.14
76 Audoin-Rouzeau (1995); Peters (1998); MacKinnon (2001) and (2004); Filean (2008); Trentacoste (2018).
77 Kron (2014) 119.
78 de Cupere et al. (2005) 1596.
79 Kron (2014) 121.
80 Kron (2014) 119.
81 Columella, *Rust.* 8.4.3. Translated by Forster (1954) 339: *Nam volatile pecus facile custodiam pastoris decipit.*
82 Goebel and Peters (2014) 601–2.
83 Columella, *Rust.* 8.7.4; Varro, *Rust.* 3.9.19–20.
84 Mart. 13.62. Translated by Shackleton Bailey (1993c) 197: *Pascitur et dulci facilis gallina farina, pascitur et tenebris. Ingeniosa gula est.*
85 Varro, *Rust.* 3.9.3; Columella, *Rust.* 8.2.3; Plin. *HN* 10.25.50. See also: Arist. *Hist. an.* 631b.
86 Plin. *HN* 10.50. This passage names two ways of gelding: either searing the legs, or searing the loins with a glowing iron.
87 De Cupere et al. (2005) 1595.
88 Mart. 13.64. Translated by Shackleton Bailey (1993c) 199: *Succumbit sterili frustra gallina marito. Hunc matris Cybeles esse decebat avem.*
89 Mart. 13.63. Translated by Shackleton Bailey (1993c) 199 with changes: *Ne nimis exhausto macresceret inguine gallus, amisit testes. Nunc mihi gallus erit.* The word *gallus* is a pun that can mean a cockerel, a Gaul, or a priest of Cybele.
90 Juv. *Sat.* 9.70–1; Hor. *Sat.* 2.2.120–1.
91 Zeuner (1963) 448.
92 Birkhead (2016) 43ff.
93 Columella, *Rust.* 8.6.1–2; Varro *Rust.* 3.9.12.
94 Thurmond (2006) 209.
95 Columella, *Rust.* 8.3.1. The same advice is repeated for pigeons, 8.7.2.
96 Dohner (2001) 404.
97 See Alpheius of Mitylene, *Anth. Pal.* 9.95, who describes a mother hen sheltering her chicks during snowfall until the cold kills her, and calls on Procne and Medea, who famously killed their children, to learn from this hen what it means to be a good mother.
98 Columella, *Rust.* 8.5.14; Geoponica 14.7.20.

99 Columella, *Rust.* 8.5.13–14; Varro, *Rust.* 3.9.10; Geoponica 15.7.8.
100 Varro, *Rust.* 3.9.11; Geoponica 14.7.2.
101 Diod. Sic. 1.74.4–5; Plin. *HN* 10.154.
102 Perry-Gal (2015) 9849.
103 Kron (2014) 119.
104 Gill (1994) int. xxiii.
105 Horsfall (1981).
106 Dembeck (1965) 200.
107 Ov. *Fast.* 1.453–4; Juv. *Sat.* 6. 535–41.
108 Lucr. 4.682–683. Translated by Rouse (1924) 329–31: *et humanum longe prae-sentit odorem Romulidarum arcis servator, candidus anser.*
109 Livy 5.47.4; Plut. *Mor. De fort. Rom.* 12; Plut. *Quaest. Rom.* 98 287c.
110 Varro, *Rust.* 3.2–9; Gell. *NA* 6.16.
111 Arist. *Hist. an.* VIII 593b. For a Roman reference, see Ael. NA 5.30.
112 Columella, *Rust.* 8.14.3. Translated by Forster (1954) 389–91: *curandum est, ut mares feminaeque quam amplissimi corporis et albi coloris eligantur. Nam est aliud genus varium, quod a fero mitigatum domesticum factum est. Id neque aeque fecundum est, nec tam pretiosum: propter quod minime nutriendum est.*
113 Plin. *HN* 10.26. Translated by Rackham (1940) 325: *Est et anseri vigil cura Capitolio testata defenso, per id tempus canum silentio proditis rebus, quam ob causam cibaria anserum censores in primis locant. quin et fama amoris Aegii dilecta forma pueri nomine Olenii Amphilochi, et Glauces Ptolomaeo regi cithara canentis quam eodem tempore et aries amasse proditur. potest et sapientiae videri intellectus his esse: ita comes perpetuo adhaesisse Lacydi philosopho dicitur, nusquam ab eo, non in publico non in balineis, non noctu non interdiu digressus.* The story of Lacydes and his faithful goose is repeated in Ael. *NA* 7.41
114 Birkhead (2011) 94.
115 Plin. *HN* 10.27. Translated by Rackham (1940) 325–7: *Nostri sapientiores qui eos iecoris bonitate novere. fartilibus in magnam amplitudinem crescit, exemptum quoque lacte mulso augetur.*
116 Petr. *Sat.* 136; Ov. *Fast.* 1.453–4.
117 Mart. 13.58. Translated by Shackleton Bailey (1993c) 197: *Aspice quam tumeat magno iecur ansere maius! Miratus dices: Hoc, rogo, crevit ubi?* See also Juv. *Sat.* 5.114–6 and Stat. *Silv.* 4.6.9–10.
118 Varro, *Rust.* 3.10.7; Columella, *Rust.* 8.14.10–11.
119 Hor. *Sat.* 2.8.88, Plin. *HN* 8.77.
120 Compare to Simulus, the peasant character of the *Moretum*, whose poverty is indicated by the lack of meat in his diet.
121 King (1999) investigates the presence of animals on Roman military sites. Though the focus is on domestic mammals, hunted and trapped species feature commonly on military sites, including a wide range of birds. German sites in particular show high numbers of birds.
122 The following description is taken from Columella, *Rust.* 8.15.1–6.
123 Columella, *Rust.* 8.15.4. Translation by Forster (1954) 399: *Nec ob hanc tamen causam totus locus silvulis occupetur, sed ut dixi, per circuitum vacet, ut sine impedimento, cum apricitate diei gestiunt aves, nandi velocitate concertent.*
124 Farrar (1998) 64.
125 Kron (2014) 125.
126 Mart. 13.52. Translated by Shackleton (1993) 193: *Tota quidem ponatur anas, sed pectore tantum et cervice sapit: cetera redde coco.*
127 Smith (1971) 43–5 notes that salmonella infection is more easily transmissible through duck eggs than chicken eggs, and bacteria is more likely to accumulate

on the shells since the ducks will return to the nest to brood while damp from swimming. Given that duck eggs are regularly and safely consumed in many cultures, however, it may rather be a result of the fact that Romans lacked true domesticated ducks, and generally gathered eggs from the wild to hatch.

128 Plin. *HN* 10.76. Translated by Rackham (1940) 391: *super omnia est anatum ovis subditis atque exclusis admiratio prima non plane agnoscentis fetum, mox incerti singultus sollicite convocantis, postremo lamenta circa piscinae stagna mergentibus se pullis natura duce.*

129 For more on zooarchaeology, Albarella (2005) provides an overview of the use of ducks and geese from Roman to medieval times.

130 Allen (2009) 20.

131 Sen. *QNat.* 1.5.6. Corcoran (1971) 49: *Alioquin, ut ait Nero Caesar disertissime, 'colla Cytheriacae splendent agitata columbae' et uariis coloribus pauonum ceruix, quotiens aliquo deflectitur, nitet.*

132 Mart. 3.58.18–19; 12.31.6. See also: Ov. *Pont.* 1.6.51.

133 Bowe (2004) 53.

134 Gaál (2017) 12.

135 Ov. *Tr.* 1.97–8; Columella, *Rust.* 8.83.

136 Cato, *Agr.* 36; Varro, *Rust.* 3.7.5; Houlihan (1986) 103.

137 Lichtheim (1957) 110.

138 See Prudent. *Hamartigenia*, 804–23 for a vision of a fowler baiting flocks of pigeons with food and catching them with various implements.

139 Mart. 15.53. Translated by Shackleton Bailey (1993c) 195: *Cum pinguis mihi turtur erit, lactuca valebis; et cocleas tibi habe. Perdere nolo famem.*

140 Varro, *Rust.* 3.8.1. It was recommended to catch turtle-doves for fattening at harvest time (late autumn) because this was when hardier and larger broods were hatched. They could then be kept into the winter.

141 Mart. 13.67. Translated by Shackleton Bailey (1993c) 201: *Inguina torquati tardant hebetantque palumbi: non edat hanc volucrem qui cupit esse salax.*

142 Husselman (1953); Lewis and Llewellyn-Jones (2018) 261–2.

143 Zeitlin (2013) 72–3.

144 Mattingly (1967) 147.

145 Gilbert (2016) 58.

146 Plin. *HN* 10.23.45; Ael. *NA* 5.21.

147 Kron (2014) 127.

148 Gilbert (2016) 57.

149 Ath. 2.58b; Macrob. *Sat.* 3.13.2.

150 Zeuner (1963) 456.

151 Mart. 13.70. Translated by Shackleton Bailey (1993c) 201: *Miraris, quotiens gemmantis explicat alas, et potes hunc saevo tradere, dure, coco?*

152 Hor. *Sat.* 2.2.23–30. Translated by Fairclough (1926) 139 with amendments: *vix tamen eripiam, posito pavone velis quin hoc potius quam gallina tergere palatum, corruptus vanis rerum, quia veneat auro rara avis et picta pandat spectacula cauda: tamquam ad rem attineat quidquam. num vesceris ista, quam laudas, pluma? cocto num adest honor idem? carne tamen quamvis distat nil, hac magis illam inparibus formis deceptum te petere esto.*

153 Hor. *Sat.* 1.2.115–16. Translated by Fairclough (1926) 29: *num esuriens fastidis omnia praeter pavonem rhombumque.*

154 Juv. *Sat.* 1.142–43. Translated by Braund (2004) 143: *poena tamen praesens, cum tu deponis amictus turgidus et crudum pauonem in balnea portas.*

155 Aristotle noted how long-lived the birds are, citing their lifespan as twenty-five years (*Hist. an.* 564a25-b9).

156 Gilbert (2016).

157 August. *CD* 21.4.
158 Taylor (2003) 195.
159 Jennison (1937) 109.
160 Plin. *HN* 10.5; Beagon (2014) 426.
161 Wilkins and Hill (2006) 150.
162 Bodson (2014) 559. Hor. *Epod.* 2.53; Petr. *Sat.* 93; Juv. *Sat.* 11.142–434; Mart. 3.58.15, 13.45.1.
163 Pliny, *HN* 10.144 comments on their pugnacious natures.
164 Johnson (1968) 10.
165 Zeuner (1963) 457.
166 Cocker and Tipling (2013) 37.

4 Fowling and Bird-Catching

Introduction

In the previous chapter, we considered how farming and aviculture intensified in response to market forces. It is worth reiterating how drastically urbanisation was changing the Roman world. At its peak around 150 CE, Rome held 1,200,000 people on eighteen square kilometres. Food was drawn from greater and greater distances to supply urban demand.[1] Feasting was common, and in this climate fowlers and farmers stood to make huge profits. Important individuals might throw a banquet upon their accession to office, or upon their arrival in the City (Suet. *Vit.* 13.2). Communal feasting was commonplace among *collegia* throughout the Empire.[2] The charter of the college of Aesculapius and Hygia in Rome (mid-second century CE) records seven dinners in its list of meals. Here, rank is shown to determine the share of food each of the sixty members received, with college leaders and patrons taking the lion's share and remaining members receiving lesser portions according to rank.[3] Martial's complaints ring all the truer for knowing that apportioning better food according to status was a candidly documented reality: 'A golden turtle dove fills you up with its outsize rump, while I am served with a jay that died in its cage'.[4] Frequent feasting in urban centres, coupled with the ways in which one could use the dinner table to reinforce status, was having as much an effect on humble fowlers as on large-scale food producers. Fashions dictated which birds were hunted to beautify the tables of nobles. In the City, an industry sprang up to service demand. Varro tells us that in Rome, butchers (*macellarii*) had reserves both within and without the City where they could obtain birds to sell at the market (Varro, *Rust.* 3.4.2). Fowlers could therefore work as itinerant vendors and sell catches themselves or journey to the City and sell to the *macellarii* depending on what suited them.[5] Not just the professional *auceps,* but also the poor could catch wild birds to make money. For example, at the turn of the first century CE, Dio of Prusa wrote of a peasant family that farmed in the Euboean hills. They were self-sufficient, and catching game and selling vegetables allowed them to make a meagre supplementary income (Dio Chrys. *Or.* 7). Since bird-catching could be done virtually anywhere, by anyone, and with simple tools, wildfowl provided an

DOI: 10.4324/9781003247906-5

important source of meat in otherwise sparse diets.[6] In wildfowl, we can measure the extremes of Roman consumption patterns and lifestyles. Yet although we might suppose that the poor and itinerant stood to gain the most from urban demand for wildfowl, wealthy elites soon constructed special enclosures wherein they could house game birds for fattening, with special emphasis on capturing migratory birds so they could sell them out of season when wild catches were no longer available.

Previous research has claimed there is little evidence to show exactly how birds were hunted in Roman times.[7] In actuality, there is an abundance of evidence available. Fowling was practised from the earliest days in Italy and there are records of birds being hunted with glue traps, nets, decoys, and slings. Thurmond notes that thanks to the migratory patterns of Mediterranean birds, eating fresh fowl was a 'feast or famine' scenario, but adds that our Roman sources fail to illuminate us on this point.[8] Again, this is untrue, for our Roman sources *do* show a keen awareness of seasonal changes in the availability of birds. The concept of migration – that birds travelled to live in more favourable climates when the seasons changed – was admittedly not fully understood. In Roman texts, we see birds hailed as harbingers of changing seasons, but awareness of where they went and why is less complete.[9] For some birds their movement was proverbial, as when Pompey criticised his enemy Lucullus' property at Tusculum, saying it was unsuitable for winter. Lucullus simply laughed in his face and asked if he believed he had less sense than cranes and storks, and did not think to change residence according to the seasons (Plut. *Vit. Luc.* 39.4). Aristotle and Pliny mention that swallows migrate in winter, retiring to nearby sunny places, although they also offered hibernation as another explanation. Blackbirds, thrushes, and starlings were said to migrate to neighbouring districts, while the turtle-dove was believed to moult and hibernate (Plin. *HN* 10.35–36). The cuckoo's annual disappearance was even blamed on it transmuting into a different bird entirely.[10] Regardless of whether bird migration was fully understood, Roman attention to seasonal fluctuations is key to understanding hunting methods and appreciating the significance behind wildfowl consumption. Neville Morley stresses the importance of ecology and its effects on trade and economics. One region will have a certain resource in abundance and a dearth of another, affecting demand for goods on a regional scale.[11] We can relate this to birds in a temporal as well as regional sense.

In the Roman period, birds were caught in many ways and for many reasons.[12] Fowling had its peak seasons, but it could be done year-round. In general terms, the easiest time to catch birds was when they migrated in autumn. Peak trapping periods were October and November, when birds gathered in huge numbers and in predictable places as they prepared to journey to warmer climates. Birds are especially fat at such times, loaded with fuel for the journey.[13] Once winter set in, fowlers hunted the Italian winter residents such as thrushes, fieldfares, and blackbirds. Palladius tells us

December to March was the best time to catch birds: 'At this time it is appropriate to set snares in thickets and berry-trees and brush to catch thrushes and other birds. This bird-catching extends right to the month of March'.[14] In summer (July-August), waterfowl such as ducks, geese, and swans moult their flight feathers and cannot fly, making them easy to corral and capture in nets.[15] Such seasonal considerations are key when investigating how wildfowl consumption could betray status and social stratification.

Legalities of Hunting

Before we get into details surrounding individual birds, it is worth exploring the laws recorded in the *Digest* that relate to bird-catching to get a sense of who hunted birds, where they were permitted to hunt, and why they hunted. One law specifies that the purchase of a catch of birds remains valid even if a fowler's efforts are unfruitful; that is, a fowler paid to bring home storks, for example, would still be paid even if no storks could be found (*Dig.* 18.1.8). This indicates that people made contracts with fowlers to supply birds for the table. Another law specified that wild birds automatically became the property of the person who caught them, except in cases where they were fulfilling a contract (*Dig.* 41.1.1). Ownership applied even if the birds had been caught on another person's land, although if a fowler trespassed without permission the owner had the right to ban him from doing so again (*Dig.* 41.1.3). Poaching does not seem to be a concept; trespass is the issue. A rescript issued by Antoninus Pius declared that fowlers had to gain permission *prior* to hunting on another person's land, which might indicate that some complained of fowlers and hunters straying onto their property (*Dig.* 8.3.16). There was no concept of having ownership over wild animals on one's land unless certain prerequisites were met. Bees swarming in a farmer's tree could not be considered his, but they became property if they were housed in his hive. A bird nesting in a tree was not his, but a pigeon that chose to nest in his dovecote was, which meant a fowler could be made liable if he caught a pigeon on another person's land (*Dig.* 41.1.5). Wild birds kept in cages were owned so long as the owner kept control over them, but ownership was lost if they escaped (*Dig.* 41.2.3). For animals universally considered wild, but which had been tamed or were in the habit of returning, ownership was retained so long as the instinct to return remained. Peacocks and pigeons were acknowledged to have wild natures, but since they always returned, the status of ownership was clear. If a bird classed as 'wild' lost its inclination to return, it could be seized by the first taker. This is in contrast to chickens and geese, which were considered to have tame natures. If chickens or geese ran or flew away, they remained the property of the owner, even if he had no idea where his flock was (*Dig.* 41.1.44, 41.1.4, 41.1.5). In contrast to the Middle Ages, there were no formal restrictions on hunting. Anyone could hunt birds in woods, meadows, or waterways, though this would not have extended to privately owned game enclosures.[16] Conceptually, wild birds belonged to all, and all were free to hunt and catch them however they wished, provided they did not commit trespass along the way.

Hunting Methods

Fowling has long been practised in the Italian peninsula, with pre-Roman peoples developing their own specialised methods of hunting. For example, the Etruscans were said to have used music when hunting, and the Tomb of the Leopards (Tarquinia, c.470 BCE) depicts a flute player surrounded by birds, a possible depiction of the Etruscan method of attracting prey.[17] In the Tomb of Hunting and Fishing (Tarquinia, c.510 BCE), we see a boy using a sling to bring down waterfowl.[18]

Figure 4.1 Fowling with a sling. Etruscan Tomb of Hunting and Fishing, c.510 BCE.

Source: Photo by Edward Blume-Poulton.

The labour of bird-catching was considered sweet because it involved no risk of personal harm and involved no dangerous weaponry (Oppian, *The Chase*, 1.57f). Swords, spears, and arrows were generally not used to hunt birds, except for the very largest like ostriches. Ancient hunters did not possess the blunt-headed arrows, or bird-bolts, that were employed by fowlers in the medieval and early modern periods. There are, in fact, few examples of ancients using arrows to hunt birds, and those that exist are tied to heroic scenes (such as the shooting contest in the *Aeneid*) where the point is to demonstrate the skill of the archers, rather than to hunt and kill a bird in an efficient manner.[19] A bow and arrow was serviceable to one who had access to expensive equipment and the training to use it, but the arsenal of the typical *auceps* consisted of nets, decoy birds, nooses, traps, and springes.[20] An epitaph for a professional fowler that demonstrates the variety of tools used runs thus:

> Craugis the huntsman, son of Ncolaidas, an Arcadian of Orchomenus, gives to thee, Pan the Scout, this serap of his old fowling net, his triple-twisted snare for the feet, his spring-traps made of sinews, his latticed cages, his nooses for the throat which one draws up, his sharp stakes hardened in the fire, the sticky moisture of the oak, the cane wet with it that catches birds, the triple cord which is pulled to close the hidden spring-net, and the net for catching by the neck the clamorous cranes.[21]

By far, the commonest and most popular tool was the *harundo*, or limed reed, which essentially functioned as a portable glue trap.[22] This was the choice for professional and recreational hunters alike, to the point that lime and reeds could personify the very spirit of fowling (Apul. *Met.* 11.8).[23] While listing the different types of *harundo*, Pliny mentions that reeds used in fowling must be of a considerable length and strength, and that the reeds best suited to the task came from Palermo (Plin. *HN* 16.66). As for hunting nets, they were made of flax, and it appears that imported flax from the Spanish provinces was best for the task. The flax of Comae in Campania had a reputation for making superb fishing and fowling nets, being incredibly strong and yet fine enough that a net large enough to encircle a wood could be passed through a ring. Each string consisted of 150 threads (Plin. *HN* 19.2). This betrays a certain sophistication and refinement to the basic technology they used.

Bird liming typically involves smearing branches or other surfaces with lime and luring birds to roost or flutter nearby until they become stuck.[24] The Roman technique of liming with a *harundo* was very different. It involved the fowler actively attempting to smear the birds' wings, causing the feathers to stick together and either forcing it to the ground or leaving the feathers stuck fast to the reed. As the adage goes, 'The bird cannot make its escape once its wings are limed'.[25] It is attested that fowlers would hide in bushes, attract birds with decoys or food, and suddenly lunge from hiding to smear the wings while the bird was distracted (Mart. 14.216). Other descriptions of the limed reed reveal that it was jointed, and could be gradually extended, rather like a fishing pole (Satyrus, *Anth. Pal.* 10.11). As part of a poetic metaphor, we have the following description:

> Thus the fowler who dispeoples the grove with his cane-rod tipped with birdlime, pursues the bird over his head with a lengthening reed, and silently tries to reach at last the topmost branches by adding a joint to his tapering rod.[26]

In Roman art, we see representations of men (sometimes Cupids) preparing the sticky lime.[27] It was then stored in a portable pot. The hunter would find a suitable place close by berries or another food source, or perhaps use a decoy to attract birds. Once in place, he would apply the lime to the end of his *harundo* and slowly, carefully poke it into the top branches of a tree, extending the reed if necessary. If a bird brushed its wings against the lime it would become stuck, and the hunter would collect his prize. The advantage of this method is that it allowed fowlers to take their prey alive.[28] Stuck feathers could be plucked off and the (mostly unhurt) bird could either be killed immediately or caged and stored alive to be eaten, kept as a pet, or sold at the market at a later date. The 'Small Hunt' Mosaic from Piazza Armerina in Sicily (fourth century CE) shows fowlers standing under a tree with limed rods upon their backs, small capes over their shoulders to act as perches for their decoy birds, and jars hanging from their belts which must contain lime.[29]

Figure 4.2 Fowlers and their decoy birds. Detail of the Small Hunt Mosaic, Piazza Armerina, Sicily. Fourth century CE.

Source: Photo by Paul Williams, Alamy Stock Photo.

According to our sources, bird lime was of thick consistency and whitish yellow in colour. It was also fireproof.[30] The lime was made from mistletoe berries. As a parasitic bush that grows on trees, mistletoe seeds are naturally sticky to help them cling to the trunk of a host tree when deposited by birds

Figure 4.3 A fowler using a *harundo* to catch a blackbird in a tree. Fourth century CE, House of the Laberii, Uthina. Tunisia.

Source: Photo by Heather Farish, Alamy Stock Photo.

or animals. This explains why the word *viscum* denotes both mistletoe and the viscous glue that could be made from the berries. The Romans observed that birds (particularly the mistle thrush, *Turdus viscivorus*) would eat the berries and spread the seeds by defecating onto trees.[31] William Turner, an authority on birds in the sixteenth century, records that mistletoe berries were still used for making lime in his day and cites the ancients on their wisdom. He quotes the following ancient proverb and explains:

> *"Turdus ipse sibi malum cacat"* – the thrush shitteth mischief for herself. She shitteth out the miscel berries well prepared in her body, and layeth them upon the tree; the berries grow into a bush, and the bush bringeth forth berries, and of the berries the fowler maketh birdlime, wherewith afterward he taketh the thrush: and so the thrush hath shitteth out her own destruction.[32]

Isidore of Seville says the same: 'The *turdela* [mistle thrush] is bigger than the *turdus* [song thrush]. It is said to beget mistletoe through its shit. Among the ancients there was the proverb, "the bird shits trouble for itself"'.[33] Mistletoe bears fruit in late autumn and winter, hence its association with

Christmas. Since thrushes were resident in Italy during winter, the berries were an important source of food for them. Oak trees likely furnished most of the mistletoe bushes used by hunters.[34]

> No longer warble, blackbird, by the oak-tree, no longer perch on the highest branch and call. This tree is thy enemy; hie thee to where the vine mounts with shady green leaves. Set thy feet on its branch and sing by it, pouring shrill notes from thy throat. For the oak bears the mistletoe which is the foe of birds, but the vine bears grape-clusters; and Bacchus loves songsters.[35]

The irony that birds were sustained by the same berries that furnished man with the means to catch and eat them was clearly not lost on the Romans. Pliny describes the process of making bird lime:

> Mistletoe berries can be used for making bird lime, if gathered at harvest time while unripe; for if the rainy season has begun, although they get bigger in size they lose in viscosity. They are then dried and when quite dry pounded and stored in water, and in about twelve days they turn rotten – and this is the sole case of a thing that becomes attractive by rotting. Then after having been again pounded up they are put in running water and there lose their skins and become viscous in their inner flesh. This substance after being kneaded with oil is bird lime, used for entangling birds' wings by contact with it when one wants to snare them.[36]

A formula for the stickiest lime involved chewing the berries to remove the skins rather than letting them rot off. Superstitious advice accompanied this recipe, with recommendations that it should ideally be gathered from an oak tree, at the new moon, without the use of iron, and without letting it touch the ground. This interesting passage suggests a quasi-magical approach to the preparation of the substance and may hint that fowlers practiced magical rituals to help ensure the success of the hunt.[37]

David Parrish catalogues how winter was represented in Roman and Late Antique art, noting how images of boar, hare, ducks, and hunters holding reeds exemplified the season due to its connection to hunting and bird-catching.[38] Based on these images and the overwhelming connection of bird-catching to winter, we can assume that the giant reed (*Arundo donax*) supplied the *harundo* of choice. This reed produces tall, straight, bamboo-like stems that reach a diameter of one to four centimetres. *Arundo donax* is traditionally harvested in winter when the plant goes dormant and has a low moisture content. It has a variety of uses and is still grown commercially in Italy and the wider Mediterranean region today.[39] The ease with which poor families could access and prepare these simple tools likely explains the *harundo*'s dominance in fowling.

Figure 4.4 Detail of the Triumph of Neptune Mosaic. Second century CE. Personification of winter holding a reed and ducks. Bardo National Museum.

Source: Photo by Erdal Şükrü Akan, Alamy Stock Photo.

Fowling was especially appropriate for young men and boys. In a Greek source, Xenophon describes a young man's dedication to bird-catching, and how he would get up on cold winter nights to lay traps and snares before the creatures were awake (Xen. *Cyr.* 1.6.39). Longus' *Daphnis and Chloe,* a pastoral novel, shows rustic boys catching birds, even saying that in the freezing winters there was little else to do but stay by the fire and make bird traps (3.3.3). The teenage Daphnis is shown liming birds in winter, and the scene demonstrates the effectiveness of the technique:

> Right in front of Dryas' farmyard grew two large myrtles and an ivy bush, the myrtles close together and the ivy between them, so that it spread its tendrils over each of them like a vine and with its intertwining leaves formed a kind of cave, and many a cluster of berries, as big as grapes, hung from the stems. So there was a crowd of winter birds around it, owing to the scarceness of food outside: many a blackbird, many a thrush, pigeons and starlings and every other winged ivy-eater ... So he made tracks for the farmyard and, after shaking the snow off his legs, set his snares, daubed long sticks with his birdlime, and sat down waiting

for birds and thinking anxiously of Chloe. Plenty of birds came, and enough were caught that he was endlessly busy collecting, killing, and plucking them.[40]

Elsewhere in the novel, it is made clear that part of the charm of fowling was that boys could provide meat for the table while having fun (2.12.4). The fact that bird-catching was a pursuit for boys and young men can also be seen in the fable of *Love and the Fowler*:

> A fowler, still a boy, was hunting birds in a woodland grove and saw winged Eros sitting on a branch of a box tree. When he noticed him, he was excited because the bird seemed a good catch. Fastening all his rods together one to another he lay in wait for Eros, who was hopping here and there. The boy grew annoyed when he met with no success. He threw away his rods and went to an old plowman who had taught him that skill; he told him the story and showed him Eros perched in the tree. The old man shook his head with a smile and answered the boy: "Stop your hunting and don't go near that bird; get far away from it; it's a dangerous creature. You will be happy so long as you don't catch him; but when you come to the measure of a man, this bird which now avoids you and has hopped away will suddenly come unbidden and land on your head".[41]

This fable is an allegory about sexual awakening. To the prepubescent boy, Cupid seems as harmless as a bird. The wise old man knows better, and warns that once he has come to manhood, he will realise that this 'bird' is, in fact, a dangerous creature that will hunt after him. It demonstrates that fowling was naturally associated with youths.

Under the Empire, professional fowlers did a roaring trade. Pompeii and Herculaneum yield beautiful wall paintings of dead fowl meant for the dinner table. In them we see mallards, chickens, dead thrushes, partridges, and a whole host of others.[42] The presence of game birds in Campanian paintings indicate that wealth and prosperity could be expressed through appetising images of both domestic and wild-caught birds.[43] Demand for wildfowl, particularly rare and exotic breeds, led men to go fowling as far afield as Numidia and Ethiopia. Reflecting on simpler times, Pliny laments that not even legendary dangers could deter men from hunting birds abroad, and in fact this made the game more prized (Plin. *HN* 19.19). Sepulchral epigrams recorded for fowlers suggest that the man who got his living by this trade was poor, but happy in his work, and that the skill was passed down through families:

> By his bird lime and canes Eumelus lived on the creatures of the air, simply but in freedom. Never did he kiss a strange hand for his belly's sake. This his craft supplied him with luxury and delight. Ninety years he lived, and now sleeps here, having left to his children his bird-lime, nets and canes.[44]

Figure 4.5 Detail of a boy hunter catching birds and fowl with a snare. Third
century CE. Carthage, Villa of the Hunters.

Source: Photo by iStock.com/TerryJLawrence.

One is struck by the emphasis that the fowler was a free man and not a slave.
Another epitaph says:

> Here, too, the birds of heaven shall rest their swift wings, alighting on
> this sweet plane-tree. For Poemander of Melos is dead, and cometh here
> no longer, his fowling canes smeared with lime.[45]

The importance of limed reeds is again highlighted. To thrive in such a
pursuit, we are elsewhere told that a talent for fowling required patience,
dedication, and a great deal of hiding in bushes (Ov. *Ars am.* 1.47).[46]

Consuming Wild Birds

With such a fantastic variety of birds on offer, we should consider how they
made their way to elite tables. Bird consumption communicated status,
but effective communication required strict adherence to the complex yet
unwritten rules that governed the 'correct' way to consume, which could
distinguish the 'true aristocrat' from someone who merely had the money to

live like one.[47] Petronius' social satire, the *Satyricon,* includes an extended scene at the dinner of the wealthy freedman Trimalchio. This freedman's constant attempts to awe and impress his guests include serving up birds, and one of the passages gives us an idea of what a sumptuous, extravagant feast might have been like:

> During the course of the game he used up all the common swearwords. While we were eating the hors d'oeuvres, a large platter was brought in holding a basket, in which there was a wooden hen with its wings spread in a circle, just as hens are accustomed to do when brooding over eggs. Two slaves at once came up and to the roaring sound of music began to hunt in the straw. They immediately drew out peahens' eggs and distributed them to the guests. Trimalchio turned his face to this staged scene and said: "My friends, I ordered a peahen's eggs to be placed under the hen. And by god I'm afraid that now they're ready to hatch. Let's test, however, whether they're still fresh enough to suck". We grabbed spoons weighing not less than half a pound and perforated the eggs which were made of fine flour. I almost threw away my portion, for it seemed to me that it had formed into a chick, but then I heard an experienced guest say: "I don't know what, but there's something good in this". I poked through the shell with my finger and found a very fat fig pecker, coated in peppered egg yolk.[48]

The joke is that peahen eggs were often hatched under hens, and Trimalchio had his cooks create fake peahen eggs, place them under a fake hen, and 'hatch' from them the *ficedula,* an even more expensive dainty. *Ficedula* translates as fig-pecker, and denotes a variety of garden warbler still known as *beccafico* in Italy today. These warblers typically subsist on insects, but switch to a fruit-based diet when they are preparing to migrate for the winter. As the name suggests, figs are a favourite of theirs, though Martial asks, with characteristic cheek: 'Though the fig nourish me, yet, since I feed on sweet grapes, why did not the grape rather give me my name?'[49] Unfortunately for the little warbler, this fruit-based diet makes them taste delicious, and their migratory preparations made it easy for fowlers to catch them in large numbers when they were at their fattest. These delicious morsels were beloved by the upper classes, and it is said that a rich boy would be brought up on dainties such as quails and fig-peckers (Juv. *Sat.* 14.7–10). A visual representation of the fig-pecker may be seen at the Villa of Oplontis. According to Martial, the *ficedula* was best enjoyed seasoned with pepper (Mart. 13.5).

Thrushes were another type of wild bird treasured for their taste. They were caught in huge numbers using nets and limed reeds. Another episode in the *Satyricon* shows the fowlers in action. Trimalchio's cook cuts open a boar, and 'From this gash thrushes flew out; fowlers were ready with limed reeds and quickly caught the birds as they flew around the dining room'.[50]

Figure 4.6 Bird pecking figs. Villa Oplontis, first century CE.

Source: Photo by the author.

The fashion of presenting a complete beast at dinner was popular during the Empire (Plu. *Mor.* 658 A). Wild boar is among the most prestigious kills for a hunter, and thrush among the most prized hauls for a fowler. Combining the two, and even hunting and catching the birds in front of the guest so the living and dead mingled in the same space, served to bring the prestige of the hunt into the dining room, though this was all, apparently, in poor taste.[51] The Latin word for thrush, *turdus,* was a catch-all term, and could refer to four different birds: the redwing (*Turdus iliacus*), the song thrush (*Turdus philomelos*), the mistle thrush (*Turdus viscivorus*), and the fieldfare (*Turdus pilaris*). Mistle thrushes are the largest and generally solitary, though they sometimes gather in groups. These were probably hunted using the *harundo.* The fieldfare is next in size and, at least today, they are far commoner. These birds gather in flocks and would have been hunted with nets. The song thrush is third in size, followed by the redwing, and these can also be hunted with nets and caught in large numbers. Blackbirds, we are told, also made fine table birds and were caught in the same manner as thrushes.[52] Martial declares: 'Among birds the thrush, if anything I decide is certain, is the prime delicacy; among quadrupeds, the hare'.[53] The thrush is elsewhere called fit to grace a rich man's table (Petr. *Sat.* 65). Thrushes were considered suitable gifts between the wealthy.[54] Ovid advises us. 'Nay too by sending a thrush or a pigeon you may witness that you are mindful of your lady'.[55] It is unclear whether such gifts were intended for the beloved's birdcage or her dinner table. Song thrushes and pigeons made delightful caged companions, but in this context one suspects the way to a lady's heart may have been through her stomach. Complaining about how particular women are, Propertius says that in the good old days, one could woo a girl by giving her simple gifts like grapes, apples, or a bird of dappled plumage, but they are no longer impressed by such dainties (Prop. 3.13.32). Thrushes also made fine gifts between friends (Plin. *Ep.* 5.2.1). The Sabine region was said to attract the largest flocks of *turdi* (probably fieldfares) which were fattened in leased enclosures nearby (Varro, *Rust.* 3.4.2). The text is ambiguous as to who owned these enclosures, but it seems likely that City poulterers leased them, preparing their birds for sale at the markets.

Thrushes do not breed in captivity, so the Roman *turdarium* – thrush-cote – was a place where thrushes and similar birds were fattened after being snared in the wild. Fieldfares, mistle thrushes, redwings, song thrushes, and blackbirds would have made up the bulk of the flock, caught in winter and held until they were ready to be sold, with birds like quails occasionally held there too (Varro, *Rust.* 3.5.2). The practice of fattening thrushes reportedly began in the late Republic. Plutarch tells us Lucullus was the trendsetter, much to the chagrin of Pompey, and he relates the anecdote that one summer's day, Pompey fell ill and his physicians prescribed that he eat a thrush. Since thrushes had all migrated from Italy at this time, the only place he could find a thrush was in the *turdarium* of the decadent Lucullus, his mortal enemy. Finding death preferable to buying into Lucullus' luxury, Pompey ordered his physicians to come up with another cure, which they did post-haste (Plut. *Vit. Luc.* 40).

Plutarch's story indicates that it was not only profitable to fatten the birds before selling them, it was also good practice to keep them in captivity so they could be sold in the warmer months when fowlers were unable to procure them from the wild. Varro and Columella describe huge structures in which thousands of birds could be kept indefinitely and fattened to order. Though they were kept plump in the cotes, twenty days before sale the necessary numbers were removed and placed in smaller coops, where they were fed intensively to make them fit for market (Varro, *Rust.* 3.5.4). It may well be that thrushes were eventually available all year round thanks to such large-scale enterprises, provided one could afford them. But while the ordinary farmer might have kept a few thrushes in a miniature cote, either for his own consumption or to make a little extra money, the massive cotes our writers speak of would only have graced villas specialising in aviculture. The presence of such enormous operations indicates how lucrative aviculture became in the first century CE, and how one could make an extravagant display by eating birds out of season.

When the practice was still relatively new, Varro recommended keeping thrushes in an enclosure that sounds very similar in design to a dovecote. It was a round, domed structure, broad but not high. To keep out vermin and predators, it was covered with plaster within and without. A steady supply of running water ensured the birds always had clean drinking water.

Wooden rods were set into the walls, and gratings were leaned against the wall to provide perches. There were no nesting boxes (the birds did not breed), and it had few windows, which kept the interior in semi-darkness. Interestingly, the door to access the cote was at the end of a curved passageway – called a *coclia* to denote the spiral shape. This would have kept light to a minimum, and would also have prevented the birds from winging to freedom when the door opened. Exactly how little light was admitted is best indicated by Varro's recommendation that the birds should not be able to see trees and birds through the windows, for the sight of them, he says, makes them grow thin from yearning. This passage should rather indicate that the darkness was intended to inhibit excessive activity and make them dull and lethargic. They were only permitted enough light to see food, water, and their perches. In this way, it was believed, they would grow fat more quickly (Varro, *Rust.* 3.5.1–6).

Death rates in these enclosures must have been high, for by Columella's time the recommended *turdarium* had evolved into something more distinct. It was still scrupulously defended from predators, but it was much more wholesome, and filled with light and fresh air. Columella is sensitive to how delicate these birds can be, and to bolster survival rates he advises that the farmer should mix newly caught birds with thrushes that had been captive for a long time. By watching the veterans, they would learn how to eat and drink within the enclosure, and it would help keep them calm as they became used to captive life. Like Varro, Columella recommends a diet of dried figs mixed with millet. In the wild, thrushes are fond of berries, and the figs had to be carefully crushed for their consumption, or ideally chewed, though Columella acknowledges this is not an expedient solution. Fig-chewers were expensive and could not be trusted to abstain from swallowing the figs they chewed. But thrushes demanded variety, and this basic diet was supplemented by beech nuts, as well as other forms of wild harvest including myrtle seeds, ivy berries, wild olive, and strawberry-tree fruit.[56] Columella's advice about thrushes stood the test of time, for Palladius adheres closely to his recommendations in the late fourth and early fifth century CE. Trial and error ensured that Varro's dank and dark enclosure was quickly redesigned in favour of something light and airy, with the walls at least partially formed by netting (Palladius 1.26).

When the fattened thrushes were finally taken to the marketplace, they fetched a fine price (Varro, *Rust.* 3.5.8). What is astonishing is that as supply increased from the late Republic onwards, prices increased too, as if they could never quite meet demand.[57] To give a sense of their value, in 301 CE Diocletian fixed their maximum price at sixty *denarii* for ten, higher than for any other songbird. However, this does not necessarily mean they were the most valuable birds on the market – fig-peckers and ortolan buntings, which are much smaller and provide only a mouthful of meat at most, went for up to forty *denarii* for ten.[58] These batches of ten were fastened to a wicker wheel called a crown (*corona*). Hence, Martial's joke: 'A crown woven of roses or of costly nard might please you, but I delight in a crown of thrushes'.[59]

Work on the early Roman site of Pollentia (modern-day Mallorca) by Alejandro Valenzuela has revealed evidence of urban consumption of thrushes. Valenzuela investigated the refuse dump of a food shop, a *popina* very similar to the eateries uncovered at Pompeii.[60] The recovered faunal assemblage consisted of different mammals, fish, and birds that had been cooked and consumed at the shop. Thrushes were among the most abundant bird species recovered. Notably, the skull, wings, and legs were recovered most commonly, the 'non-meaty' parts that represent food waste. In addition to these, a high proportion of sterna were recovered from the dump, which Valenzuela attributes to the use of a particular cooking method wherein the sternum is removed and the bird is 'butterflied' so it can be roasted flat on a grill. It is impossible to tell whether these birds were fattened, but this faunal assemblage at least shows the context in which they were consumed – at a food shop – and how they were cooked – flat, on a grill, in a way that would have preserved moisture while facilitating quicker cooking at the same time.[61]

Thrush-cotes containing thousands of birds produced another asset: dung. Varro states thrush-cotes produced the best dung, which was suitable both as fertiliser and as fodder for pigs and cattle (Varro, *Rust.* 1.38.2). In contrast, Columella places thrush dung third on his list after pigeon and

Figure 4.7 Dead thrushes with herbs nearby, ready for cooking. Naples Archaeological Museum, inv. 8634.

Source: Photo by the author.

chicken dung (Columella, *Rust.* 2.14.1). Pliny, who read both testaments on bird dung, is driven to muse on morality:

> Marcus Varro gives the first rank to thrushes' droppings from aviaries, which he also extols for fodder of cattle and swine, declaring that no other fodder fattens them more quickly. If our ancestors had such large aviaries that they supplied manure for the fields, it is possible to be hopeful about our own morals![62]

Keeping aviaries and dining regularly on birds were inextricably connected with excess and decadence, and this is another example of how bird-keeping grew in popularity and sophistication to satisfy the burgeoning luxury trade in the late Republic and early Empire.

Recreational Fowling and Rare Birds

As a leisure activity, bird-catching was principally enjoyed by landowners who could afford to keep a few acres for game, and who also had the free time to devote to such pleasures (Plin. *Ep.* 2.8.1). Ovid tells us that hunting quadrupeds afforded the greatest pleasure, but that, 'Tis a milder pleasure (yet a pleasure it is) to seek a humble prize by snaring birds with net or reed'.[63] Fowling ranked below hunting but above fishing as a recreational pursuit. Big game hunting was dangerous and brought the greatest prestige, as we see when Propertius writes to his girlfriend admitting that he might not be manly enough to take on a lion or a boar, but at least he can snare a bird or catch a hare (Prop. 2.19.21–4). Horace describes hunting activities carried out in the colder months and affirms that hunting birds was a secondary delight to the chase because it was less thrilling and dangerous. Importantly, however, despite its lower status it was still a perfectly acceptable pursuit for men of his standing. This is in contrast to Greek thought, which disapproved of free men hunting birds as it was beneath their dignity. For them, hunting was only acceptable if it was against game that required dogs and horses to pursue (Pl. *Leg.* VII 823b–824a). Horace's description of the winter hunt is worth exploring further:

> But in wintertime, when thundering Jove brings masses of rain and snow, he hunts fierce boars from here and there with packs of hounds into the nets that are spread in their path, or with smooth rods he stretches baggy nets to catch greedy thrushes, and with a snare he takes a timid hare and a migrant crane – choice prizes.[64]

The crane was a passage visitor in winter and difficult to catch, so its alleged sweetness as a prize is probably due to its rarity. Romans sometimes kept demoiselle cranes for their beauty.[65] We have a report of cranes being displayed in the arena, where they allegedly fought one another.[66] It is more likely that this was a display of their mating dance, which looked like fighting to ancient eyes. A study of zooarchaeological finds from central Europe (near Hungary) reveals that crane bones are found in much greater abundance on sites from the Roman period, sharply increasing from the Iron Age before dropping off again on Byzantine sites. It has been suggested that this directly correlates to Romans keeping cranes as pets or using them as food, though we should be careful not to generalise the findings to the rest of the Empire.[67] Until the twentieth century, cranes nested in Hungary, which is not typical of Italy.[68] Hungarian peasants did not breed the birds, but they were able to collect young cranes in the breeding season and keep them as pets. They served as guards, signalling the arrival of intruders with the sound that gave them their onomatopoeic names in most European languages (*grus, grue, grulla, Kranich, trana*, crane, *zhuravl, daru*, etc.).[69] Roman pet or ornamental cranes may have done the same. The enduring legend that cranes appointed sentries who held stones in their feet to keep them awake, since they would drop them if they dozed, may have its origin in practices such as these (Plin. *HN* 10.59). Dionysius' work *On Birds,* which was probably written in the first century CE, describes various fowling techniques (3.11). He lists two odd ways to catch cranes; the first was to fill a hollowed gourd with lime and place a beetle inside. Attracted by the buzzing, the crane stuck its head into the gourd and became blinded and immobilised by the lime. The second method involves snaring using a noose trap. The first method seems rather bizarre, but the second method is sound, since Virgil describes winter as the season for snaring cranes. In the *Greek Anthology*, Antipater also refers to noose snares for cranes.[70] More usual were net traps (Babrius 13).

Literary evidence shows that crane was eaten at feasts, though some frowned on killing the bird.[71] Reportedly, crane meat tastes foul and must be prepared thoroughly before it becomes palatable.[72] This is reflected in the way the Romans fattened cranes and had recipes dedicated to correctly cooking and seasoning them. Apicius' method of tenderising tough crane flesh consisted of boiling the crane whole, except for the head, which remained outside of the pot. It was then wrapped in a hot towel and the head was pulled off in a way that drew the tough sinews with it, leaving only palatable meat and bones behind.[73] Apicius' crane recipe also implies that the dish was valued for its visual appeal rather than its flavour. Like the peacock, taste had nothing to do with demand for the bird. It was meant to make a sensational banquet centrepiece and advertise the capabilities of the host in procuring such a rare and impressive bird.

The stork was in similar straits as the crane. In the *Satyricon,* the following quotation against luxury was recited, apparently written by Publilius:

The walls of Mars crumble beneath the gaping jaws of luxury. To please your palate the peacock clad in Babylonian golden plumage is fed in cages, for you the guinea hen, for you the capon; even the stork, the beloved foreign guest, devotion-filled, graceful-stepping, castanet-dancer, winter's exile, warrant of warm weather, has made its nest in the cooking pot of your worthlessness.[74]

While cranes were winter visitors in Italy, storks were summer residents. This passage reveals that the revulsion towards eating storks was centred on the fact that, as Varro notes, they bred when they arrived in Italy, and therefore could only be caught while nesting (Varro, *Rust.* 3.5.6). Whether the Romans ate the young or simply trapped the parents or the chicks or both is unclear, but the repeated mention of the nest implies the chicks were stolen (Hor. *Sat.* 2.2.49–50). Pliny tells us:

> Cornelius Nepos, who died in the principate of the late lamented Augustus, when he wrote that the practice of fattening thrushes was introduced a little before his time, added that storks were more in favour than cranes, although the latter bird is now one of those most in request, whereas nobody will touch the former.[75]

Part of the joke in the *Satyricon* passage may have been that the freedman was inveighing against a form of excess that was no longer fashionable or acceptable anyway – as Pliny says, eating storks had long been abandoned. The distaste for the slaughter of storks in the wild may be related to Roman attitudes towards hunting. Hunting was encouraged because it improved stamina and bravery, but there was a general rule against slaughtering the newly born offspring of harmless species, and by extension the mothers that cared for them. These were left for Diana.[76] One wonders if the loss of appetite for stork was effected by a humane impulse, or whether the fad simply died naturally when another took its place. It is noteworthy that storks are often shown killing snakes in Roman art.[77] This motif is based on real behaviour. In Thessaly, storks were protected because they kept the viper population under control.[78] Storks were also symbols of piety. The stork was called *pia avis* – the pious bird (Ambrose, Hex. 5.16.53–4). It was common lore that storks fed and cared for their parents when they grew old.[79] They were auspicious if seen at nuptial auspices because they 'married' and raised children together (Ael. *NA* 1.44). Striking use of the pious stork imagery comes from coinage for the Antonine Party in Cisalpine Gaul that supported Lucius Antonius, who took up the cause of those dispossessed by Octavian's settlement of veterans. Lucius, consul in 41 BCE, associated himself with Pietas to show support for his brother. On the *aureus* minted in that same year is the goddess Pietas depicted holding a rudder and cornucopia with a stork at her feet. On the obverse is the head of Antony.[80] It was observed that storks always came back to the same nest when they returned from migration (Ael. *NA* 3.23). This is borne out by modern observation; storks might not mate for life, but they are loyal to their nests. They are also comfortable nesting in urban areas and probably nested on columns and roofs, where their return was noted each spring. As a comparison, swallows (*Hirundo rustica*) are also summer residents that nested frequently on Roman houses. Such behaviour caused them to be seen in an extremely positive light, with sources betraying a sentimental attachment to these feathered guests.[81] Storks were held in esteem for their gentle, faithful natures, and for the fact that, unlike cranes, they did not harm crops (Babrius 13). We might account for the squeamishness around eating storks to the positive view Romans took of the birds, and the fact they shared their houses with them.

A taste for flamingo tongues was another infamous fad (Plin. *HN* 10.133). Martial says: 'My ruddy wing gives me a name, but my tongue is a treat to epicures. What if my tongue were to tell tales?'[82] Pliny credits Apicius with the creation of this fad. There are in fact two recipes relating to flamingo (6.6.1–2). Both are sauces that can be served with the whole bird, so we can be assured that it was not only the tongue that was enjoyed. In Juvenal a whole large flamingo is served at an extravagant meal.[83] Flamingos live in the wetlands of southern Europe and once lived on the Tiber meadows too.[84] They were rare and beautiful birds, and when the Emperor Caligula established a cult to his own godhood, he named flamingos and other rare birds as acceptable sacrifices to himself. Later he is recorded sacrificing a flamingo with his own hands (Suet. *Calig.* 57). There can be no surer sign that the flamingo was a coveted status symbol. Presumably the birds were netted wild in Italy and abroad, though Martial claims that a friend's estate, stocked with all manner of rare birds, boasted red-winged flamingos (Mart. 3.58.14). Given the Romans' skill at constructing duck ponds, there is no question that they could have created a suitable habitat for the birds, but we have no evidence that this ever became common practice. Consuming flamingo was a type of excess that came under fire multiple times. In condemning tones, Vitellius was accused of eating flamingo tongue along with pheasant and peacock brains (Suet. *Vit.* 13). In the *Life of Elagabalus*, the emperor was accused of eating flamingo brains and parrot heads (SHA, *Heliogab.* 20.6). When describing the antics of particularly despised emperors, it is not enough for them to indulge in the eating of luxurious birds. They also have to eat only the brains, or only the tongue, in order to generate additional outrage. This act of eating only the choicest parts of the choicest animals was part of the stereotyped image of the tyrant's luxury and gluttony.[85] The act of killing so many precious birds for a scanty morsel was a display of wealth and power, pure and simple.

Finally, distinct from the hunting of other birds was the hunting of ostriches, a dangerous and thrilling pursuit. Pliny opens his book on birds in the *Natural History* with a fairly accurate description of the ostrich, linking it to Africa or Ethiopia and claiming it is taller and faster than a man on horseback (Plin. *HN* 10.1–2). The ostrich does indeed stand over two metres tall and can outpace horses with ease, making it sporting quarry for a

Figure 4.8 Detail from Sarcophagus, end second century CE. Capitoline Museum, Palazzo Nuovo, inv. 307.

Source: Photo by Edward Blume-Poulton.

hunter.[86] The Gladiator-Emperor Commodus fought ostriches in the arena. According to Herodian, he would shoot them with crescent-shaped arrows. This decapitated them, and the headless bodies would run on for a time, to the amusement of spectators (Herodian, 1.15.3–6). The existence of such crescent arrows is substantiated by carvings on a sarcophagus that depict Cupids shooting at ostriches with crescent arrows.

Dio gives another version, stating that on one occasion the emperor decapitated an ostrich with a sword. Taking up the head, he approached the senators (Dio among them) and smiled eerily at them, sending the message this was what he intended to do to them (Dio Cass. *Epitome* 72.10.3). Compared to a bear or a lion, ostriches might not seem particularly dangerous, but they are formidable creatures. If provoked, they lash out on clawed feet with enough force to disembowel or break bones. That ostriches were hunted in the wild or in private game enclosures is clear from iconographic evidence. Hunting scenes often depict an ostrich among big game animals like leopards and deer. According to Aelian, they were hunted on horseback and chased in wheeling loops until they became exhausted, whereupon they were speared. Another method was to surround an ostrich's nest with spears, so that when the parent bird returned to her young she would injure herself trying to reach them, allowing the hunter to take easily both mother and chicks. Both the birds and their eggs were eaten, and the stones taken from their stomachs (which they swallow to grind food in their gizzards) were sold as charms to aid digestion (Ael. *NA* 14.7). The idea that Pliny relates, and which survived well into the early modern period, that ostriches are capable of digesting anything, including iron, likely came from observation of it swallowing stones and other seemingly indigestible objects to aid its gizzard. Ostrich bones and eggshells are commonly found on North African sites in the Greco-Roman period.[87]

There is no definite evidence that ostriches were kept permanently in Italian aviaries, but the possibility is there. They had been imported for Roman shows since at least Plautus' time (Plaut. *Persa*, 198). Amusingly, it was first called *marinus passer* – sea sparrow. Of course, what was meant was that is was not a sea bird, but a bird *from* overseas.[88] Later, the Greek name 'strouthokamelos' took its place – 'camel sparrow'.[89] If the *Life of Elagabalus* is to be believed, the young emperor served ostrich heads at banquets, sometimes hundreds at a time, and made ten ostriches a prize for guests in a lottery (SHA, *Heliogab.* 22, 1; 28, 4; 30, 2). Aelian, who lived around this time, describes the ostrich accurately and remarks upon its flightlessness, its running speed, and its thick, fluffy feathers (Ael. *NA* 2.27).

Dubious though such sources may be, it is not too much to assume that ostrich imports were flourishing, and that there was room in Roman aviaries or game enclosures for ostriches, either to hunt, to eat, or to show off to guests. Even in the early fifth century CE, we have reports of ostriches being shipped from Cyrene to Rome (Synesius, *Ep.* 134). The ostrich was probably eaten only rarely, although its eggs were enjoyed. Apicius gives us two recipes (6.1.1–2), and these seem to be the earliest written sources for the eating of ostrich.[90]

Other prestige game birds include the *tetrax*, or *tarax*, usually identified as the black grouse (*Lyrurus tetrix*) or the enormous capercaillie (*Tetrao urogallus*).[91] Nemesianus gives a vivid picture of a slave tottering under the weight of these enormous birds. He goes on to describe how snipe (likely *Scolopax rusticola*) were hunted:

> When the woodland everywhere is despoiled of its green honours, make straight for the deep forest, mounted on the snow-white housing of your steed. The snipe is an easy and an agreeable prey. You will find it no larger in body than Venus' doves. It feeds close to the edge of embankments, by the wash of the water, hunting tiny worms, its favourite fare.[92]

Hunting birds such as these required special forays into the woods and mountains, often on horseback, and the hunt itself was considered sporting and enjoyable, contributing to the birds' prestige.[93]

Decoys

Already alluded to is the use of decoy birds. Xenophon mentions decoy birds used by a young fowler, which were left in the open to attract birds while the fowler lay hidden, waiting to jerk the nets and trap the birds (Xen. *Cyr.* 1.6.39). The decoy birds employed were numerous. As has been mentioned, captured owls were used to attract birds through 'mobbing' behaviour. Aelian describes the scene, seeing owls as witches that use a kind of magic to summon birds, even beguiling their human captors, who carry them around like pets or charms, sometimes on their shoulders.[94] Martial describes a scene where birds are drawn by song: 'The bird is deceived not only by rods but by song, as the cunning reed lengthens in the silent hand'.[95] Partridges were useful as decoys and both sexes could attract other partridges through their garrulous calls (Ael. *NA* 4.16). The Romans distinguish between three types of partridge, but they possibly had more than that (Ael. *NA* 4.13). Rock partridges (*Alectoris graeca*) and red-legged partridges (*Alectoris rufa*) are both natives of Italy, with the rock partridge being the easiest to tame. Grey partridges are more common in northern Europe, and Chukar partridges (*Alectoris chukar*) may have been imported from the eastern part of the Empire. For the Greeks, the rock partridge was common on the mainland, while the Chukar was the resident on the Aegean Islands and in Turkey. Rock and Chukar partridges are visually similar, but the ancients noted the differences in their cries.

Pliny describes how a single male decoy partridge could attract a whole flock of belligerent males. Around breeding time, a decoy female would also attract other females who wanted to hustle her out of their territory (Plin. *HN* 10.60). Due to their use as decoys and fighting birds, they were sometimes derided as simple, lusty, and pugnacious creatures. Aelian, while praising the virtues of the monogamous, affectionate pigeon, compares them unfavourably to partridges for their sexual licence and lack of self-control (Ael. *NA* 3.5). Nevertheless, partridge hunting would have been a profitable exercise, since the bird was expensive and considered a dainty among the wealthy: 'This bird is only rarely placed on Roman tables, and only often if you're accustomed to splashing in fancy swimming pools'.[96] Recorded in the *Greek Anthology* are a number of mournful epitaphs for favourite cock-partridges. Though we should be wary of calling decoy birds pets, fowlers obviously grew attached to their beautiful – and valuable – hunting companions. Apparently, these creatures often met their end in the jaws of a household cat.[97] Babrius records a fable where a poor fowler was making a meal of mint and celery when a friend visited unexpectedly. He had not caught anything recently, so had no meat to offer his guest:

> So he started to kill a speckled partridge which he had tamed and kept as a decoy for use in hunting. The partridge begged the fowler not to kill him, saying: "Henceforth, sir, how will you manage your net when you hunt? Who will bring together for you a flock of sharp-eyed, gregarious birds? To what songster's tune will you fall asleep?" So he let go the partridge and decided to seize upon a bearded cockerel.[98]

The cockerel pleads his usefulness due to his knowledge of the hours of the day, but the fowler decides that this is not reason enough to deny his friend a decent meal.

Inquisitive birds could be caught with oil-traps. Aelian tells us that when men wanted to catch jackdaws, they would approach where flocks were feeding and arrange basins full of oil. A curious jackdaws would approach, settle on the rim, and look at its reflection. Seeing itself, it would attempt to reach the supposed other bird, and in doing so scatter oil on itself, rendering it unable to fly.[99] A similar method worked on quails. During the mating season, a noose and mirror were set up so the bird would run headlong into the snare as it attempted to fight its reflection (Ath. 393a.).

According to Pliny, quails were not much esteemed as a foodstuff. He cites a belief that they fed on poisonous plants, making it risky to eat one (Plin. *HN* 10.69). The presence of quails meant for the table in Roman art might indicate that most paid little heed to this advice. Fattened quails certainly fetched a good price.[100] Their annual migratory arrival in huge numbers was anticipated and observed closely.

> Thrushes do not rear their young here and there as do the other migratory birds, storks in the field, swallows under the roof, and though their name (*turdi*) is masculine, there are in fact females too; nor is the case otherwise as regards blackbirds (*merulae*), though they have a feminine name, there are also males. Again, birds being partly migratory, as swallows and cranes, and partly indigenous, as hens and doves, thrushes belong to the former class, the migratory, and fly yearly across the sea into Italy about the time of the autumnal equinox, and back again whence they came about the spring equinox, as do turtle-doves and quail at another season in vast numbers. The proof of this is seen in the near-by islands of Pontiae, Palmaria, and Pandateria; for when they arrive in these at the first migration, they remain there for a few days to rest, and do the same when they leave Italy for their return across the sea.[101]

Sheer exhaustion from their long journeys made them easy prey at this time, and they could be caught in the thousands by stretching nets along the coastline.[102] That Varro advised keeping them with thrushes probably indicates that farmers held onto the birds until they migrated away from Italy, and sold their fattened birds at a high price when wild-caught quails were no longer available. Eating fattened stock was not just a matter of consuming something that was tastier than anything an ordinary person could procure from the wild. It was about eating something that had become rare and expensive because it was no longer seasonally available.

Figure 4.9 Mosaic of cat catching a quail. The various birds and fish here give the idea of bounty and plenty. Naples Archaeological Museum, inv. 9993.

Source: Photo by the author.

Hawks and Falcons

It is worth noting that one form of hunting that the Romans did *not* have was falconry.[103] The sport of hawking and falconry was so popular in medieval and early modern Europe that we might find it surprising the tradition did not stretch back to the classical world; indeed, if this fact were pointed out to medieval peoples, they would have found it surprising too, since their art and literature portray ancient nobles with raptors on their hands.[104] Pictorial evidence exists to suggest the Assyrians may have hunted with hawks or falcons.[105] The earliest literary reference to hunting with birds of prey in the classical world comes from Aristotle:

> In the part of Thrace once named as belonging to Kedripolis men hunt the small birds in the marsh in partnership with the hawks. The men hold sticks and stir the reeds and brushwood to make the small birds fly, while the hawks from above appear overhead and chase them down. In fear they fly down again to the ground; the men strike them with the sticks and take them, and give the hawks a share in the prey: they throw them some of the birds and the hawks catch them.[106]

Pliny appears to repeat Aristotle's tale:

> In a part of Thrace above Amphipolis, men and hawks have a kind of partnership for catching birds. The men chase the birds from the woods and rushes, while above the hawks fly and drive them down; the captives are then divided between the fowlers and the hawks.[107]

Though this represents a planned and co-ordinated hunting effort that utilises hawks, Claus Dobiat points out it cannot be termed falconry in the modern sense, which employs a trained bird.[108] Nevertheless, it is an effective means of hunting, and we have descriptions of such methods being successfully employed in the Middle Ages and the Renaissance. Quails, larks, partridges, and other small fowl could be taken in this manner. A sixteenth-century description runs thus:

> Finding themselves pursued by the hounds and spanels, (they) are enforst to trust to their wings, and to take to the ayre; and being there, finding themselves, molested by the Falconers and Hobbies, do make their choyse and election to become prey rather to the dogs, or seek mercy among the horse legges, and so be surprised alive, than to affie to the curtesie of the cruell Hobbies, and to be taken in their cruell talons, where they are most assured to dye the death.[109]

This is a more sophisticated plan of attack than the one devised by the Thracians, but it shows clearly how fowlers could take advantage of the birds' instinctive fear of hawks, which was so strong that it prevented them from taking wing even when faced with other dangers. Merely holding a hawk up to view can paralyse a lark.[110] The hawks made them such easy prey for the fowlers that they could simply walk up and club them to death. While Pliny seems to record this as a kind of Thracian oddity, one of Martial's epigrams called *Accipiter* – 'Hawk' – suggests Romans at least occasionally used hawks in fowling: 'He was a pirate to birds; now as the fowler's servant he deceives them and grieves that they are not caught for himself'.[111] This implies the hawk was caged as a decoy bird. As with the owl, a hawk can inspire mobbing behaviour in small birds, especially in the nesting season when they are more defensive. Apart from this example, we do not get any indication that the Romans enjoyed raising, taming, or hunting with falcons or hawks as nobles did in medieval Europe. Dobiat demonstrates that the predilection for falconry that swept across Europe only began in the late Empire, citing two pieces of ancient evidence, one of a Paulinus of Pella in Gaul who, in last decade of the fourth century, wrote that when he was young desired to own a 'well-shaped' hunting bird, and another of a Sidonius Apollinarius, also from Gaul, who reported trained birds of prey in the mid-fifth century CE.[112] Earliest undisputed depictions of European falconry come from a Byzantine site called *Villa of the Falconer* in Argos, fifth century CE.[113] The cool indifference of the ancients towards hawking and falconry is remarked upon as early as 1531 by the humanist Thomas Elyot.[114] It might seem odd that the Romans never bonded with raptors, but when we consider the references to nets fashioned for the purposes of keeping hawks away from valuable poultry, we might conclude that hawks, kites, and falcons were generally seen as pests. Farmers were more interested in keeping their flocks safe from these predators than bonding with them.[115] When interpreting dreams, Artemidorus advises that hawks and kites symbolise robbers and highwaymen (Artem. *On.* 2.20). This can be explained by the fact that kites, hawks, and falcons not only attacked living stock but also were known to make off with meat from sacrifices or meat from the marketplace (Ael. *NA* 2.47). Pigeon-keepers would use a dove as bait to trap and kill hawks that threatened their flocks (Varro, *Rust.* 3.7.7). Terence says that people do not bother to catch birds like the hawk and kite that 'do us harm' – *male faciunt* (Ter. *Phorm.* 331–2). Furthermore, a real contempt was felt for birds of prey that ate other birds, as falcons and hawks commonly do. The image of the innocent dove fleeing a brutal hawk was a common one employed in art, fable, and poetry.[116] The Roman dislike of raptors betrays something fundamental to their thinking; they valued their domestic flocks too much to show any interest in keeping or hunting with predatory birds as medieval falconers did.

Conclusion

This overview of Roman fowling touches on many echelons of Roman society. On the one hand, it gives us a glimpse of how the improverished *auceps* could turn a profit by catching birds, and how a subsistence farmer could take advantage of local and seasonal availabilities to catch birds for his own consumption using relatively simple tools. On the other hand, we see how the ingenuity of Roman businessmen allowed them to take advantage of these same seasonal availabilities to corral wild birds in large numbers so they could fatten them and sell them out of season when demand was high and wildfowlers no longer had access to game. Roman elites exhibited demand for many different types of wild bird, with certain species rising and falling in popularity according to the latest fad. Thrushes were the most popular of the wild game birds and an enormous industry sprang up to meet urban demand for these delicious little birds, which apparently retained their popularity throughout the Empire. We have seen how hunting birds was a recreational pursuit that could be respectably enjoyed by elites, but which was not as prestigious as hunting dangerous game. By examining different hunting methods we can appreciate that, although the tools and methods varied considerably, on the whole hunting birds was within the means of even the poorest citizens. With the *harundo* functioning as the tool of choice, anyone could procure sticky lime and a reed and go hunting. What really mattered was investing time and patience in the pursuit.

Attention to seasonal fluctuations in bird populations grants us the most illuminating insight into the practice of wildfowling, as we begin to understand the power in the display of a statesman eating thrushes out of season, or in the way migratory preparations make birds easier to catch or better tasting due to accumulation of fat for the journey.

Notes

1 Hoffman (2014) 41.
2 Varro, *Rust.* 3.2.16 names feasts of the *collegia,* as well as public banquets and triumphs, as key occasions on which one can make a fortune by selling birds.
3 Kron (2015) 164–5.
4 Mart. 3.60. Translated by Shackleton Bailey (1993a) 231 with amendments: *Aureus inmodicis turtur te clunibus implet, ponitur in cauea mortua pica mihi.*
5 Frayn (1993) 73.
6 Chandezon (2015) 139.
7 Watson (2002) 358.
8 Thurmond (2006) 208.
9 Gill (1994) 287.
10 Arist. *Hist. an.* 8.16.600A16; Plin, *HN,* 10.70. See Plin. *HN* 10.11 for the cuckoo.
11 Morley (2007) 20.
12 Kron (2008).
13 Birkhead (2014) 14.
14 Palladius 13.6. Translation by the author: *tempore hoc per humiles silvas et bacis fecunda virgulta ad turdos ceterasque aves capiendas laqueos expedire conveniet. Hoc usque in Martium mensem tendetur aucupium.*
15 Zeiler (2013) 379–81.
16 Fischer (2013) 260.
17 Keller (1975) 50.
18 Lulof and Van Kampen (2011) 102.
19 Verg. *Aen.* 5.485ff. See also Soph. *Phil.* 285–92. For an allegorical tale of a man using a bow and arrow to kill an eagle sent from Zeus, see Bianor, *Pal. Anth.* 9.223.
20 Verg. *G.* 1.139–40; Ov. *Rem. am.* 501–2; Nemes. *Versus de aucupio.*
21 Antipater, *Anth. Pal.* 6.109, translated by Paton (1916) 359: Γηραλέον νεφέλας τρῦχος τόδε, καὶ τριέλικτον ἰχνοπέδαν, καὶ τὰς νευροτενεῖς παγίδας, κλωβούς τ' ἀμφίρρωγας, ἀνασπαστούς τε δεράγχας, καὶ πυρὶ θηγαλέους ὀξυπαγεῖς στάλικας, καὶ τὰν εὔκολλον δρυὸς ἰκμάδα, τόν τε πετηνῶν ἀγρευτὰν ἰξῷ μυδαλέον δόνακα, καὶ κρυφίου τρίκλωστον ἐπισπαστῆρα βόλοιο, ἄρκυν τε κλαγερῶν λαιμοπέδαν γεράνων, σοί, Πὰν ὦ σκοπιῆτα, γέρας θέτο παῖς Νεολάδα Κραῦγις ὁ θηρευτάς, Ἀρκὰς ἀπ' Ὀρχομενοῦ.
22 Prop. 4.2; Bion, *Idylls,* 4; Artem. *On.* 2.19.
23 Similar sentiment is found in Oppian's *The Chase* (1.71–6).
24 Alciphron's *Letters of a Farmer* (Letter 27, iii.30) describes this method. In winter, with little else to do, the farmer spies blackbirds and thrushes in the snow. He takes bird lime from his pot and smears the branches of a fruit tree. Before long, multitudes of birds are hanging from the branches, caught by wing, head, and foot.
25 Ov. *Ars am.* 1.391. Translated by Mozley (1929) 39 with amendments: *non avis utiliter viscatis effugit alis.* A similar metaphor is employed in Seneca's *De Ira* (3.16.1), indicating that the more a bird struggled against lime, the more entangled it became.

26 Sil. *Pun.* 7.674–7. Translated by Duff (1934) 385: *ut, qui viscata populatur harundine lucos, dum nemoris celsi procera cacumina sensim substructa certat tacitus contingere meta, sublimem calamo sequitur crescente volucrem.*

27 Parker (1988) 204.

28 Rhianus, *Anth. Pal.* 12. 142 describes a man holding a blackbird he has caught with lime that is still alive and struggling noisily.

29 Compare to a late first century BCE, *oscillum* from the House of Caecilius Iucundus, Pompeii, that shows a fowler brandishing a *harundo* and lunging from hiding to smear a bird.

30 See, respectively, Oppian, *The Chase,* 1.64–6; Arist. *Mete.* 385b; Aen. Tact. 34. According to Aeneas the Tactician, bird lime was an important resource during sieges, as it could be used to prevent the enemy from setting wooden objects alight.

31 Verg. *Aen.* 6.205–6; Plin. *HN* 16.93.

32 Turner, *A New Herball* Vol. 2 (1562), taken from Chapman and Tweddle (1995) 598. Later in this passage, Turner gives a recipe from his own day of lime made from holly bark collected at midsummer. I have not found any ancient examples of the holly recipe.

33 Isid. *Etym.* 12.7.71. Translation by the author: *Turdela quasi maior turdus; cuius stercore viscum generare putatur. Vnde et proverbium apud antiquos erat, 'Malum sibi avem cacare'.* See also Serv. *Aen.* 6.205.

34 Athen. 451d calls the lime 'oak-sweat'.

35 Marcus Argentarius, *Pal. Anth.* 9.87. Translated by Paton (1917) 47: Μηκέτι νῦν μινύριζε παρὰ δρυΐ, μηκέτι φώνει κλωνὸς ἐπ' ἀκροτάτου, κόσσυφε, κεκλιμένος· ἐχθρόν σοι τόδε δένδρον· ἐπείγεο δ', ἄμπελος ἔνθα ἀντέλλει γλαυκῶν σύσκιος ἐκ πετάλων· κείνης ταρσὸν ἔρεισον ἐπὶ κλάδον, ἀμφί τ' ἐκείνῃ μέλπε, λιγὺν προχέων ἐκ στομάτων κέλαδον. δρῦς γὰρ ἐπ' ὀρνίθεσσι φέρει τὸν ἀνάρσιον ἰξόν, ἁ δὲ βότρυν· στέργει δ' ὑμνοπόλους Βρόμιος. Reluctance to kill blackbirds is recorded elsewhere in the Greek tradition because of their beautiful songs. See *Pal. Anth.* 9.76, 9.343.

36 Plin. *HN* 16.94. Translated by Rackham (1945) 549: *Viscum fit ex acinis qui colliguntur messium tempore inmaturi; nam si accessere imbres, amplitudine quidem augentur, visco vero marcescunt. siccantur deinde et aridi tunduntur ac conditi in aqua putrescunt duodenis fere diebus, unumque hoc rerum putrescendo gratiam invenit. inde in profluente, rursus malleo tusi, amissis corticibus interiore carne lentescunt. hoc est viscum pinnis avium tactu ligandis oleo subactum cum libeat insidias moliri.*

37 Plin. *HN* 24.11. See also Ar. *Av.* 1077–83 and Bonner (1925) 210.

38 Parrish (1994); Parrish (2003) 238. See page 248 for a particularly striking personification of winter as a hunter holding a reed and ducks: detail of the Four Seasons Mosaic located in Argos, Greece, fifth century CE. For the iconography of the seasons more generally, see Hanfmann (1971); Kranz (1984); Parrish (1984).

39 Angelini et al. (2005); Bentini and Martelli (2013).

40 Longus, *Daphnis and Chloe,* 3.5–6. Translated by Henderson (2009) 109–11: Πρὸ τῆς αὐλῆς τοῦ Δρύαντος ἐπ' αὐτῇ τῇ αὐλῇ μυρρίναι μεγάλαι δύο καὶ κιττὸς ἐπεφύκει, αἱ μυρρίναι πλησίον ἀλλήλων, ὁ κιττὸς ἀμφοτέρων μέσος, ὥστε ἐφ' ἑκατέραν διαθεὶς τοὺς ἀκρεμόνας ὡς ἄμπελος ἄντρου σχῆμα διὰ τῶν φύλλων ἐπαλλαττόντων ἐποίει, καὶ ὁ κόρυμβος πολὺς καὶ μέγας ὅσος βότρυς κλημάτων ἐξεκρέματο. ἦν οὖν πολὺ πλῆθος περὶ αὐτὸν τῶν χειμερινῶν ὀρνίθων ἀπορίᾳ τῆς ἔξω τροφῆς· πολὺς μὲν κόψιχος, πολλὴ δὲ κίχλη, καὶ φάτται καὶ ψᾶρες καὶ ὅσον ἄλλο κιττοφάγον πτερόν. ... Δρόμῳ οὖν πρὸς τὴν αὐλὴν ἔρχεται καὶ ἀποσεισάμενος τῶν σκελῶν τὴν χιόνα τούς τε βρόχους ἔστησε καὶ τὸν ἰξὸν ῥάβδοις μακραῖς ἐπήλειψε καὶ ἐκαθέζετο τὸ ἐντεῦθεν ὄρνιθας <ἀναμένων> καὶ τὴν Χλόην μεριμνῶν.

ἀλλ᾿ ὄρνιθες μὲν καὶ ἦκον πολλοὶ καὶ ἐλήφθησαν ἱκανοί, ὥστε πράγματα μυρία ἔσχε συλλέγων αὐτοὺς καὶ ἀποκτιννὺς καὶ ἀποδύων τὰ πτερά·

41 Bion, Fr. 13 *Stobaeus*. Translated by Hopkinson (2015) 535–7: Ἰξευτὰς ἔτι κῶρος ἐν ἄλσεϊ δενδράεντι ὄρνεα θηρεύων τὸν ὑπόπτερον εἶδεν Ἔρωτα ἐσδόμενον πύξοιο ποτὶ κλάδον· ὡς δὲ νόησε, χαίρων ὤνεκα δὴ μέγα φαίνετο τὤρνεον αὐτῷ, τὼς καλάμως ἅμα πάντας ἐπ᾿ ἀλλάλοισι συνάπτων τᾷ καὶ τᾷ τὸν Ἔρωτα μετάλμενον ἀμφεδόκευε. χὠ παῖς, ἀσχαλάων ὅκα οἱ τέλος οὐδὲν ἀπάντη, τὼς καλάμως ῥίψας ποτ᾿ ἀροτρέα πρέσβυν ἵκανεν ὅς νιν τάνδε τέχναν ἐδιδάξατο, καὶ λέγεν αὐτῷ καί οἱ δεῖξεν Ἔρωτα καθήμενον. αὐτὰρ ὁ πρέσβυς μειδιάων κίνησε κάρη καὶ ἀμείβετο παῖδα· "φείδεο τᾶς θήρας, μηδ᾿ ἐς τόδε τὤρνεον ἔρχευ. φεῦγε μακράν· κακόν ἐντι τὸ θηρίον. ὄλβιος ἔσσῃ εἰσόκε μή νιν ἕλῃς· ἢν δ᾿ ἀνέρος ἐς μέτρον ἔλθῃς οὗτος ὁ νῦν φεύγων καὶ ἀπάλμενος αὐτὸς ἀφ᾿ αὑτῶ ἐλθὼν ἐξαπίνας κεφαλὰν ἔπι σεῖο καθιζεῖ".

42 Guidobaldi and Esposito (2012) 102, 276–7. These pieces are now held in the National Archaeological Museum of Naples, inv. 8759, 8753, and 8647.

43 Watson (2002) 357.

44 Isidorus of Aegae, *Pal. Anth.* 7.156. Translated by Paton (1916) 89: Ἰξῷ καὶ καλάμοισιν ἀπ᾿ ἠέρος αὐτὸν ἔφερβεν Εὔμηλος, λιτῶς, ἀλλ᾿ ἐν ἐλευθερίῃ. οὔποτε δ᾿ ὀθνείην ἔκυσεν χέρα γαστρὸς ἕκητι· τοῦτο τρυφὴν κείνῳ, τοῦτ᾿ ἔφερ᾿ εὐφροσύνην. τρὶς δὲ τριηκοστὸν ζήσας ἔτος ἐνθάδ᾿ ἰαύει, παισὶ λιπὼν ἰξὸν καὶ πτερὰ καὶ καλάμους.

45 Mnasalcas of Sicyon, *Pal. Anth.* 7.171. Translated by Paton (1916) 99: Ἀμπαύσει καὶ τῇδε θοὸν πτερὸν ἱερὸς ὄρνις, τᾶσδ᾿ ὑπὲρ ἀδείας ἑζόμενος πλατάνου· ὤλετο γὰρ Ποίμανδρος ὁ Μάλιος, οὐδ᾿ ἔτι νεῖται ἰξὸν ἐπ᾿ ἀγρευταῖς χευάμενος καλάμοις.

46 See also Anon. *Anth. Pal.* 9.209. Here a fowler expresses his impatience with a bird that keeps eluding him.

47 Morley (2007) 48. See also Veyne (1961) and Edwards (1993).

48 Petr. *Sat.* 33. Translated by Schmeling (2020) 123: *Interim dum ille omnium textorum dicta inter lusum consumit, gustantibus adhuc nobis repositorium allatum est cum corbe, in quo gallina erat lignea patentibus in orbem alis, quales esse solent quae incubant ova. Accessere continuo duo servi et symphonia strepente scrutari paleam coeperunt, erutaque subinde pavonina ova divisere convivis. Convertit ad hanc scenam Trimalchio vultum et: 'Amici, ait, pavonis ova gallinae iussi supponi. Et mehercules timeo ne iam concepti sint. Temptemus tamen, si adhuc sorbilia sunt'. Accipimus nos cochlearia non minus selibras pendentia, ovaque ex farina pingui figurata pertundimus. Ego quidem paene proieci partem meam, nam videbatur mihi iam in pullum coisse. Deinde ut audivi veterem convivam: 'Hic nescio quid boni debet esse', persecutus putamen manu, pinguissimam ficedulam inveni piperato vitello circumdatam.*

49 Mart. 13.49. Translated by Shackleton Bailey (1993c) 193: *Cum me ficus alat, cum pascar dulcibus uvis, cur potius nomen non dedit uva mihi?*

50 Petr. *Sat.* 40. Translated by Schmeling (2020) 139: *ex cuius plaga turdi evolaverunt. Parati aucupes cum harundinibus fuerant, et eos circa triclinium volitantes momento exceperunt.*

51 Chandezon (2015) 138.

52 Varro, *Rust.* 3.5.1–2; Hor. *Sat.* 2.8.91; Hor. *Ars P.* 458–9.

53 Mart. 13.92. Translated by Shackleton Bailey (1993c) 211: *Inter aves turdus, si quid me iudice certum est inter quadripedes mattea prima lepus.* See also 13.51.

54 Hor. *Sat.* 2.5.10; Plin. *Ep.* 5.2.1.

55 Ov. *Ars am.* 2.269–70. Translated by Mozley (1929) 85: *Quin etiam turdoque licet missaque columba te memorem dominae testificere tuae.*

56 Columella, *Rust.* 8.10.1–6; Plin. *HN* 17.6.

57 Johnson (1968) 45.

58 Diocletian, *Maximum Price Edict*, 4.27, 34, 36.

59 Mart. 13.51; see also 3.47.10. *Texta rosis fortasse tibi vel divite nardo, at mihi de turdis facta corona placet.*

60 Holleran (2012) 142.

61 Valenzuela (2018).

62 Plin. *HN* 17.6. Translated by Rackham (1950) 35: *M. Varro principatum dat turdorum fimo ex aviariis, quod etiam pabulo boum suumque magnificat, neque alio cibo celerius pinguescere adseverat. de nostris moribus bene sperare est si tanta apud maiores fuere aviaria ut ex his agri stercorarentur.*

63 Ov. *Rem. Am.* 207–8. Translated by Mozley (1929) 193: *lenius est studium, studium tamen, alite capta aut lino aut calamis praemia parva sequi.* Oppian, *The Chase*, 47f elucidates the differences between the three types of hunting, with big game hunting touted as most impressive.

64 Hor. *Epod.* 2.29–36. Translated by Rudd (2004) 275: *at cum tonantis annus hibernus Iovis imbris nivisque conparat, aut trudit acris hinc et hinc multa cane apros in obstantis plagas aut amite levi rara tendit retia turdis edacibus dolos pavidumque leporem et advenam laqueo gruem iucunda captat praemia.*

65 Zeuner (1963) 474.

66 Dio (Epitome) 66.25.

67 Bartosiewicz (2005) 260.

68 Bartosiewicz (2005) 262.

69 Bartosiewicz (2005) 262.

70 Verg. *G.* 1.307; *Anth. Pal.* 6.109.

71 Hor. *Sat.* 2.8.87; Mart. 13.74.

72 Albarella and Thomas (2002) 23.

73 Bartosiewicz (2005) 263; Apicius 6.213.

74 Petr. *Sat.* 55. Translated by Schmeling (2020) 173: *Luxuriae ructu Martis marcent moenia. Tuo palato clausus pavo pascitur plumato amictus aureo Babylonico, gallina tibi Numidica, tibi gallus spado. Ciconia etiam, grata peregrina hospita pietaticultrix, gracilipes, crotalistria, avis exul hiemis, titulus tepidi temporis, nequitiae nidum in caccabo fecit modo.*

75 Plin. *HN* 10.30. Translated by Rackham (1940) 331: *Cornelius Nepos, qui divi Augusti principatu obiit, cum scriberet turdos paulo ante coeptos saginari, addidit ciconias magis placere quam grues, cum haec nunc ales inter primas expetatur, illam nemo velit attigisse.*

76 Bodson (1983) 315.

77 Juv. *Sat.* 14.74; Plin. *HN* 10.62.

78 Bodson (1983) 314; Thomson 1988.

79 Arist. *Hist. an.* ix 615b 23; Ar. *Av.* 1355–8.

80 Carson (1978–81) 1.75

81 Ov. *Ars Am.* 2.149–50; Ael. *NA* 1.52, 1.58.

82 Mart. 13.71. Translated by Shackleton Bailey (1993c) 201: *Dat mihi pinna rubens nomen, sed lingua gulosis nostra sapit. Quid si garrula lingua foret?*

83 Juv. *Sat.* 9.139.

84 Dembeck (1965) 205.

85 Alföldi-Rosenbaum (1972) 16.

86 Laufer (1926) 24.

87 MacKinnon (2013) 175

88 Bodson (2014) 557.

89 Arnott (2007) 227–30. See Plin. *HN* 10.1, Sen. *Constant.* 17.1, Petr. *Sat.* 137.4.

90 Alföldi-Rosenbaum (1972) 14.

91 Nemes. *Versus de aucupio* 1–18; Plin. *HN* 10.56.

92 Nemes. *Versus de aucupio* 19–24. Translated by Duff (1934a) 515: *cum nemus omne suo viridi spoliatur honore, fultus equi niveis silvas pete protinus altas*

exuviis: praeda est facilis et amoena scolopax. corpore non Paphiis avibus maiore videbis. illa sub aggeribus primis, qua proluit umor, pascitur, exiguos sectans obsonia vermes.

93 Grouse are among the birds suitable for Caligula's godhood: Suet. *Calig.* 52.4

94 Ael. *NA* 1.29. The 'Small Hunt' mosaic from Piazza Armerina shows men with decoy birds on their shoulders. We can assume some had tethered owls, which no doubt alarmed passers-by.

95 Mart. 14.216. Translated by Shackleton Bailey (1993c) 323: *Non tantum calamis, sed cantu fallitur ales, callida dum tacita crescit harundo manu.*

96 Mart. 13.65. See also 13.76, where it is preferred not for its taste, but because it is expensive.

97 *Anth. Pal.* 7.203, 204, 205, 206.

98 Babrius 124. Translated by Perry (1965) 161: ὥρμησε δὴ πέρδικα ποικίλον θύσων, ὃν ἡμερώσας εἶχεν εἰς τὸ θηρεύειν. ὁ δ᾽ αὐτὸν οὕτως ἱκέτευε μὴ κτεῖναι· "τὸ λοιπόν, <ὦ τᾶν>, δικτύῳ τί ποιήσεις, ὅταν κυνηγῇς; τίς δέ σοι συναθροίσει εὐωπὸν ἀγέλην ὀρνέων φιλαλλήλων; τίνος μελῳδοῦ πρὸς <τὸν> ἦχον ὑπνώσεις;" ἀφῆκε τὸν πέρδικα, καὶ γενειήτην ἀλεκτορίσκον συλλαβεῖν ἐβουλήθη.

99 Ael. *NA* 4.30. This is corroborated by Greek sources, from which Aelian may have taken the information. It may have been a Greek hunting method rather than a Roman one. See Ath. 393ab; Dionysius, *On Birds*, 3.18–19.

100 Varro, *Rust.* 3.5.2. They were fattened with thrushes and ortolans.

101 Varro, *Rust.* 3.5.7. Translated by Boyd Ash (1934) 451 with amendments: *Non ut advenae volucres pullos faciunt, in agro ciconiae, in tecto hirundines, sic aut hic aut illic turdi, qui cum sint nomine mares, re vera feminae quoque sunt. Neque id non secutum ut esset in merulis, quae nomine feminino mares quoque sunt. Praeterea volucres cum partim advenae sint, ut hirundines et grues, partim vernaculae, ut gallinae ac columbae, de illo genere sunt turdi adventicio ac quotannis in Italiam trans mare advolant circiter aequinoctium autumnale et eodem revolant ad aequinoctium vernum, et alio tempore, turtures ac coturnices immani numero. Hoc ita fieri apparet in insulis propinquis Pontiis, Palmariae, Pandateriae. Ibi enim in prima volatura cum veniunt, morantur dies paucos requiescendi causa itemque faciunt, cum ex Italia trans mare remeant.* See also Diod. Sic. 1.60.

102 Cocker and Tipling (2013) 56–7.

103 Contra. Watson (2002) 358, who interprets a vague etching as depicting a man with a tethered falcon on his wrist.

104 For example, in Chaucer's *Troilus and Criseyde*, the prince of Troy rides forth to the Greek camp 'with hauk on honde' (book 5, line 65). See Oggins (2004) 112.

105 Epstein (1943) 498–9.

106 Arist. *Hist. an.* 620b. Translated by Balme (1991) 309: ἐν δὲ Θρᾴκῃ τῇ καλουμένῃ ποτὲ Κεδρειπολιὸς ἐν τῷ ἕλει θηρεύουσιν οἱ ἄνθρωποι τὰ ὀρνίθια κοινῇ μετὰ τῶν ἱεράκων· οἱ μὲν γὰρ ἔχοντες ξύλα σοβοῦσι τὸν κάλαμον καὶ τὴν ὕλην ἵνα πέτωνται τὰ ὀρνίθια, οἱ δ᾽ ἱέρακες ἄνωθεν ὑπερφαινόμενοι καταδιώκουσιν· ταῦτα δὲ φοβούμενα κάτω πέτονται πάλιν πρὸς τὴν γῆν· οἱ δ᾽ ἄνθρωποι τύπτοντες τοῖς ξύλοις λαμβάνουσι, καὶ τῆς θήρας μεταδιδόασιν αὐτοῖς· ῥίπτουσι γὰρ τῶν ὀρνίθων, οἱ δὲ ὑπολαμβάνουσιν.

107 Plin. *HN* 10.10. Translated by Rackham (1940) 307: *In Thraciae parte super Amphipolim homines et accipitres societate quadam aucupantur: hi ex silvis et harundinetis excitant aves, illi supervolantes deprimunt rursus; captas aucupes dividunt cum his.* See also Ael. *NA* 2.42. See Plin. *HN* 10.18 for a story about a maiden in Sestos who raised a young eagle and hunted with it until she died and the bird immolated itself on her pyre. It is a quaint story but not concrete enough to act as evidence for widespread falconry.

108 Dobiat (2013) 348.

109 Turberville, *Book of Faulconrie* (1575) 54. See Spenser, *Faerie Queene*, 3.7.33 for a poetic description.
110 Harrison (1956) 70.
111 Mart. 14.216. Translated by Shackleton Bailey (1993c) 323 with amendments: *Praedo fuit volucrum: famulus nunc aucupis idem decipit et captas non sibi maeret aves.*
112 Dobiat (2013) 348.
113 For images and an explanation of the site's significance, see Akerström-Hougen (1974).
114 Sir Thomas Elyot, *The Book Named the Governor*, 18.
115 Kites are considered 'bad beasts' that carry off chickens: Plaut. *Poen.* 1292–3.
116 Gaál (2017) 10.

5 Pets and Pleasure

Introduction

Now that we have covered the raising, hunting, and consumption of birds, we can consider how birds as pets or objects of pleasure conferred status or otherwise communicated social meaning in ancient Rome. For a villa owner, the pursuit of pleasure was as much a motivation for keeping birds as the pursuit of profit.[1] The country villa was a place where *otium* (leisure) dominated, as opposed to the City, where *negotium* (business) ruled.[2] Visual representations reflect the sensorial feast that would have characterised Roman *villae*, the cacophony of birdsong from the multitude of avian guests that visited – and indeed, were encouraged to visit – their gardens.[3] Birds either penned or wild brought satisfaction and joy through song or visual beauty.

A custom-built aviary was one way of deriving pleasure from birds, but another way involved cultivating a garden full of wild birds that freely came and went. Romans were garden-loving people, and a large part of this was tied up in the appreciation of birds and song. Just as no vision of the Garden of Eden is complete without birds to inhabit it, so too was the perfect rustic idyll imagined alive with birdsong. Tibullus describes his vision of the Elysian fields thus: 'But me, for I have been ever pliable to gentle Love, shall Venus' self escort to the Elysian fields. There never flags the dance and song. The birds fly here and there, fluting sweet carols from their slender throats'.[4] Closer to home, the anonymously written *Elegy for Maecenas* outlines what a joy it is to listen to birdsong in the garden: 'He chose rather the shady oak, the falling waters, the few sure acres of fruit-bearing soil. Honouring the Muses and Apollo in luxurious gardens, he reclined babbling verse among the tuneful birds'.[5] From the late Republic onwards, Rome was a city of gardens – ringed by them, with other smaller gardens within the bounds of the City. There were temple groves, gardens in house courtyards, gardens at baths, roof gardens, gardens at inns and small taverns, and outside the City there were funerary gardens too. Many people kept their own gardens, facilitated by the Augustan water program, and the poor who lived in *insulae* still had access to public gardens.[6] The passion for gardens and nature found expression in Roman art.[7] Through the first century BCE and first century

DOI: 10.4324/9781003247906-6

CE in elite and sub-elite house in Rome and in Campania, garden scenes flourished on wall paintings and panels. The most realistic depictions garnered the highest praise, while inaccurate or deliberately playful renditions were met with disapproval (Vit. *de Arch.* 7.5.3–4). Therefore, we may use garden scenes in Roman art as evidence of what their real gardens looked like. The Roman house was a canvas on which nature could be recreated.[8] Such was the Roman fidelity to nature that Pliny even records anecdotes of birds being fooled by realistic paintings of grapes (Plin. *HN* 35.23, 35.65–6, 35.95). The passion for bucolic scenes in the art should be seen as an attempt to bring the pleasures of nature, and the pleasure of birds and birdsong, inside their own houses.

Pliny names Spurius Tadius of the Augustan age as the man who first introduced the fashion of painting walls with garden scenes and snapshots of rural life. All elements of nature were painted, including scenes of fishing, fowling, and gathering grapes (Plin. *HN* 35.37). According to Wilhelmina Jashemski, these garden paintings celebrated the real gardens of a garden-loving culture.[9] By extension, they were symptomatic of a bird-loving culture. Birds were common as decorative motifs in art, or as 'filling elements'.[10] They were indispensable to *hortus* scenes and most outdoor scenes.[11] Fountains and birds were seemingly essential parts of every garden painting.[12] Frescoes reveal that the bird population in Roman gardens was diverse and abundant. While it is important to recognise that art does not necessarily reflect reality, the accuracy with which various species were depicted is nevertheless compelling. Doves, pigeons, blackbirds, thrushes, buntings, flycatchers, golden orioles, and warblers, as well as larger birds such as ibises, peacocks, partridges and pheasants have all been successfully identified in Roman paintings.[13] In other forms of art, they repeated favourite imagery, such as drinking doves, a cat attacking birds, herons fighting snakes, Leda with swan-Zeus, and Ganymede with eagle-Zeus.[14] The original creator of the drinking doves mosaic, so popular because doves were kept as pretty pets, was Sosos of Pergamon, who designed it for the Attalid palace at Pergamon (Plin. *HN* 36.184). The work inspired copies all across the Mediterranean. The most famous Roman example is the Doves Mosaic from the Villa of Hadrian at Tivoli, now held in Rome's Capitoline Museum.[15]

Birds and Gardens

Widely considered the most impressive and beautiful garden mural from ancient Rome is Livia's Garden Room at Prima Porta. This a useful case study to consider since it involves the imperial family, who were necessarily preoccupied with exhibiting status and exclusivity. The Garden Room represents an attempt to give the viewer an immersive, three-dimensional view of a garden, replete with no less than 69 birds, of various species and in a multitude of different poses.[16] The verdant garden painting may be linked to the botanical imagery of the Ara Pacis, suggestive of peace and prosperity.[17] It is thought that this was an underground dining room, intended to be used in the summer months when it became too hot to lounge in real gardens.[18] Livia's garden room takes realism to the extreme in one way while bending reality in others. Different types of vegetation which naturally flower at different times of the year bloom and bear fruit all at once in this painting.[19] Similarly, the different species of birds present all have different migratory patterns, and yet are present at the same time. The tame bird in its cage perhaps reminds the viewer that this is a depiction of nature, but one that is better than anything nature could provide, since it has been shaped by human hands.[20] While the bird is undoubtedly a songster, the painting is too faded to make out any more than that. Some speculate that the bird is a nightingale.[21] Nightingales perish quickly in captivity, however, and only sing for a few weeks in spring. A song thrush is another option. They sing most months of the year, and as winter residents in Italy, they were rare and therefore valuable in summer. Many gardens and dining rooms must have featured caged songsters to provide music, but since the cages were wicker they have left no archaeological trace.[22] This is nature but improved upon to best suit the human viewer.

Landscape paintings were intended to provide a multisensory experience. Philostratos describes roses that have been painted with scent intact and invites people to listen for the lowing of cattle and shepherd's pipes as they

Figure 5.1 Caged bird in Livia's Garden Room, held in Palazzo Massimo alle Terme.
Source: Photo by Edward Blume-Poulton.

admire artificial scenes (Philostr. *Imag.* 1.2, 1.6, 1.12). The presence of so many small songbirds in the garden room invites the viewer to conjure up an auditory landscape as they admire it, and lends credence to the idea that a caged songbird was often a feature at soirées. Reeder describes the Garden Room as giving the illusion of being in the interior of a grotto and looking out into a surrounding grove. She compares this to the description of Varro's aviary at Casinum, where the diner seated in the central *tholos* looked out beyond the netting designed to keep the birds inside.[23]

The areas affected by the eruption of Vesuvius provide the most information about the Roman love of gardens. Latium and Campania, like most of Italy, were packed with farmhouses and villas in which Roman farmers lived and worked.[24] Farming was intensive in these areas, and gardens too were plentiful. The contrast between a garden intended for pleasure and traditional agriculture sometimes led to moral tension.[25] Horace deplores the changing attitudes towards land use and the way luxury buildings were constructed at the expense of productive agriculture. He yearns for the good old days of Romulus and Cato the Elder, who upheld traditional farming (Hor. *Carm.* 2.15). Excavations at the Villa of Poppaea reveal how nature was shaped in non-traditional ways. Over a dozen gardens, parks, and planted areas have been discovered in the residence.[26] The rooms are as immersive as Livia's garden room, depicting water, plants, and foliage alongside birds and

Figure 5.2 A Campanian birdbath. Villa Oplontis, first century CE.

Source: Photo by Edward Blume-Poulton.

birdbaths. Many of the birds of Oplontis have faded, making it difficult to identify them accurately, but in the garden scenes small warblers and songbirds seem to be favoured, perhaps to help the viewer imagine the auditory landscape that the birds would have provided. The House of the Orchard in Pompeii is another example of an idyllic garden landscape complemented by a multitude of birds. The sheer number depicted in all these garden scenes, the attention to detail, and the way they were carefully painted on top of the foliage suggest that they were made by specialised painters.[27]

It is well-known that the Romans were adept at constructing water features. At villas we often find both real fountains and painted ones, so we can assume that there were living counterparts to the menagerie of painted birds on the wall.[28] The prevalence of birds drinking from fountains in art shows that they were specially placed to attract birds.[29] In the hot Campanian summers, the real fountains would have been swarming with birds. Herons and egrets would have been especially lovely visitors, probably the largest wild birds one could hope to entice into the garden. It is possible that the Roman predilection for bathing helped prompt them to leave out baths for their feathered visitors, and that they derived a sense of pleasure or kinship from watching the birds splash around in their miniature *thermae*. A decorative motif used in the Pompeian bathhouse is a splashing duck – happy ducks were something Romans could relate to.

Birds were sometimes turned into water features too. In the section on Automata in *Pneumatics,* Hero of Alexandria writes of Roman fountains and describes an unusual owl fountain. In this fountain, a number of fake birds would 'sing' until an owl turned its head to look at them. Allegedly this was recreated sometime before 1580 in Renaissance Italy at the Villa d'Este, Tivoli, which proves that the plans are feasible.[30] In a previous chapter we considered the Romans' low opinion of the owl, and this fountain is a delightful illustration of that attitude. Pneumatic blackbirds are also attested in Vitruvius (Vitr. *de Arch.* 10.7.4.4).

What does all this tell us about the Roman temperament? These elite sites indicate that gardens full of water features and birds were intended to provide nothing more than pleasure. Only the wealthiest – and critically, the imperial family – could afford to dedicate significant land and resources to non-productive purposes, and this was reproduced in art to intensify the effect. While we might be tempted to say that pleasure gardens and aviaries were simply a means of advertising power, wealth, and land ownership, the Roman, and particularly the Campanian, love of birds seems to go beyond this. To illustrate this, we can look at one person who dwelt on a second storey on the Via dell'Abbondanza in Pompeii, who converted his or her balcony into a tiny aviary roughly two metres square. The three windows were covered with netting, and nine intact watering pans for birds were found on the balcony along with fragments of others. Jashemski points out how this tiny aviary, tucked into an upstairs apartment on a busy street, speaks of a genuine love of birds.[31] The impulse to entice and keep songbirds was not one monopolised by the wealthy, and it was not always motivated by a desire to advertise status. Aviaries were also kept on a small scale, secreted in urban apartments, apparently simply for the joy the birds brought their owners. We see this impulse again when we look at pet birds, which could bring their owners prestige or simply pleasure.

Pest Birds

Though sweet songbirds were welcome in the Roman garden, to quote Thomas Hardy, what is good for God's birds is bad for God's gardeners, so we should consider what measures the Romans took to keep pesky birds *out* of their gardens and fields. Not everyone had the luxury of dedicating land to non-productive purposes, and not everyone could enjoy the sight of wild birds in their garden. What happened when birds did not bring pleasure, but rather pestilence, to the garden? A prayer directed to Ceres and the Earth runs thus: 'Forbid the birds, pests of the tilled land, to devastate the fields of corn with their destructive flocks'.[32] Priapus, also called Mutunus Tutunus, is an unmistakable Latin deity who promoted fertility and protected from the Evil Eye. He also had the task of keeping the household garden safe from its most common desecrators – namely, thieves and birds. To secure his protection, the rustic Roman would set up a wooden statue of him in the garden, which functioned both as a shrine and a scarecrow. There are many references to the Priapus scarecrow in literature. It was said, 'to the fruit-laden gardens is given red Priapus as watch, to scare the birds with cruel billhook'.[33] He was, 'the Crimson One who by his lewd image scares the timid birds'[34] or 'crimson Priapus, glory and guard of gardens'.[35] It is not the sort of statue we would put in our gardens today, but this scarlet, sickle-wielding wooden Priapus with his fearsome crotch was dearly beloved by many Roman families. A poem called *Priapea* describes Priapus as the guardian of the poor man's garden and rustic cottage, and warns the would-be thief to beware the farmer's wrath as well as his own. His guardianship was entreated with sacrifice, and the statue was kept clean and repainted regularly. As the year progressed, his family would wreathe the statue with garlands made of seasonal produce. Horace's eighth satire tells an amusing story about a wooden Priapus, which begins thus:

> Once I was a fig-wood stem, a worthless log, when the carpenter, doubtful whether to make a stool or a Priapus, chose that I be a god. A god, then, I became, of thieves and birds the special terror; for thieves my right hand keeps in check, and this red stake, protruding from unsightly groin; while for the mischievous birds, a *harundo* set on my head affrights them and keeps them from lighting in the new garden.[36]

The phrase 'new garden' may mean freshly planted in this context, the object being to prevent birds eating seeds or sprouts. This passage differs from the others in that it tells us that Priapus' enlarged genitals and the sickle in his right hand were meant to frighten human intruders, but the birds were instead frightened by a *harundo* on his head – a limed reed. We cannot imagine that the *harundo* was particularly frightening to birds, and was most likely magical or symbolic in nature. The *Priapea* indicates how effective these statues were at scaring birds: '(...) and often by shouting have we driven away the old raven and enthusiastic jackdaw who would, with horny beak, peck your sacred head'.[37] Birds become used to scarecrows if they are not moved or altered regularly, and this poem shows that in spite of Priapus' fearsome crotch and limed reed, they took no notice of him. If you wanted to keep birds away from your garden, your crops, and even your scarecrow, you had to do it yourself. In the midst of imparting sage advice to farmers, Virgil instructs them to scare birds with noise, which implies that they shouted and used rattles to spook pest birds (Verg. *G.* 1.156). A sepulchral epigram in the Greek Anthology informs us that men employed to protect crops from birds would do so armed with a leather sling (Antip. Sid. *Anth. Pal.* 7.172). If a man had money, he could employ a bird-scarer to keep his crops safe, while in poorer families this task probably fell to the children. Sometimes other magic was invoked, as Pliny tells us that he heard there was a certain plant (its name unknown) which, if planted in the four corners of a field, would deter sparrows and starlings, the scourge of Roman fields, from entering.[38] Before sowing, prayers were offered up to protect the seed from disease, beasts, and birds.[39] In contrast to the imperial family and other elites who could afford to entice birds into their gardens and construct ponds and fountains for them, small-scale farmers worked hard to keep birds *out* of their precious plots of land and away from their produce. Romans appealed to Priapus for help in keeping their gardens safe from thieving birds and employed more practical measures to this effect too. There was a firm distinction drawn between delightful songbirds, welcome in ornamental gardens, and pest birds, unwelcome in the fields and gardens where families grew food. The act of appreciating wild birds and taking pleasure from their appearance on one's land was something not everyone could afford, hence the elite preoccupation with pleasure gardens.

Pleasure Aviaries

As if it were not enough to dedicate time and precious resources to non-productive pleasure gardens, the fashion for ornamental aviaries took things to the next level. Here, wild birds were not only tolerated in the garden, but special enclosures were built for the purposes of exhibiting birds. Roman tradition from the elder Cato through to Varro, Cornelius Nepos, and Pliny the Elder sniped at excessive household expenditure, classing it as *luxuria*, a vice of excess and folly. Cato boasted of his lack of stuccowork; Varro sneered at Lucullus for the fad of dining in picture galleries; Lucullus was generally derided as excess personified. For all their moralising, however, it was impossible to escape the reality that *luxuria* was a social necessity in a stratified and competitive society.[40] A man of rank and dignity needed a house that reflected his social standing, which could admit and entertain guests, and provide hospitality as appropriate. A Roman house expressed social standing through decoration and quality. If it became fashionable to own a pleasure aviary, one could not afford to fall behind.

Any discussion of Roman aviaries must necessarily include Varro's description of the *ornithon* at his villa in Casinum.[41] This was a large, imposing structure with netted colonnades to keep the throngs of songbirds penned inside, and it was set around a duckpond (Varro, *Rust.* 3.5.8–17). According to tradition, M. Laenius Strabo was the inventor of the pleasure aviary, and Varro modelled his estate on this prototype. Huge aviaries were intended to show off architecture as well as exotic and extensive collections of birds. Some aviaries were used as dining rooms. Varro describes the pleasure aviary of Lucullus at Tusculum which was intended to serve as a dining room in which one could eat birds while living birds flew about overhead. As one might expect, dining inside an aviary was not a particularly wholesome experience. Fluttering birds might please the eye, but their dung offended the nose. In theory, it was beautiful, a feast that used birds to tickle all the senses and bring delight through song, taste, and appearance. In practice, this dining room was apparently dank and filthy (Varro, *Rust.* 3.4.3). A failed experiment, one might think, in trying to maximise the pleasure one could derive from watching and keeping birds.

A more detailed description of Varro's own *ornithon* runs as follows. Walking along a stream in the villa, one would come to find an aviary of 72 by 48 feet. At the end was added a domed structure. In the rectangular section was a path between fish basins enclosed by a peristyle. The outer ring was made of stone columns, the inner ring of dwarf trees. This peristyle contained all manner of birds that were fed through rope netting that covered the entire peristyle. A rivulet supplied them with water. The *tholos* was netted with gut (to give a better view than a rope) and the trees behind had the lower branches trimmed to provide shade without blocking all light. In the colonnade were mainly songbirds like blackbirds or nightingales. Brackets attached to the columns served as perches. This surrounded a pool linked to the fish basins in which ducks dabbled and played. One could watch the ducks within this space while the songbirds wheeled above.[42] The pond had an island in the middle and a border about a foot wide, along which were 'docks' that served as duck shelters. On the island was a rotating platform from which food and drink could be served to *conviviae*. The text is ambiguous as to the identity of the *conviviae*, the 'guests'. Are we to assume that this island was where humans dined, even despite Varro's mention of how unpleasant it was to dine in Hortensius' smelly aviary, or is *conviviae* a playful name for the ducks? C.M.C. Green argues that the ducks are the true guests. They own the aviary, and it is set up to deliver food to them.[43] In either case, it is striking that ornamental ducks and other waterfowl were so central to pleasure aviaries. Small songsters above were complemented by ducks splashing and playing in the water below. Deriving pleasure from birds in such a way could only be accomplished by the very wealthy, and it was intended as part of display. Visitors were invited to enjoy the owner's garden and aviary, and marvel at how much he could afford to dedicate to trivial pursuits. We have seen how a small-time landowner could ill-afford such an extravagance, but there was still a drive to derive pleasure from bird ownership in more subtle ways, such as keeping birds as pets.

Pet Birds

This section explores those birds that were kept not merely because they provided profit or were pleasing in shape or song, but because they provided a form of intimate companionship. This can reveal a great deal about Roman sentimentality, but it is also useful since the decision to keep a particular pet, and the ability to care for it, are defined by one's means and status. Whether consciously or not, we choose to surround ourselves with animals that communicate how we view the world and our place in it.[44] Birds of all types were highly desirable as pets. In fact, in Latin literature, there are more references to pet birds than all other kinds of pet put together.[45]

The motivations for keeping a pet are varied and complicated. Caring for and thinking about animals expresses social factors as much as the act of consuming them.[46] Standards of care and attitudes towards different pets also varied.[47] What a Roman might consider a high standard of care may not actually coincide with what is best for the animal. All of this must be taken into consideration as we explore companion birds. Complicating the matter is that there is no word for pet in Latin the way it exists in our vocabulary today. Animals were more generally classed as wild or tame, kept for work or pleasure.[48] The phrase that best expressed the idea of keeping a pet was *in deliciis habere* – literally, 'to have as a delight'.[49] This betrays the thinking behind it; a pet was an animal that served no function except to bring delight to its owner. It is fascinating that those who spent small fortunes on acquiring pet birds were seen as somewhat foolish, but they were met with more tolerance than the gluttons who ate anything that hopped or fluttered:

> Though I should regard those people who pay great sums in copper and silver for the pleasure which their pets give them merely because they own and possess them, as less insufferable than those who clear of all their birds the River Phasis in Pontus and the pools of Lake Maeotis in Scythia; nay, they are now in their drunkenness belching forth birds brought from the Ganges and from Egypt![50]

Terms of endearment were derived from sparrows, hens, quails, ducks, doves, swallows and jackdaws, indicating a fondness for these birds.[51] The Greeks

Figure 5.3 Children playing with birds. Piazza Armerina, Sicily. Fourth century CE.
Source: Photo by Damian Byrne: Alamy Stock Photo.

could be similarly sentimental about pet birds. Exotic birds made fine gifts for kings and potentates (Ael. *NA* 13.25, 13.18). Socrates had his pigeons (Pl. *Tht.* 197c). Penelope had her geese (Hom. *Od.* 19.536–7). Antipater of Sidon describes the tomb of a housewife decorated with the carving of a goose to represent her care over the home (*Anth. Pal.* 7.425). Such depictions of women alongside poultry and waterfowl suggest that domestic birds were suitable companions for women.[52] Many Roman artistic representations of pet birds are based on Greek originals, betraying how the two cultures held similar attitudes. Studies of Greek art have shown that women and children are more likely to be shown with pet birds, probably because they spent more time at home.[53] In the Roman context, pet birds were most frequently in the company of children (Figure 5.3).

Studying pet-keeping among Roman children is particularly illuminating. Parents today take it for granted that pet-keeping is good for the socialisation and education of a child. Caring for an animal inculcates a sense of personal responsibility while providing comfort and companionship. But how conventional was it for Romans to keep pets, and how did it factor into the upbringing of children? What was the reasoning behind giving them pets? Looking at the evidence, we have mentions of birds, dogs, cats, goats, sheep, rabbits, and geese as standard companions.[54] Children of both sexes kept pets from earliest childhood, from when they were *infantes* to when they were teenagers.[55] Hellenistic sculptures of children with pets were

Figure 5.4 Boy strangling a goose. Roman copy of the bronze Greek original, c. 220
     BCE. Held in the Glyptothek.

Source: Photo by the author.

copied across the Roman world. Baby boys wrestling geese were popular.[56]
There were also sculptures of boys with puppies and girls holding doves.[57]
The Roman appreciation for, and reproduction of, these statues should
indicate that it was normal for both Roman and Greek children to play with
pets, and that keeping animals was a part of regular upbringing. Children
were also given toys in the shape of animals to play with, including roosters
and ducks.[58] Roman clay rattles in the shape of various domestic birds have
been recovered.[59]

   The association between children and animals likely has practical roots.
In Tamara Lewit's investigation of the roles of children in agriculture in the
Roman world, she discovered that young children, both free and enslaved,
were typically assigned 'fool-proof' work that was suited to their age and
strength, including gleaning, gathering fodder, and caring for small, docile
animals like donkeys, sheep, goats, and poultry.[60] Difficult, dangerous
work, or work that required precision and experience, such as reaping and
ploughing, were left to the adults. If caring for small animals like birds was
widely held to be the responsibility of children, this provides insight into

why birds and children were seen to go together, and also blurs the line between pet birds and domestic poultry.[61]

Pets were commonly included as decorations on children's funerary monuments and sarcophagi.[62] The marble sarcophagus rose to prominence as a means of burial at some point in the late first century CE, supplanting cremation.[63] Sarcophagi were not always personalised; sculptors tended to employ the same motifs relentlessly.[64] When it came to children, they were usually shown in the company of birds or dogs.[65] If we opt for a literal interpretation of the images, we might say they depict the dead child's pets. If we opt for a symbolic interpretation, we might say the puppy represents fidelity and the doves represent love and innocence, but we could still argue that those symbolic images were used because artists naturally associated children with birds and dogs due to how commonly they were kept as pets.[66] The images on sarcophagi are often bittersweet: a dead boy feeds grapes to a bird as he must have done in life. A dead girl clutches a pigeon to her chest just as the images of living children do. Sometimes cupids gambol with birds in fanciful scenes around the rim of the child's coffin. The image of a dead boy situated between his loving parents is shown with two birds on his shoulders.[67] Because birds were an

Figure 5.5 Marble grave stele of a little girl holding doves, c. 450–440 BCE. This motif is common in Greek and Roman art.

Source: Photo by the Metropolitan Museum of Art. Fletcher Fund, 1927. Inv. no. 27.45.

integral part of a child's life from the moment they were born, it is fitting that they became their companions in death.[68]

Perhaps because children were given birds when they were very young, it appears that as they grew older it became less acceptable for them to dote on their pets. A teenage boy could not neglect his education in favour of playing with animals, as we see in the story of a blithe young man who is mad for birds and spends all his time whistling to his blackbirds and nightingales and teaching his pets to talk instead of focusing on his own schooling. What is the world coming to, the author asks, when his birds are more eloquent than he is! (Philostr. *VA*, 6.36). In the *Satyricon*, the rustic firefighter Echion says: '([My son is] a clever lad and made of good quality, even if he has an almost unhealthy interest in birds. I've already killed three of his goldfinches and said that a weasel ate them'.[69] Devotion to birds was a lovely trait in young children, but part of the maturing process involved putting aside such sentimental pursuits. This is not to say that keeping birds was unacceptable in teens and adults, merely that it had to be enjoyed in moderation, lest one fall victim to idleness and luxury.

Figure 5.6 Boy with a gosling. First century CE. Copy of a Greek original from the second century BCE. Held in the Naples Archaeological Museum, inv. 6110.

Source: Photo by the author.

Domestic poultry were the most common pets.[70] In Pompeii and Herculaneum, faunal remains of chickens, geese, ducks, quails, pigeons, turtle doves and partridges have been recovered.[71] For wealthier children, these might have been companion animals alone. For poorer children, caring for a flock of hens and collecting eggs each morning were useful things they could do from their earliest days, and they might choose a special favourite.[72] If the family had a natural pond on their property or a garden with water features, they might keep pet ducks, which were depicted with boys in art.[73]

Then there were pigeons, suitable for children of both sexes. In one of Fronto's letters, we hear how his infant grandson has begun to show a fondness for pet chickens, sparrows, and pigeons, just as he himself did as a lad (Fronto, *Ep.* 1.12). Art, too, suggests that children were very young when given birds. Most often they are little more than toddlers clutching birds in their chubby fists.[74] Goslings, ducks, chickens, and pigeons are most often seen with the very young, perhaps because they are harmless and easy to handle. As the child grew older, they might be given more exotic or delicate pets that required more care, as indicated in a joke in Plautus where Tyndarus says he has been given a 'crowbar', 'just as patrician boys are given jackdaws or ducks or quails to play with'.[75] If you could provide your child with pets that were expensive and difficult to procure, so much the better. Pliny the Younger describes the funeral of a child: 'The boy used to possess a number of Gallic ponies for riding and driving, also dogs of all sizes, and nightingales, parrots and blackbirds; Regulus had them all slaughtered round his pyre. That was not grief, but a parade of grief'.[76] Even at his own son's funeral, this man was able to make a spectacle of his wealth by slaughtering expensive pet birds.

We saw above that aristocrats kept caged songbirds, beautifully illustrated by the image from Livia's Garden Room. The nightingale is, of course, the best songster, but keeping them in captivity is a difficult task. Pliny waxes poetic about their beautiful song, but Tim Birkhead points out that although nightingales have been coveted as pets for millennia, they make poor cage birds. Most individuals perish within a day or two of capture. Those that survived provided only ephemeral delight, as the males sing for just a few weeks each spring.[77] There was an added danger – caged nightingales were at risk of dying every autumn. As migratory birds, they attempt to act out their migration while confined and batter themselves against their cage bars for several weeks, going through the entire journey in a series of frantic motions.[78] Those who wanted singing nightingales would have to buy them from fowlers each spring. It would be a very rare bird that survived more than a year or two in captivity. Part of the prestige of owning a nightingale was probably connected to the fact that they had to be procured from the wild each spring if one wanted ready access to their song.

Pliny's discussion of nightingales suggests he believes the birds could not sing so well unless they had been trained by humans. Therefore, 'trained' nightingales fetched a similar price to that of slaves. A white nightingale was sold for an unprecedented 600,000 sesterces to grace the birdcage of Empress Agrippina.[79] As children, Britannicus and Nero had talking starlings and nightingales. Plutarch also mentions talking starlings. These birds can indeed be taught to speak, but talking nightingales are more doubtful.[80] Agrippina also possessed a talking thrush; again, this is dubious. The species may have been misidentified, the seller may have duped the imperial family, or the stories might be simple fabrications, symptomatic of the desire to possess the rarest and most fabulous birds. The ability to own and display exotic creatures such as albino or leucistic birds communicated prestige. Possessing wonders bestowed wonder status on rulers and cities, and this principle was extended to aspiring individuals among the elite who sought out particularly rare, talented or unusual birds.[81] Imperial interest in acquiring such birds clearly indicates this.

Goldfinches were another popular bird. Pretty and intelligent creatures, they are full of charm and personality and are harmless even to toddlers. They whistled to their owners and could perform little tricks, one of which involved pulling on a piece of string to reach a treat (Plin. *HN* 10.116). This string-pulling trick is an extension of its natural way of handling grass stems, which it will pull through its feet to reach the seeds at the tip.[82] During the Italian Renaissance, artwork often depicted the infant Jesus and other children holding a goldfinch. The bird had a rich symbolic meaning in art, but youngsters did keep them as pets so it was natural to equate goldfinches with children. When we look at fat Medici children holding goldfinches, we should imagine Roman youngsters doing the same.

Fighting Birds

There is a real tenderness in the way Romans speak of birds that suggests they admired many because they were sweet and harmless: 'The swallow is free from men's attack because he is gentle, and the Chaonian bird has towers he may inhabit'.[83] Yet it would be a mistake to assume all interactions with beloved birds were sweet-natured. Bearing in mind that this is a time when beast hunts were popular entertainment, it is perhaps unsurprising that many young boys were encouraged to keep fighting cocks, which they would battle to the death. According to Pliny, sometimes fights did not end until both cocks were dead.[84] For any owner who loved his bird, and especially for any boy, this could cause heartbreak.

Written and iconographic evidence for Roman cockfighting is not as abundant as in Greece, but it should not be argued that they did not practise the sport at all.[85] Zooarchaeological evidence from the Roman Castellum at Velsen in the Netherlands, for instance, revealed the town produced an exceptionally high percentage of cockerels to hens. Similar results were found at the Romano-British towns of York, Dorchester, and Silchester. Such finds could be explained also by a preference for roosters in ritual and sacrifice, but at Silchester at least, iron cock-spurs were also recovered.[86]

Artificial cock-spurs have also been found in Cornwall and Baldock in Hertfordshire. In the latter case, the iron spur was found still attached to the cock's leg.[87] Of course, regional differences must be taken into consideration. Based on Caesar's observation that Britons did not eat cocks, but used them for ritual and entertainment purposes, the evidence for urban cockfighting in Britain may be more indicative of how native cockfighting practices remained popular under Roman rule. Nevertheless, in the Italian context there is still enough evidence to confirm cockfighting was a Roman sport. Pompeii yields several representations of cockfights on mosaics and wall paintings.

It is well attested that Greeks loved cockfighting and encouraged their male children to take up the sport. Cocks were often given to teenage boys as love tokens by older male suitors. Athens was also mad for quails and quail fighting, to the point where Socrates was quoted as (controversially?) declaring that he would rather have a good friend than the best fighting quail or fighting cock.[88] It was apparently so normal to go about one's business with a quail in tow that Plutarch relates how Alcibiades stopped to address the Athenian Assembly with a quail tucked under his arm. The bird was startled by sudden applause, escaped, and was pursued on Alcibiades' behalf by many eager audience members.[89] They also battled partridges. Partridge fighting was not as common in Rome, but the Emperor Alexander Severus was said to enjoy the sport (SHA. *Alex. Sev.* 41). Aelian gives several accurate descriptions of partridge fights that tell us it existed in the Roman context (Ael. *NA* 4.1). Cockfighting was bound up with notions of masculinity, warfare, sexual prowess, and victory. Battling cocks was seen as a way to imprint such virtues on impressionable youths. Anthropological studies have shown that wherever cockfighting is practised, it is usually crucial to the definition of masculinity within that culture. There is a close identification between men and their roosters, and the hyper-sexed, hyper-aggressive rooster symbolises what it means to be a man. Cockfighting has been found to be more common in patriarchal societies, especially where domestic violence and violence directed at women are relatively high.[90] We should consider the popularity of cockfights symptomatic of the negative masculine values that dominated the Greco-Roman world. Columella states the Romans had not the same passion for the sport as the Greeks. When it came to chickens, the principal aim was to use them to establish a source of income for a hardworking *paterfamilias,* not profit some trainer who was likely to lose his whole livelihood gambling on a single fight (Columella, *Rust.* 8.2.5). Yet as much as this disapproval shows that Romans were not on the whole fond of cockfighting, we can nevertheless see it was practised. Through the interlocutor Solon, Lucian refers to the law that all men of military age should watch cockfights and quail fights (Luc. *Anach.* 36–7). This ruling in sixth century BCE Athens must still have made sense to men of Lucian's day, indicating Romans also saw cockfighting as a way of instilling in men and boys the tenacity and aggression of roosters. Herodian comments that the rivalry between the emperor Severus' sons Caracalla and Geta went back to earliest childhood, when they battled fighting cocks. In the *Satyricon*, we see Encolpius winning sexual favours from a beautiful boy by giving him a pair of fighting cocks, indicating that cockfighting was connected to male homosexuality as in Greece (Petr. *Sat.* 86). Plutarch records that Antony and young Octavian battled quails and cocks. Antony always lost, emblematic both of their rivalry and of Octavian's ultimate victory (Plut. *Vit. Ant.* 33). Quails and partridges were usually kept as either decoys or prize fighters rather than as tame companions.[91] Ovid laments that Corinna's gentle parrot should die prematurely when quails can live through countless fights to attain old age (Ov. *Am.* 2.6.27–8). Pliny describes the cry of a quail during a fight, the cry of a partridge before, and the cry of a triumphant rooster afterwards (Pliny, *HN* 11.268). In a personal letter, Fronto admits that in his old age he has become fond of partridges, a trait obvious to anyone who knows him even a little (Fronto, *Ep.* 1.12). These written sources indicate that cockfighting was an acceptable pursuit for young men and boys, but among citizen men, it was a low-class pursuit. A Pompeiian mosaic shows children involved in fights. As two roosters battle,

Figure 5.7 A man and a boy are on either side of this cockfight. Naples Archaeological Museum, inv. 9982.

Source: Photo by iStock.com/dmitriymoroz.

a man and a boy stand on the side of the victor, the boy holding a palm aloft. On the side of the loser, another man turns away, and a boy covers his eyes as if he is weeping.

Bradley posits that exposure to cockfighting in childhood would have helped to prepare Roman children for the large-scale bloodletting they would witness in adult life, whether through acts of sacrifice, in battle, or at the beast hunts.[92] The violence and bloodshed that accompany cockfights are extreme. In every fight, at least one bird would be seriously mutilated or killed. Crops could be slit open, eyes gouged out, bones broken, abdomens split, and spectators would cheer all the more upon seeing an injured bird's persistence when afflicted with hideous wounds. This was a male-oriented event, with male birds and male spectators, and it celebrated male virtues.[93] A boy having his pet mutilated and killed before his eyes would help turn him into a man – or, like the boy in mosaic, simply drive him to tears. Such activities were a normal part of growing up, even for imperial boys, which casts a shadow over other interactions with childhood pets. The oft-reproduced statues of toddlers wrestling geese and manhandling pigeons can be taken as indications that children were not always gentle with animals, nor were they reprimanded for being cruel or rough.[94] It was so normal and endearing for boys to engage in rough and tumble activity with delicate birds that it became a playful motif. At the Villa Poppaea there is a fountain figure of a boy gripping what appears to be a gosling by the neck; originally, water would have squirted from its squawking beak.[95] Cockfighting was

Figure 5.8 Mosaic of a cockfight from Pompeii, first century CE. Held in Naples Archaeological Museum, Santangelo Collection (s.n.).

Source: Photo by the author.

thick with social meaning; it was an acceptable pursuit for boys, but an adult citizen male could not engage in such activities without risking association with profligacy, the lower classes, and foreigners.

Talking Birds

The traditional association of pet birds with children came with the expectation that one would not allow such sentimental pursuits to continue into adulthood. While it was acceptable to keep pets, one could not be perceived as *in aves morbosus* – bird-crazy. A poem by Martial satirises how sentimental people became about their strange and exotic pets. Disturbingly for us, slaves are included in this category:

> If my Flaccus delights in a long-eared fennec, if Canius enjoys a sombre Ethiopian, if Publius is a-fire with love for a tiny lapdog, if Cronius adores a long-tailed monkey that resembles him, if a destructive ichneumon charms Marius, if a jay that can speak your name pleases you, Lausus, if Glaucilla twines a clammy snake about her neck, if Telesilla gave a tomb to a nightingale, why should not anyone who sees these freaks pleasing their owners not love the face of Cupid's Labyrtas?[96]

One phenomenon that is worth exploring is the sudden fever for rare and talking birds that swept over the Empire. Clever birds were most coveted, as were birds of unusual appearance or colour. When aediles exhibited exotic animals at festivals, strange and beautiful birds were often put on display.[97] In Varro's time, these included the parrot, and also white blackbirds (Varro, *Rust.* 3.9.17). White blackbirds were apparently found on Mt Cyllene in Arcadia and nowhere else.[98] Whether or not white blackbirds really were abundant in Arcadia, it is certain that leucism and albinism are among the commonest plumage aberrations, and blackbirds with white patches are far from unusual in Europe.[99] It is also possible that 'white blackbirds' merely referred to ring ouzels (*Turdus torquatus*), which are almost identical to blackbirds save for a white patch on the breast, and comparatively rare on the Italian peninsula.[100]

Aelian speaks of priests and royalty in India teaching their native parrots and mynahs to talk, which means that techniques for training birds to speak doubtless first developed there. It is worth noting, however, that there is a dearth of references to talking birds in the classical world prior to the Roman period.[101] It seems Aristotle alone discusses talking birds when he mentions the parrot (Arist. *Hist. an.* 504b, 597b). By contrast, the Romans not only had talking parrots, but talking crows and ravens as well. This indicates that Romans may have developed techniques for schooling birds independent of other cultures, using their own native corvids. Certainly, if we track the evidence, we see that in the late Republic and early Empire, talking birds were greeted with astonishment.

When [Caesar Augustus] was returning to Rome on top of the world after his victory at Actium, one of those who ran to congratulate him was holding a raven that he had taught to say, "Hail Caesar, the victorious commander." Marveling at the dutiful bird, Caesar bought it for 20,000 sesterces. The trainer's confederate, who had gained nothing from this generous act, swore to Caesar that the man had another raven, too, which Caesar asked to be shown. When it was brought out it spoke the words it had been taught: "Hail the victorious commander, Antony." Nothing fazed, Caesar thought it sufficient that the trainer divide the gift with his mate. When he was similarly greeted by a parrot, he ordered its purchase and, admiring a jay with the same skill, he bought it too. Seeing this, a poor shoemaker was moved to teach a raven to give the same salute: but after he'd spent his last penny on the bird—which remained mute—he kept saying, over and over, "My effort and my money, down the drain." At length, however, the raven began to repeat the greeting it was taught; but when Augustus heard it as he was passing by, he said in response, "I have greeters of that sort in abundance at home." The raven still remembered hearing his master's complaint, and so ended by saying, "My effort and my money, down the drain." That made Caesar laugh, so he had the bird purchased at a price higher than all the rest.[102]

The value and rarity of talking birds in the Augustan period are clear. A little earlier than this, the tragic actor Claudius Aesopus paid a whopping 100,000 sesterces for a meal made from the tongues of talking parrots, believing they would endow him with eloquence. The price testifies to their rarity, but interestingly, such shenanigans caused Pliny in the next century to accuse him of cannibalism (Plin. *HN* 10.141–142). To kill a bird that could talk was considered an abominable thing to do, let alone to kill and *eat* it. This is clearly illustrated in the following tale of a famous talking raven. The story goes that when Tiberius was emperor, a raven chick hatched from a nest on the top of the Temple of Castor and Pollux and flew down to a nearby cobbler's shop, where the cobbler adopted it and taught it to speak. From then on, every morning it would fly onto the platform that faces the Forum and salute Tiberius, Germanicus, Drusus, and the Roman people before it returned to the shop. It performed this feat every morning for several years and garnered some celebrity for it. Then one day the cobbler's neighbour, stirred by jealousy (or perhaps anger at the bird befouling his stock) killed the raven. This caused such an outrage that he had to flee the district and was eventually murdered. The people thought the murder of a clever bird was worth avenging – more so than the deaths of illustrious men such as Scipio Aemilianus, Pliny comments acidly. To top it off, the bird was given a public funeral. It was carried on a bier with flute-players and hundreds of mourners following in procession. The date was 28 March, 36 CE.

Pliny ends the story with a tale of a famous talking crow in his own day. Originally from Spain, it was noted for its pure black feathers (a carrion crow, rather than the hooded crow common to Italy) and its impressive vocabulary (Plin. *HN* 10.121–3). By Pliny's day it was not enough that a bird could speak. To be remarkable, it had to show loquacity that was impressive in comparison to the many other chatterers around it.

These colourful stories show that lowly cobblers could possess wonderfully talented birds. Common crows and ravens were turned into valuable companions through care and attention: 'Birds are taught to talk in private and where no other utterance can interrupt, with the trainer sitting by them to keep on repeating the words he wants retained, and coaxing them with morsels of food'.[103] When it came to teaching birds, there was one phrase the patriotic Roman would always have them repeat: 'A parrot, I shall learn from you the names of others; this I have learned to say by myself: "Caesar, hail!"'[104] Talking crows and ravens were so common that Martial could complain: 'You never say good day, Naevolus, you always return it, though even a raven often says it first!'[105]

Jays (*Garrulus glandarius*) were among the common talking birds, called *picae*. *Pica* has been popularly and incorrectly translated as magpie for a long time now, and the mistake is even encoded in the magpie's scientific name, *Pica pica*. The Loeb translation of Book X of Pliny's *Natural History* by H. Rackham, one of the most readily accessible ancient sources on birds in the ancient world, repeats this mistake, informing readers that magpies are famous chatterers that thrive best when fed on acorns. Taking this translation at face value leads one to conclude that Pliny is spouting nonsense. Translated correctly as a Eurasian jay, the passage makes perfect sense. It is true that in some contexts the word *pica* can refer to the common magpie, but its default meaning is jay. The magpie was apparently something of a rarity in Italy until the first century CE, when it underwent a sudden expansion in territory and numbers.[106] Pliny says: 'The kinds of *pica* called *varia* (pied), and distinguished for their long tail, though hitherto rare, have lately begun to be seen between the Apennines and Rome'.[107] Thus *pica* means jay, while *pica varia* denotes the magpie specifically. *Pica* may have been used interchangeably without the qualifying adjective, so we should pay attention to context when translating. In Ovid's fable about nine sisters turned into birds, for example, *picae* refers to jays rather than magpies, because the sisters are guilty of the incessant chattering and mimicry for which jays are notorious (Ov. *Met.* 5.294–5, 669–78). Their fondness for attention and love of learning words are also characteristic of a mimic, making jay the acceptable translation in Pliny's passage (Plin. *HN* 10.118–119). They are such bold little creatures that they can be befriended in the wild if one has morsels of food on hand. Jeremy Mynott corrects this long-held mistake, although he is not the first scholar to puzzle over how to identify Pliny's *picae*. In 1544, the naturalist William Turner had to figure out that *pica* meant jay too![108]

Jays are acknowledged as excellent mimics in Greek sources, being capable of reproducing sounds of human speech and activity in the wild.[109] Comparing the different musical notes of birds, Aelian deems the jay 'talkative' (Ael. *NA* 6.19). A Roman pet jay appears in a story passed on to Plutarch, allegedly by multiple eyewitnesses. In the city of Rome, a lowly barber possessed a jay which reproduced not only human speech, but also imitated the cries of beasts and the sound of instruments. One day, a mighty trumpet blast and accompanying applause from a crowd caused the bird to fall silent, and it remained silent for a very long time. Apparently, the jay was meditating, and showed self-discipline in doing so, for the story concludes that the bird finally let forth its own spectacular rendition of those trumpet-blasts (Plut. *Mor. De soll. an.* 973c). Though we might doubt the details of the story, we can take it as evidence that jays were often kept as pets, particularly by the poor, and that their skill in mimicry was renowned. In the *Satyricon* we get a vision of a henpecked husband when Trimalchio's wife Fortunata is described as a *pica pulvinaris* – literally, a jay on a cushion meant for the image of a deity. This charming expression might come from spoilt pet jays being notorious for their demanding natures (Petr. *Sat.* 37.7). Martial's poem about the *pica* tells us it was common to hang a jay in one's house, where it could greet guests: 'A chattering jay, I greet you as "lord" with a clear voice. If you did not see me, you would say I am no bird'.[110] But in the *Satyricon*, we get the following image: 'Over the doorway hung a golden cage, inside which was a dappled magpie (*pica varia*) that greeted all those entering'.[111] This is probably meant to satirise the freedman Trimalchio's ostentatious luxury. No doubt it was more fashionable to possess a *pica varia* – rarer and more difficult to train – than an ordinary *pica*. As mimics, jays will repeat what they hear, but a magpie can only be taught to speak with great effort.

Among the rarest speaking birds was the parrot, accessible only to those who could afford it. The species was introduced from India, and its origins are traced to 327 BCE and the campaigns of Alexander the Great. Upon his return from the east, he displayed beautiful green parrots as part of his train, which are today called alexandrine parakeets in his honour.[112] After his death, trade with India continued, and parrots continued to make their way into Europe, where they proved popular both as pets and ornamental birds. They were always associated with India and the exotic east, even after hundreds of years had passed since they were first introduced. African greys and Senegal parrots were theoretically within the trading range of the Roman Empire at its height, but there is no firm evidence that Romans kept African varieties, as parrots were always described and depicted as green, Indian birds, so *psittacus* should be taken to mean either the alexandrine parakeet (*Psittacula eupatria*), the rose-ringed parakeet (*Psittacula krameria*) or possibly the plum-headed parakeet (*Psittacula cyanocephala*).[113] Allegedly, Emperor Elagabalus fed parrots and pheasants to his lions, and even ate parrot heads (SHA. *Heliogab.* 20.6, 21.2). Whether this is true, it can be taken as an indication of how rare and valuable the birds were, and how it was treated as a shocking act to kill them so wantonly.

Aristotle calls parrots Indian birds, says they are good mimics, and declares them to be outrageous after they have drunk wine (Arist. *Hist. an.* 7.597b.25–9; 8.614a). Pliny repeats this description:

> Above all, birds imitate the human voice, parrots indeed actually talking. India sends us this bird; its name in the vernacular is *siptaces*; its whole body is green, only varied by a red circlet at the neck. It greets its masters, and repeats words given to it, being particularly sportive over the wine. Its head is as hard as its beak; and when it is being taught to speak it is beaten on the head with an iron rod—otherwise it does not feel blows. When it alights from flight it lands on its beak, and it leans on this and so reduces its weight for the weakness of its feet.[114]

Here we must take issue with a few of these assertions. Its habit of drinking wine may be due to it being released at dinner parties, where it would crawl over the couches and eat as it pleased, perhaps attempting to drink from cups or deliberately being given alcohol as a joke. But wine is not good for parrots, and alcohol can poison them.[115] Melior's parrot, which died suddenly after seeming fit and healthy at a dinner party, might have been killed by alcohol poisoning, or perhaps by some other common food they find toxic.

> Parrot, chief of birds, your master's eloquent delight, Parrot, skilled mimic of human tongue: who cut short your murmurs by so sudden a fate? Yesterday, poor bird, you joined our meal, about to die. We saw you sampling the grateful table's gifts, wandering from couch to couch, past midnight. And you had talked to us, given us your practiced words.[116]

Then there is Pliny's assertion that a parrot must be beaten if it is to learn words. This is blatantly untrue. Teaching a parrot to speak depends on intimacy and trust. Training *cannot* be done through intimidation or physical violence or it will drive the bird to terror and psychosis.[117] Parrot trainers may have used a rod, but not for the reason Pliny describes. When training a bird with a powerful, crushing beak like the alexandrine parakeet, it can be advisable to keep a wooden rod on hand. This rod acts as a perch for the bird, and if the bird becomes aggressive it can be used to push it away and deflect the crushing bites. The bird is never hit with the rod; the trainer uses it merely to ensure their own safety. If Pliny saw firsthand a trainer brings forth a parrot at a dinner party wielding a rod, he may have simply misunderstood its purpose. He almost talks about the parrot as if it were a little slave, and assumes that, like slaves, they were beaten when they misbehaved.

Figure 5.9 Detail of mosaic found on the Aventine Hill, second century CE. Rome
        National Museum. Parrots often appeared in paintings, mosaics, and on
        jewellery.

Source: Photo by the author.

Pliny imagines that the parrot navigated with its beak because it had weak
feet, but parrots are adept climbers and simply use their beaks for grip and
balance as they wander about. Though owners often brought them out for
their entertaining shenanigans at dinner parties, these men did appear to
value them for their companionship in private: 'He, saluter of kings that
spoke Caesar's name, would play the role of sympathizing friend or again be
a lightsome dinner companion, so ready to return words shown. When he
was released, dear Melior, you were never alone'.[118] Women kept parrots
too. Ovid writes a poem dedicated to his mistress Corinna's dead parrot,
which supposedly died saying goodbye to her. 'His bones are covered by a
mound – a mound such as fits his body's size – on which a scant stone bears
a legend that just fits the space: "you may judge from my very monument my
mistress loved me well. I had a mouth was skilled in speech beyond a
bird."'[119] The birdcage in the House of Livia shows us that Romans typically made cages from wood or wicker. Parrots could chew their way out of
such enclosures, so had to be kept in metal cages instead. Melior's parrot
was housed in a splendid cage of silver and ivory (Stat. *Silv.* 2.4.11–12). The
curious belief that parrots and turtle-doves enjoyed a special friendship may
be attached to how they were caged (Plin. *HN* 10.207). As beloved pets, they
were often kept in the same aviary (Ov. *Am.* 2.6.10–14). In what must be a
portrait of pets, a mosaic depicts two parrots drinking with a dove.[120]

Figure 5.10 Pet parrots housed with a pigeon. Pompeii, Naples Archaeological
Museum, inv. 9992.

Source: Photo by the author.

As for other talking birds, another exceptional Indian speaker, the mynah,
was present in the Roman Empire. A mynah is identified in the garden room of
the House of the Bracelet at Pompeii.[121] Analysing a passage from Aelian,
Thompson interprets a mysterious, starling-sized, docile, talking bird as a
description of a mynah (Ael. *NA* 16.3). Unlike parrots, they did not respond
well to captivity, which may be why the parrot remained the preferred bird
despite the superior loquacity of the mynah. In the case of the talking blackbird
mentioned earlier, a mynah might again be the culprit (Ael. *NA* 8.24).

In a climate where birds were coveted for beauty, rarity, and cleverness,
the Romans developed astoundingly effective methods for teaching birds to
speak. While foreign parrots and mynahs were beloved by elite men and
women alike, and often provided entertainment at dinner parties, lowly
shopkeepers could turn common native birds like crows and ravens into
marvellous companions that were the envy even of the imperial family.
Literary evidence suggests that talking birds became increasingly common
from the time of Augustus. Chattering jays hung from gilded cages in grand
estates or roamed about as sweet companions with lowlier owners. Teaching
a bird to talk provided one with both the pleasure of a bond with the animal

as well as the opportunity to mimic the opulence of the upper classes and their predilection for acquiring strange birds.

Other Companion Birds

Far and away the most common and popular pet bird was the pigeon. The Greeks and Romans both considered doves the gifts of lovers. In the *Metamorphoses*, Acis tries to woo Galatea by promising her bear cubs instead of the customary pair of doves (Ov. *Met.* 13.833). Theocritus' fifth idyll tells us young men typically caught the birds themselves and would become contrary and sulky if they did not receive a kiss for their efforts (Theoc. *Id.* 5.96, 132–3). Encolpius buys a pair of doves to win favours from a beautiful boy (Petr. *Sat.* 85). The birds were, of course, sacred to Aphrodite/Venus, and symbolised friendship, fidelity, and good fortune in love (Artem. *On.* 2.20). Martial brags that the dove of his friend Stella surpasses even the sparrow of Catullus (Mart. 1.7). Not only were they farmed in dovecotes and kept as companions, but feral birds existed in ancient cities just as they do today. Aelian differentiates between timid wild stock that lives in the countryside and the tame, fearless stock that swarmed

Figure 5.11 Drinking doves mosaic from Pompeii. Note the degree of plumage variation that comes with selective breeding. Naples Archaeological Museum, inv. 114281.

Source: Photo by the author.

freely about one's feet in the cities (Ael. *NA* 3.15). It would seem feral pigeons have been an essential part of any Italian city since antiquity. Even despite the way doddering pigeons are always getting underfoot, Aelian calls them the most temperate and loving of birds (Ael. *NA* 3.5). Pigeon-fancying was a common indulgence. A handsome breeding pair of pigeons typically cost 200 sesterces, but an unusually fine couple could fetch up to 1,000 sesterces in Varro's time (Varro, *Rust.* 3.7.10). In Columella's time, some paid 4,000 for a pair – a ludicrous sum (Columella, *Rust.* 8.8.10). Such fine birds were distinct from the commercial flocks meant for producing eggs and squabs.

One cannot mention pigeons without discussing their use as messenger birds. It does not seem to have been common practice, but it was not entirely unknown to the ancients either. Aelian relates the tale that the Olympic winner Taurosthenes of Aegina sent a pigeon from Elis to carry news home of his victory (Ael. *VH*, 9.2). The detail that he chose a hen who had been brooding on eggs adds a note of authenticity to the practice. Brooding hen birds are indeed the swiftest since they can be counted upon to return to their eggs with utmost urgency. In Varro's time, it was common for the masses to release pigeons at the theatre, which then flew home (Varro, *Rust.* 3.7.7). He does not elaborate on the reason. Perhaps it was a way of informing the household that the spectacle had finished, and that the owner was on his way home, rather like a courtesy phone call today.[122] The only other account of Romans using pigeons to communicate comes from Frontinus. The story goes that in 43 BCE, when Decimus Brutus was besieged by Antony in Mutina, pigeons took messages to Brutus from the consul Hirtius. In this instance, it was not their homing instincts that the Romans exploited. Hirtius' strategy was to starve the birds and shut them in the dark. He would then tie a message around their necks and release them close to the city walls. Seeking light and food, the birds sought the highest buildings, where they were trapped by Brutus, who improved upon this strategy by deliberately setting food in certain spots and training the pigeons to alight there (Frontin. *Str.* 3.13.7–8). More sophisticated methods of communicating with pigeons were employed by the Assyrians and Egyptians.[123] It is important to note that the only birds that can be used as messengers are those that will reliably return to their own nests when released. One must take the bird away from its nest and keep it caged until the time comes to send the message. It is not a matter of training, merely of exploiting instinct. In a fascinating and delightful twist, it seems that pigeons were not the only birds used for this. Pliny relates that a man of knightly rank from Volterra, Caecina, used to catch swallows and take them with him to Rome. He would use the bird to communicate the outcome of chariot races, painting the winning colour on them before releasing them. Pliny goes on to say that Fabius Pictor employed the same trick when a Roman garrison was besieged by Ligurians. A swallow taken from her chicks was smuggled out for him to indicate by means of knots tied to a thread on its foot how many days it would be until help arrived (Plin. *HN* 10.70). Swallows were in an interesting category. They do not seem to have been caged or considered pets, but they were regarded with an affection that could be considered companionate. Varro observes that when swallows returned in spring they nested *in tecto* – literally, 'under the roof' (*Rust.* 3.5.7). This is usually translated as 'under the eaves', a mistaken interpretation as the Roman word for 'eave' is *suggrunda*, while *tectum* is roof.[124] There is a very good chance that when the ancients, both Greek and Roman, say the birds nested under their roofs they really do mean inside their houses and other structures, and not on the outer walls. As the early anthropologist James George Frazer explains, typical houses had no glass in their windows, only shutters that were closed at night and open during the day. The roof beams were usually exposed, so swallows and house martins could easily have entered through the windows and nested on the wooden beams.[125] Since the shutters were closed at night, the swallows would have roused the household at first light by twittering impatiently to get out. There are even descriptions of swallows twittering around the heads of slumbering men and women at dawn; in one case, a man complains of swallows waking him from a sexual dream.[126] Such behaviour explains why Aelian says the birds share a house with men, and why men were expected to extend Homer's laws of hospitality to the swallow – that is, befriend the guest who shares your table and send him on his way when he wants to go.[127] Pliny observes that swallows defied usual categorisation and were, paradoxically, wild and domestic at the same time (Plin. *HN* 8.82). Untamed, yet companions in the home, they were sacred to household gods and under their protection (Ael. *NA* 10.34).

Another bird kept as a pet was the jackdaw (*Coloeus monedula*), a bird smaller than a crow with black feathers and an ashy grey patch around its head. We have heard that jackdaws were among the birds given to patrician boys, but there are notably few Roman examples of pet jackdaws when compared to their popularity in Greece.[128] Readers of Aristophanes will recall that the first scene in *The Birds* shows Euelpides with a jackdaw perched on his wrist, which he purchased from the market for a single obol. In the Etruscan record, there is a unique fourth century BCE askos in the shape of a jackdaw that is believed to represent a favourite pet. The bird has a protective *bulla* necklace around its neck, of the kind usually worn by Etruscan children, and holds a white pebble in its mouth.[129] Aelian records that in Sparta a jackdaw fell in love with a boy by virtue of his beauty (Ael. *NA* 1.6). It is worth noting that jackdaws, like geese, are especially susceptible to sexually imprinting on humans when they are hand-raised.[130] Aelian also tells us that the inhabitants of Thessaly, Illyria and Lemnos viewed jackdaws as benefactors and encouraged their presence because jackdaws kept the locust population in check (Ael. *NA* 3.12). The Veneti of northern Italy had a different view. Every year they sought a truce with the jackdaws and left out honey cakes as a way of dissuading the little birds from digging up their newly-sown fields. They would summon the birds – huge flocks of them – with loud calls, and the birds would inspect the gifts on offer. If they rejected the cakes, famine was sure to follow (Ael. *NA* 17.16). They were proverbially fond of gold, probably due to the bird's attraction to anything that shines or sparkles. Their reputation as unrepentant thieves belongs largely to the Latin tradition rather than the Greek.[131] *Graculus* was one name for them. Another was *monedula,* derived from *moneta* – money. In Ovid's Metamorphoses a greedy nymph is transformed into a jackdaw (Ov. *Met.* 7.465–8). Despite these beliefs about their cheeky, thievish, and sometimes destructive temperaments, the birds were still viewed in a largely positive light.

The purple swamphen (*Porphyrio porphyrio*) deserves mention even though it was more of an ornamental bird than a pet, simply because it was never eaten. Pliny accurately describes its habit of eating by clutching its food in one foot (Plin. *HN* 129). Aelian describes its love of dust baths, its nervousness, the way it was primarily kept as a pet in opulent households, and finally adds the curious superstition that if the mistress of its house committed adultery, it would hang itself.[132] George Jennison posits that this myth may have its origin in the bird's notorious shyness. In the presence of an interloping stranger, it could injure itself in a panic.[133]

Figure 5.12 Purple swamphen. Their purple feathers gave them tremendous value as ornamental birds. Naples Archaeological Museum, inv. 8644.

Source: Photo by the author.

It must have been viewed as exceedingly beautiful, for Aelian goes on to contrast it with the peacock, saying that, although the peacock was not spared from the cooking pot, he has never heard of anyone eating a purple swamphen. Men took pleasure in looking at it and caring for it alone. The esteem for the bird's beauty was connected to the fact its plumage was, of course, rare and royal purple, a colour that was the ultimate expression of status and power.[134] That the Romans preferred purple plumage in birds is shown by a passage in Oppian, where he declares that pigeon breeders would put scraps of purple fabric next to a sitting hen in order to induce her to hatch purple-plumed offspring (*The Chase,* 1.350ff). Considering how few qualms the Romans had about eating birds, it must be that the purple swamphen's colour meant it was too valuable to eat.

The *passer*

We come at last to what is perhaps the most famous pet bird in the ancient world – Lesbia's *passer*, immortalised by the poet Catullus in two poems. One describes his mistress Lesbia playing with her pet bird to divert herself from amorous thoughts, while the other is a lament for the creature's un-timely death.[135]

> Sparrow, my lady's pet, with whom she often plays whilst she holds you in her lap, or gives you her fingertip to peck and provokes you to bite sharply, whenever she, the bright-shining lady of my love, has a mind for some sweet pretty play, in hope, as I think, that when the sharper smart of love abates, she may find some small relief from her pain – ah, might I but play with you as she does, and lighten the gloomy cares of my heart![136]

And now the lamentation for its death:

> Mourn, ye Graces and Loves, and all you whom the Graces love. My lady's sparrow is dead, the sparrow my lady's pet, whom she loved more than her very eyes; for honey-sweet he was, and knew his mistress as well as a girl knows her own mother. Nor would he stir from her lap, but hopping now here, now there, would still chirp to his mistress alone. Now he goes along the dark road, thither whence they say no one returns. But curse upon you, cursed shades of Orcus, which devour all pretty things! Such a pretty sparrow you have taken away. Ah, cruel! Ah, poor little bird! All because of you my lady's darling eyes are heavy and red with weeping.[137]

The identity of the *passer* in Catullus 2 and 3 has been a subject of con-troversy for hundreds of years.[138] Archibald Geike declared in 1912 that it must have been a thrush, not a sparrow, for a capricious beauty like Lesbia could never dote on a nasty little sparrow.[139] The blue rock thrush (*Monticola solitarius*) was a favourite alternative identification.[140] Jennison, in 1937, suggested: 'Lesbia's *passer* was small and desirable, eminently tame and loving, and piped to his mistress (...) this should be the beautiful piping bullfinch'.[141] The bullfinch identification was taken up by Jocelyn Toynbee and survives as a popular identification to this day, even appearing in the Oxford Classical Dictionary.[142] Others believe that the *passer* is not a bird at all, but rather a sexual euphemism. This view became popular in the late twentieth century and remains an important part of modern discussions about the *passer* poems.[143] More recently, opinion has moved towards a more critical and circumspect approach in favour of sparrows.[144] On the subject of Lesbia's *passer,* Mynott appraises the difficulties inherent in identifying birds in the ancient world and settles on the solution that *passer* could function as vernacular for any small bird.[145] In this section we shall investigate the *passer* poems by reconstructing the Roman cultural view of sparrows and asking whether sparrows were commonly kept as pets.

The place of sparrows in the modern world is far removed from the classical experience, with sparrows today seen in a broadly negative light across the globe due to their status as pests and vectors for diseases.[146] In contrast to our views, sparrows were held in esteem in the ancient Mediterranean. They had a special connection with the erotic, evident from Sappho's *Hymn to Aphrodite* where she playfully describes the goddess riding in a chariot drawn by sparrows (*strouthoi*). Some choose to translate *strouthoi* as 'swans' or 'doves',[147] plainly disliking the association of Aphrodite with such common birds, but sparrows suit the love goddess well.[148] These birds are prolific and their sexual habits are easily observable, making them perfect symbols of fecundity and lechery.[149] In *Lysistrata* (723–4) a sex-starved woman is said to be ready to fly off on a *strouthos*.[150] In Rome, the birds were also considered salacious and said to love carnal pleasure.[151] 'Sparrow' could be a saucy pet name (Juv. *Sat.* 9.54). Venus was similarly surrounded by lusty sparrows, as in the following description from Apuleius: 'Sparrows follow in the train of the goddess's chariot, frisking about with merry chirping; and all the other kinds of songbird too proclaim the goddess's approach by delightfully sounding their sweet melodies'.[152] One is here reminded of Catullus inviting 'Venuses and Cupids' to mourn the passing of Lesbia's sparrow. *Passer* could also be a term of endearment, and apparently in quite a wholesome sense. One example involves Marcus Aurelius addressing Gratia, the daughter of his tutor Fronto.[153] Along with swallows, sparrows served as domestic familiars in Roman houses. The two birds are depicted together in Roman art.[154] The domestic role of the sparrow is also mentioned in the Bible (Psalm 84:3) in a passage about the faithful yearning for the house of God. The link between sparrows, swallows, and the home is due to the fact that the birds nest in or on human houses.[155] The connection with beloved swallows allows us to extrapolate that Romans had few qualms with sharing their homes with sparrows, and that nesting and cohabitation inspired a greater depth of feeling. From these examples that associate *passeres* with Venus, the home, and objects of affection, we can conclude that the general Roman cultural view of sparrows was positive. Any disbelieving knee-jerk reaction to the image of Lesbia doting on a sparrow should be tempered by an appreciation of the fact that the Romans saw sparrows very differently to ourselves.

When it comes to pet *passeres*, there are a handful of references. In Apuleius' *Metamorphoses*, sparrows are listed among various young or weak household animals like kids, chicks, and puppies that must be carried when moving to a new home.[156] Pliny the Younger refers obliquely to 'little sparrows' and 'little doves' caged as pets.[157] In a passage already explored, Fronto says of his grandson: 'He is also devoted to little birds; he delights in chickens, young pigeons, and sparrows. I have often heard from those who were my tutors and masters that I had from my earliest infancy a passion for such things'.[158] In Apuleius we have a picture of *passeres* being a regular part of the household, while Fronto indicates that it was both normal and encouraged to give them to children for play. House sparrows are abundant and live alongside humans, so acquiring captive sparrows would have been a simple task. We even have descriptions of bird-catchers going after sparrows' nests, presumably to procure eggs or chicks (Ael. *NA* 4.38), and Galen says that sparrows which nest in buildings had tough flesh (*Alim. Fac.* 3.18), both of which indicate that the birds were eaten and sold at markets. In such a context where households had access to sparrows and children regularly played with them, it is perfectly feasible for Lesbia to have had a pet sparrow, but considering the link between birds and children elucidated above, her devotion to it can be construed as childish and emotional (Figure 5.13).

Now that we have shown *passeres* were kept as pets, we should analyse whether Lesbia's *passer* exhibits behaviour typical of a sparrow. There are a few clues to betray its identity. It is depicted as nestling in Lesbia's lap, nibbling at her fingers and chirping to her – *pipiare*.[159] This is a rare verb worth noting because although it can be translated as chirp, cheep, or pipe, it cannot be translated as 'sing'.[160] This spells trouble for some of the proposed alternative translations of *passer*.[161] The blue rock thrush is certainly a beautiful bird that becomes deeply attached to its owner,[162] but it does not chirp – it warbles and sings, and it is much larger, almost the size of a blackbird. It is more likely to have been classed as a *turdus* than a *passer*. As for the bullfinch, these birds do not have naturally tuneful songs, but if hand-raised and whistled to, they can learn to perform striking melodies. However, we have no evidence that Romans tamed bullfinches. Evidence of the method of taming and 'whistling bullfinches' only appears to stretch to the Middle Ages.[163] The inclination to identify *passer* as bullfinch stems from authors of the early twentieth century who were discussing Catullus at a time when bullfinches were familiar, popular, and coveted pets.[164]

The most striking trait of the *passer* is its devotion to Lesbia. While it is true that sparrows generally do not make amiable pets, especially when contrasted against alternatives, there is still a way that a sparrow could behave as Catullus describes. Sparrows taken from the wild are fragile and difficult to train, but a hand-reared sparrow would exhibit deep attachment to Lesbia. That is, if Lesbia herself reared a sparrow chick, it would be tame,

Figure 5.13 Passer on a wall fragment, second or third century CE. As with the poem, this nondescript brown figure defies concrete categorisation according to modern understandings.

Source: Photo by the Metropolitan Museum of Art. Gift of Henry G. Marquand, 1892, no. 92.11.10.

affectionate, and devoted to her. This is perhaps even intimated in the way Catullus says the bird knew Lesbia as well as a girl knows her own mother.[165] Raising a sparrow chick would be a demanding task, but if accomplished successfully it would engender such behaviour as fluttering around and on Lesbia, and only bothering to chirp for her. It would also have sexually imprinted on Lesbia. We are here reminded of the story that Empress Livia nursed a hen's egg in her bosom, foretelling her unborn child's sex by hatching out a rooster.[166] Even if that particular story is a fabrication, it would seem that it was a practice common to women and girls, for in the same passage Pliny goes on to wonder if this method of hatching birds' eggs was what led to the invention of artificial incubation and the use of fire to keep eggs warm.[167] We therefore have evidence that high-born ladies could hatch birds' eggs and raise the chicks if they were so inclined. Although at first glance it may not seem that a sparrow could behave in the way Lesbia's *passer* does, we must remember that hand-rearing and imprinting could easily account for this.

The last task is to ask to what the word *passer* could refer. We shall deal with the obvious first: was the word *passer* an obscenity? There is some indication that *passer* could function as a euphemism for *mentula*, though it is not particularly convincing.[168] *Strutheum* was a Greek loan that functioned as obscene, and *passero* and *passera* function as obscenities in modern Italian.[169] The strongest example in Latin comes from a sexual scene in Apuleius: "*"Teneo te," inquit "teneo, meum palumbulum, meum passerem"*" – 'Finally she said, "I am holding you, I am holding you, my little dove, my sparrow" (Apul. *Met.* 10.22).[170] Most of the sexual energy attached to the word seems to be derived from its known connection to Venus rather than the fact it was a blatant obscenity, however. The pre-existing erotic symbolism of the sparrow allows Catullus to be playful, which might be why he says playing with the bird diverts Lesbia from amorous thoughts.[171] But an obscene interpretation is, on the strength of it, not particularly compelling, especially since extended allegories are not found anywhere else in Catullus.[172]

Leaving aside possible obscenities, we shall examine which birds fell under the umbrella of *passer*. We can say generally that *passer* and *strouthos* both referred to sparrows. Aristotle describes only one *strouthos*, a bird that dusts itself and washes, copulates swiftly, and has males with black heads – *Passer domesticus* (Arist. Hist. an. 633b.4–5; 539b33; 613a29–b2). Pliny writes of *passeres* as amorous little birds that have black heads and hop along the ground, again *Passer domesticus* (Plin. *HN* 107, 111). Where things become strange is when we consider that in Greek, the ostrich was the *strouthocamelos* – camel sparrow.[173] In Latin the ostrich was *marinus passer* – sparrow from overseas. It seems *passer/strouthos* could function as a word interchangeable with 'bird' itself. But though it has the general meaning of bird, *passer* primarily indicated little brown birds.[174] In Roman paintings, brown birds that elude identification still look out at us.[175] Dunnock, twite, linnet, tree sparrow, house sparrow, Italian sparrow – all would have fallen under the *passer* umbrella.[176] Nevertheless, *Passer domesticus* remains the foremost identification, and though this word occasionally functioned as obscene the usage was rare.

On the balance of evidence, the identity of Lesbia's sparrow is most likely the common house sparrow (*Passer domesticus*) or the Italian sparrow (*Passer italiae*). It is clear that the Romans kept and delighted in sparrows, and there is no compelling reason to discount the idea that Lesbia kept one. Sparrows were one of many bird species beloved as companion birds in the Roman world, and Lesbia represents a typical sentimental portrait of one such bird owner.[177]

Conclusion

Studying birds as pets and as pleasure-givers delivers great insight into Roman social values. Elites, especially the imperial family, cultivated gardens and aviaries full of birds that provided no tangible value beyond their beauty. While small-scale farmers entreated Priapus and brandished rattles to protect precious productive plots from birds, elites could afford to invite birds into their garden and enjoy the sight and sound of them, even reproducing them in art to compound the effect. Elites consistently acquired rare and remarkable birds. They caged songbirds to provide music, sought out talking birds to amaze guests, and collected foreign birds as an expression of wealth. At the same time, low-class peoples were also acquiring birds. Without access to expensive foreign talkers like the parrot, they sought out common, native birds like crows and made them extraordinary through patient instruction. They too kept birds on a small scale for pleasure and companionship, though in general one had to be careful not to show too great an attachment to one's pets or one would risk ridicule. Pet birds were principally associated with children, with girls often shown playing with pigeons while boys battled cockerels or engaged in rough-and-tumble games with geese and ducks. Sentimental attachment to birds or indulging in bird battling was acknowledged as a part of growing up. Romans kept rare birds, beautiful birds, singing birds and talking birds. They were prepared to spend fortunes just for the pleasure of possessing a particular pet and they had advanced methods for training and housing them. When their beloved companions died, like Lesbia they would mourn or even erect monuments for them, betraying a deep sentimental core to the bird-keeping culture.

Notes

1 Littlewood (1987) 13.
2 Favro (2010) 161.
3 Favro (2010) 162.
4 Tib. 1.3.57–60. Translated by Postgate (1913) 209: *Sed me, quod facilis tenero sum semper Amori, ipsa Venus campos ducet in Elysios. Hic choreae cantusque vigent, passimque vagantes dulce sonant tenui gutture carmen aves.*
5 *Elegiae in Maecenatem*, 1.33–6. Translated by Duff (1934b) 125: *maluit umbrosam quercum lymphasque cadentes paucaque pomosi iugera certa soli: pieridas Phoebumque colens in mollibus hortissederat argutas garrulous inter avis.*
6 Jones (2016) 25.
7 Bergmann (2002) 88.
8 Carroll (2015) 533.
9 Jashemski (1993) 11.
10 Harden (2014) 31.
11 Harden (2014) 37.
12 Jashemski (1979) 81.
13 Bowe (2004) 52.
14 Harden (2014) 37.
15 Harden (2014) 55.
16 Farrar (1998) 155.
17 Kellum (1994) 224.
18 Neudecker (2015) 392.

19 Carroll (2015) 538.
20 Carroll (2015) 538–41.
21 Reeder (2001) 88.
22 Jashemski (1979) 107.
23 Reeder (2001) 36.
24 Kron (2017) 108.
25 Pagan (2016) 14.
26 Carroll (2015) 536.
27 Farrar (1998) int. XVI.
28 Neudecker (2015) 393.
29 Watson (2002) 357.
30 See Farrar (1998) 96 for a detailed description of how the device operated.
31 Jashemski (1979) 108.
32 Ov. *Fast.* 1.683–4. Translated by Frazer (1931) 51: *neve graves cultis Cerialia rura cavete agmine laesuro depopulentur aves.*
33 Tib. 1.18. Translated by Cornish (1913) 195: *Terreat ut saeva falce Priapus aves.*
34 Ov. *Fast.* 1.400. Translated by Frazer (1931) 31: *quique ruber pavidas inguine terret aves.*
35 Ov. *Fast.* 1.415. Translated by Frazer (1931) 31: *ruber, hortorum decus et tutela, Priapus.*
36 Hor. *Sat.* 1.8.3–7. Translated by Fairclough (1926) 97 with amendments: *Olim truncus eram ficulnus, inutile lignum, cum faber, incertus scamnum faceretne Priapum, maluit esse deum. deus inde ego, furum aviumque maxima formido; nam fures dextra coercet obscaenoque ruber porrectus ab inguine palus, ast inportunas volucres in vertice harundo terret fixa vetatque novis considere in hortis.*
37 App. Verg. *Priapea.* 4.11–13. Translation by the author: *abegimusque voce saepe, cum tibi senexve corvus impigerve graculus sacrum feriret ore corneo caput.*
38 Plin. *HN* 18.45; Ael. *NA* 17.41.
39 Scullard (1981) 68.
40 Wallace-Hadrill (1994) 4.
41 For discussion, see Fuchs (1962).
42 Littlewood (1987) 14–15. Varro, *Rust.* 3.5.8- 17; reconstruction drawing in Van Buren and Kennedy (1919).
43 Green (1997) 442.
44 Reitz and Wing (2008) 286.
45 Johnson (1968) 98; Jashemski (1979) 107.
46 Ingold (2008).
47 MacKinnon (2014) 328.
48 Clark (2007) 139.
49 Cic. *Div.* 1.76; Sen. *Apocol.* 13.3.
50 Columella, *Rust.* 8.8.10. Translated by Forster (1954) 367: *Quamquam vel hos magis tolerabiles putem, qui oblectamenta deliciarum possidendi habendique causa gravi aere et argento pensent, quam illos qui Ponticum Phasim et Scythica stagna Maeotidis eluant; iam nunc Gangeticas et Aegyptias aves temulenter eructant.*
51 Bradley (1998) 537.
52 Calder (2007) 69.
53 Lazenby (1949) 249.
54 Rawson (2003) 130.
55 Bradley (1998) 526–27.
56 Many examples have survived. A third century BCE mime by Herodas (4.20–34) mentions such a sculpture. Pliny (*HN* 34.84) speaks of Boethus, a second century BCE artist who made a bronze sculpture of a boy strangling a goose.

57 Bradley (1998) 536.
58 Bradley (1998) 538.
59 For images of fourth century CE examples, see Lamberton and Rotroff (1985) 7, 9.
60 Minding goats, sheep or donkeys: Var. *Rust.* 2.10.1, 3.17.6; Ov. *Fast.* 4.511 Hor. *Epod.* 2.39; Columella, *Rust.* 7.1.2; Apul. *Met.* 7.15–28. Minding poultry: Columella, *Rust.* 8.2.7. Collecting fodder for animals: Plin. *HN.*13.130–13
61 Lewit (2022).
62 Bradley (1998) 528; Tammisto (1997) 35.
63 Koorthojian (2015) 286.
64 Koorthojian (2015) 291.
65 Rawson (2003) 353.
66 Bradley (1998) 529.
67 A particularly bittersweet example is an Augustan-era funerary relief found on the Via Cassia. The dead boy is flanked by thrushes as his parents bid him farewell and give him fruit for the journey. Vatican Museum, inv. 2167.
68 Bradley (1998) 528.
69 Petron. *Sat.* 46. Translated by Schmeling (2020) 153 with amendments: *Ingeniosus est et bono filo, etiam si in aves morbosus est. Ego illi iam tres cardeles occidi, et dixi quia mustella comedit.*
70 Plaut. *Asin.* 3.3.666; Plin. *Pan.* 26.7; Apul. *Met.* 8.15.
71 Cooley (2014) 245.
72 Lewit (2022).
73 Jashemski (1993) 153, 154, 165, 232.
74 See the following sculptures: Vatican Museum, inv. 2709, 2774.
75 Plaut. Capt. 1002–3. Translation by de Melo (2011) 613: *quasi patriciis pueris aut monerulae aut anites aut coturnices dantur quicum lusitent.* In Latin, 'crowbar' is *upupa*, a word that also means hoopoe.
76 Plin. *Ep.* 4.2.3–4. Translation by Radice (1969) 245. *Habebat puer mannulos multos et iunctos et solutos, habebat canes maiores minoresque, habebat luscinias psittacos merulas: omnes Regulus circa rogum trucidavi. Nec dolor erat ille, sed ostentatio doloris.*
77 Birkhead (2011) 173.
78 Birkhead (2014) 33.
79 Plin. *HN* 10.84; Fògen (2014) 225.
80 Plin. *HN* 10.120; Plut. *Mor. De soll. an.* 978A.
81 Beagon (2014) 433.
82 Birkhead (2011) 106.
83 Ov. *Ars am.* 2.149–50. Translated by Mozley (1929) 77: *At caret insidiis hominum, quia mitis, hirundo, quasque colat turres, Chaonis ales habet.*
84 Plin. *HN* 10.47; see also Plut. *Mor. De frat. Amor.* 487E-F.
85 *Contra.* Morgan (1975) 121, who posits that cockfighting iconography does not reflect daily practice but had a more complex symbolic meaning.
86 Serjeantsen (2000); Serjeantsen (2009) 329.
87 Hingley (2006) 261.
88 Pl. *Lysis*, 211. See also: Xen. *Mem.* 1.6.14; Ar. *Av.* 1298–9.
89 Plut. *Vit. Alc.* 10. The man who retrieved it and gave it back to Alcibiades was the sea captain Antiochus. The two remained friends from then on.
90 Marvin (1984) 60–70; Dundes 1994; Cobb (2003) 69–83; Sykes (2014a) 86–87.
91 Lazenby (1949) 249.
92 Bradley (1998) 555.
93 Dundes (2007) 292.
94 Calder (2001) 71.
95 Bergmann (2008) 197.

96   Mart. 7.87. Translated by Shackleton Bailey (1993b) 143 with amendments: *Si meus aurita gaudet lagalopece Flaccus, si fruitur tristi Canius Aethiope; Publius exiguae si flagrat amore catellae, si Cronius similen cercopithecon amat; delectat Marium si perniciosus ichneumon, pica salutatrix si tibi, Lause, placet; si gelidum collo nectit Cadilla draconem, luscinio tumulum si Telesilla dedit: blanda Cupidinei cur non amet ora Labyrtae qui uidet haec dominis monstra placere suis?*

97   Rawson (1985) 257.

98   Pliny, *HN* 10.87. Pliny copies the Greek tradition here. See also Paus. 8.17.3.

99   Birkhead (2014) 117.

100 Gooders (2001) 238

101 Aelian, *NA*, 8.18; Fògen (2014) 226.

102 Macrob. *Sat.* 2.4.29–30. Translated by Kaster (2011) 359 with amendments: *Sublimis Actiaca victoria revertebatur. occurrit ei inter gratulantes corvum tenens, quem instituerat haec dicere: 'ave Caesar victor imperator.' miratus Caesar officiosam avem viginti milibus nummum emit. socius opificis, ad quem nihil ex illa liberalitate pervenerat, adfirmavit Caesari habere illum et alium corvum, quem ut adferre cogeretur rogavit. adlatus verba quae didicerat expressit: 'ave victor imperator Antoni.' nihil exasperatus satis duxit iubere illum dividere donativum cum contubernali. salutatus similiter a psittaco, emi eum iussit. idem miratus in pica hanc quoque redemit. exemplum sutorem pauperem sollicitavit ut corvum institueret ad parem salutationem, qui impendio exhaustus saepe ad avem non respondentem dicere solebat, 'opera et impensa periit.' aliquando tamen corvus coepit dicere dictatam salutationem. hac audita dum transit Augustus respondit, 'satis domi salutatorum talium habeo.' superfuit corvo memoria, ut et illa quibus dominum querentem solebat audire subtexeret: 'opera et impensa periit.' ad quod Caesar risit emique avem iussit quanti nullam adhuc emerat.*

103 Plin. *HN* 10.120. Translated by Rackham (1940) 369–71: *docentur secreto et ubi nulla alia vox misceatur, adsidente qui crebro dicat ea quae condita velit ac cibis blandiente.* See also Fògen (2014) 224.

104 Mart. 14.73. Translated by Shackleton Bailey (1993c) 261: *Psittacus a vobis aliorum nomina discam: Hoc didici per me dicere CAESAR AVE.*

105 Mart. 3.95.1–2. Translated by Shackleton Bailey (1993a) 257 with amendments: *Numquam dicis have sed reddis, Naeuole, semper, quod prior et coruus dicere saepe solet.*

106 Arnott (2007) 150.

107 Plin. *HN* 10.78. Translated by Rackham (1940) 343: *nuper et adhuc tamen rara ab Appennino ad urbem versus cerni coepere picarum genera quae longa insignes cauda variae appellantur.*

108 Evans (1903) 145.

109 Porph. *Abst.* 3.2; Arist. *Hist. an.* 615b 19f.

110 Mart. 14.76. Translated by Shackleton Bailey (1993c) 263 with amendments: *Pica loquax certa dominum te voce salute: si me non videas, esse negabis avem.*

111 Petr. *Sat.* 28. Translated by Schmeling (2020) 115 with amendments: *Super limen autem cavea pendebat aurea in qua pica varia intrantes salutabat.*

112 Wills (2017) 101–05.

113 Tammisto (1997) 82; Boehrer (2004) 3. Watson (2002) 394 points to evidence of an African grey parrot in a statue, but this is doubtful.

114 Plin. *HN* 10.114. Translated by Rackham (1940) 367: *Super omnia humanas voces reddunt, psittaci quidem etiam sermocinantes. India hanc avem mittit, siptacen vocat, viridem toto corpore, torque tantum miniato in cervice distinctam. imperatores salutat et quae accipit verba pronuntiat, in vino praecipue lasciva. capiti eius duritia eadem quae rostro; hoc, cum loqui discit, ferreo verberatur*

radio: non sentit aliter ictus. cum devolat, rostro se excipit, illi innititur levior-emque ita se pedum infirmitati facit.

115 Boehrer (2004) 4.
116 Stat. *Silv.* 2.4.1–8. Translated by Shakleton Bailey (2015) 123: *Psittace, dux volucrum, domini facunda voluptas, humanae sollers imitator, Psittace, linguae, quis tua tam subito praeclusit murmura fato? hesternas, miserande, dapes moriturus inisti nobiscum, et gratae carpentem munera mensae errantemque toris mediae plus tempore noctisvidimus. affatus etiam meditataque verba reddideras.*
117 Boehrer (2004) 5.
118 Stat. *Silv.* 2.4.29–33. Translated by Shakleton Bailey (2015) 125: *ille salutator regum nomenque locutus Caesareum et queruli quondam vice functus amici, nunc conviva levis monstrataque reddere verba tam facilis, quo tu, Melior dilecte, re-clusonumquam solus eras.*
119 Ov. *Am.* 2.6.59–63. Translated by Showerman (1914) 403: *Ossa tegit tumulus—tumulus pro corpore magnus—quo lapis exiguus par sibi carmen habet: colligor ex ipso dominae placuisse sepulcro. ora fuere mihi plus ave docta loqui.*
120 Watson (2002) 393.
121 Watson (2002) 359.
122 Another explanation may relate to the way *plaudere* meant the clap of hands as well as the clap of wings, so the clap of the pigeons' wings could have been used to give additional applause at the end of a performance.
123 Jennison (1937) 104.
124 P.G.W. Glare (ed), *OLD²* (2012), 'suggrunda' and 'tectum'.
125 Frazer (1891) 1–3.
126 Agathias Scholasticus of Myrina, *Anth. Pal.* 5.237; Ael. *NA* 9.17.
127 Ael. *NA* 1.52; Hom. *Od.* 15.72–4.
128 Arist. *Gen. an.* 756b22–3; Theophr. *Char.* 21.6. Aesop's seventh fable, *The Eagle and the Jackdaw*, even features a shepherd catching a foolish jackdaw. His first instinct is to clip its wings and give it to his children as a pet.
129 De Puma (2013) 220.
130 Birkhead (2011) 98.
131 Cic. *Flac.* 76; Plin. *HN* 10.77.
132 Ael. *NA* 3.42
133 Jennison (1937) 17.
134 Cocker 2013, 179.
135 See Pomeroy (2003) for how it fits with other poetic lamentations for the death of a pet.
136 Catull. 2. Translated by Cornish (1913) 2: *Passer, deliciae meae puellae, quicum ludere, quem in sinu tenere, cui primum digitum dare appetenti et acris solet incitare morsus cum desiderio meo nitenti carum nescio quid lubet iocari et solaciolum sui doloris, credo, ut tum grauis acquiescat ardor: tecum ludere sicut ipsa possem et tristis animi leuare curas!*
137 Catull. 3. Translated by Cornish (1913) 5. *Lugete, o Veneres Cupidinesque et quantumst hominum venustiorum. passer mortuus est meae puellae, passer, deliciae meae puellae, quem plus illa oculis suis amabat. nam mellitus erat suamque norat ipsam tam bene quam puella matrem; nec sese a gremio illius movebat sed circumsiliens modo huc modo illuc ad solam dominam usque pipiabat. qui nunc it per iter tenebricosum illud unde negant redire quemquam. at vobis male sit, malae tenebrae Orci quae omnia bella devoratis! tam bellum mihi passerem abstulistis. o factum male! o miselle passer! tua nunc opera meae puellae flendo turgiduli rubent ocelli.*

138 Gaisser (2007) 305–40 brings together a good range of responses to the *passer*, going as far back as the early modern period. Many scholars in the early twentieth century opted to identify the *passer* as a bird, but not a sparrow. See Geike (1912), Havelock (1929), Jennison (1937), and Thompson (1936). See also Andre (1967) and Toynbee (1973). For leading figures advocating the obscene interpretation, see Giangrande (1975), Nadeau (1984), Hooper (1985), Mulroy (2002), and Cocker (2013). Goold (1983) provides a commentary on these views, while Jocelyn (1980) and Jones (1998) offer the strongest arguments against the obscene *passer* view. Genovese (1974) argues that the *passer* can be taken in multiple ways. Adams (1982) 31–2 compiles obscene uses of *passer* in Latin.

139 Geike (1912) 197.

140 Andre (1967) 120.

141 Jennison (1937) 117.

142 Toynbee (1973) 278; Hornblower and Spawforth (2012) 1118.

143 Giangrande (1975), Nadeau (1984), Hooper (1985), Mulroy (2002), Cocker (2013). See Goold (1983) 4 for commentary.

144 Arnott (2007) 227–8.

145 Mynott (2018) 139–42.

146 See Global Invasive Species Database (2021), species profile: *Passer domesticus*. See also Anderson (2006) 270.

147 For discussion, see Castle (1958) 71 and Zellner (2008). See Nagy (2020.12.18) and Nagy (2020.12.25) for images.

148 On Catullus and Sappho's sparrows, see Brenk (1980) 712–3 and Ingleheart (2003) 555–6.

149 Horapollo 2.115; Xen *Ephes* 1.8.2.

150 Putz (2014) 67.

151 Plin. *HN* 10.107; Cic. *Fin.* 2.75.

152 Apul. *Met.* 6.6. Translated by Hanson (1996) 267: *currum deae prosequentes gannitu constrepenti lasciviunt passeres, et ceterae quae dulce cantitant aves melleis modulis suave resonantes adventum deae pronuntiant.*

153 Apul. *Met.*, 10.22, Fronto, *Ep.* 4.6.2, Plaut. *Asin.* 666, Plaut. *Cas.* 138.

154 See Mynott (2018) 169. See plate 3.11 on this page for a visual representation.

155 Romans classed birds that raised their chicks in Italy or abroad separately. See Varro, *Rust.* 3.5.7. Isid. *Etym.* 12.7.1 calls sparrows indigenous birds because they do not migrate.

156 Apul. *Met.* 8.15.

157 Plin. *Ep.* 9.25.3.

158 Fronto, *Ep.* 1.12. Translated by Haines (1920) 173. *Avicularum etiam cupidissimus est; pullis gallinarum columbarum passerum oblectatur, quo studio me a prima infantia devinctum fuisse saepe audivi ex eis qui mihi educatores aut magistri fuerunt.*

159 P.G.W. Glare (ed), *OLD*² (2012), 'pipio' and 'pipo'.

160 In Columella, *Rust.* 8.5.14 it refers to chicks peeping within their eggs. The word was also applied to children. See Ter. *De monog.*16. For discussion, refer to Mynott (2018) 140.

161 Jennison (1937) 117, Innes (1952) 78.

162 Fordyce (1961) 88–9.

163 Birkhead (2014) 68.

164 Birkhead (2011) 238–43.

165 On this imagery, see Johnson (2003) and Vinson (1989).

166 Pliny, *HN* 10.154; Suet. *Tib.* 14.

167 Romans had sophisticated incubation techniques and regularly managed and manipulated egg hatching in chickens, ducks, peafowl, geese, and other barnyard birds. See: Columella, *Rust.* 8.5; Varro, *Rust.* 3.9.

168 Adams (1982) 31–32.
169 Green (2005) 213.
170 Translation by Hanson (1989) 211. *Teneo* can also function as a sexual verb in some contexts. See Adams (1982) 181.
171 See Mart. 11.6 for comparison, where *passer* is used unambiguously as a euphemism.
172 Jones (1998) 188ff.
173 For full discussion and sources, refer to Arnott (2007) 227–30.
174 Aët. 11.11 specifically lists a *passer* that is the smallest of birds besides the wren. Isid. *Etym.* 12.7.68 simply says *passeres* are small birds.
175 Tammisto (1997) provides a catalogue of birds in Roman mosaics. The garden scenes from the *triclinium* of the Villa of Livia, now held in the Palazzo Massimo, are full of little brown birds. Sparrows are common in Campanian wall paintings, with The House of the Golden Bracelet at Pompeii offering clear examples. See also inv. 9661 and 2870 at the Naples Archaeological Museum.
176 See Mynott (2018) 139–42 for discussion.
177 Green (2022).

Conclusion

This book has taken a broad approach to the topic of birds in Roman life and myth to demonstrate the many ways that birds can shape and inform our understanding of the past. The potential for future research is self-evident, and the ambitious scope of this project has left us with as many questions as answers. We can expand on many of the topics covered here to make new or more incisive inquiries. The focus on augury and auspices left scant room to consider birds in Roman religion more broadly. We can ask why certain gods were seen to have companion birds, or investigate the use of birds as sacrificial offerings. An account of the diverse rules recorded in literature that recommend offering only certain birds to certain deities would be invaluable when interpreting faunal remains recovered from ritual deposits. One topic in particular that is ripe for investigation is the place of birds in Roman magic and medicine. Here and there, this book has mentioned the magical practices in Pliny's bird lore, but there are swathes of literature concerning how birds should be used in magic or for the purposes of healing and medicine. Domestic poultry played a huge part in ensuring the health and vitality of many poorer Romans. The Galenic and Hippocratic texts are rife with cures and advice about which birds should be eaten or avoided depending on one's ailment. A surplus cockerel was a necessary sacrifice to Aesculapius, the god of health, while runny eggs or broth made from the flesh of an old rooster could help nurse one back to health. An investigation of this advice when compared to what we know about husbandry practices, augural lore, and seasonal availabilities of birds could be truly eye-opening.

When considering future research, the methodologies employed in this research could easily be applied to other cultures and time periods. Birds are intrinsic to the expression of every human culture, whether we are conscious of it or not. The presence, use, and consumption of birds particularly betray the existence of social stratification and inequality. The tremendous value of archaeo-ornithology to this endeavour is abundantly clear. Faunal remains can be catalogued and interpreted to shed light on how societies organised themselves or communicated social or spiritual meaning. Cross-checking with evidence from art, literature, and zoological studies leads us to discoveries that challenge the way we see the past as well as the way we see birds. Meat-eating is often used to communicate wealth as well as one's moral or spiritual convictions. Our systems of classification around which animals are acceptable to eat and which are not, how old they should be when slaughtered, and whether they should be intensively fattened are just as strange and arbitrary as the Romans', but sometimes it takes looking at past societies to gain a new perspective. The potential for cross-cultural studies and reception studies is especially vibrant. It is fascinating to see later medieval and early modern authors interact with Roman literature on birds and shape it to their own ends. Similarly, it is incredibly informative to investigate why two cultures might view the same bird and its behaviour in different or similar ways. There are endless questions one could ask about how and why humans interact with birds the way we do.

In a world that currently sees many iconic bird species under threat from climate change, deforestation, and destructive agricultural practices, it is worth remembering how important birds are to ourselves and our sense of identity as well as to ecosystems and the health of the planet. We can see echoes of our own behaviour in the practices of the Romans. We assign deep symbolic value to certain bird species. Pet and ornamental birds are highly sought after today just as they were 2,000 years ago. Demand for live exotic birds sees endangered creatures captured, trafficked, and sold to people of means. Excessive human predation for sport, pleasure, or food are serious problems.[1] When we study the faunal remains of a Roman hen from the height of the Empire, we see a creature engineered to be bigger, fatter, and a more productive layer. We can deduce from this something about the farming practices and foodways dominating the Empire at this time. Our own relationship with poultry reveals as much about us. Our table birds are stocky, meaty, and incredibly fast growing. Chickens are raised en masse and slaughtered at around six weeks of age to service our fast-food systems. We may well wonder what future archaeologists will make of the vast heaps of chicken bones in our landfill.[2] Considering the many controversies surrounding caged egg production and intensive poultry farming, we might ask whether our antecedents can teach us how to manage our poultry farms more effectively. The Romans were, after all, the first to intensively raise flocks for profit. Their systems, though not always humane, were usually less wasteful. They did not raise flocks in isolation, but rather alongside other crops and animals, feeding food waste to the birds and collecting their dung to spread on fields. Today, it is common practice for male chicks to be culled upon hatching on egg farms. Conversely, Romans kept the excess males and raised them to be table birds, since their animals were dual-purpose. Our laying hens are typically despatched at around two years old, once they have passed peak productivity. Romans would have used these older, less productive hens as incubators and mothers. Though I do not argue that we should implement such practices today, it is enough to say that there is value in studying how ancient societies coped with the task of producing a food surplus for a burgeoning urban population, and how they managed waste and avoided soil depletion. With the agricultural sector under fire from animal rights and environmental groups, it becomes more important than ever to consider different perspectives when we ponder future directions for food producers.[3] It is well worth looking to the past to see where societies have grappled with similar problems, and whether they might offer solutions, or at the very least hold a mirror up to our own behaviour.

Throughout this book, it has been demonstrated that the most effective way to study bird-human relations is to approach the issue with a basic understanding of bird behaviour. In augural lore, taking a bird's eye view can help to demystify strange and arcane laws around how signs were communicated. Understanding the advantages of using caged fowl allows us to account for the existence of the so-called sacred chickens in military auspices. In the field of aviculture, we can appreciate the sophistication of Roman farming methods by comparing their recommendations to what we know of best practice in husbandry today. An investigation of fowling methods is incomplete without attention to migratory patterns and flocking behaviour, which determine how and when one can most effectively snare birds, and when they fetch the best prices at the market. Studying bird behaviour also helps us avoid rabbit holes of quibbling, such as about what the *passer* really was. It is important that we take off our own cultural goggles and remind ourselves that Romans saw birds in very different ways to ourselves. Where we overlook sparrows and pigeons as pests, Romans typically saw them as sweet, companionate animals or associates of Venus. Where we see vultures as scary or ugly, to the Romans they were pure and beautiful messengers of divine will. When treating the matter of animals in the ancient world it is critically important to lay aside our personal biases so we can accurately interpret what the sources are telling us. On this point, some translators still choose to mistranslate bird names so that passages will sound better or more intuitive in English, such as when Romulus' vultures are transfigured into eagles or Venus' sparrows are turned into swans. This does a tremendous disservice to those who cannot read the original Greek or Latin, and we ought to ask why this is considered acceptable when it alters the social and literary meaning so much.

It has been shown that birds are an effective tool for pinpointing the existence of inequality in food systems. This is true for the ability to raise and farm certain animals, but also in the ability to eat fattened birds, young birds, or birds that are not seasonally available. Consumption patterns provide a window into all the complex social meanings surrounding diet, particularly how elites could jockey for power and position through banqueting and the procurement of rare and expensive birds. The trends in bird consumption powerfully illustrate wider economic trends of the Empire. The transitional period at the end of the Republic and the flourishing of profit-driven agriculture are all amply demonstrated by the increasingly sophisticated and intensive methods of Roman poultry farming. With regard to wildfowl, elites could demand birds that were not seasonally available, hire fowlers on a contract to procure certain types of game for them, and purchase birds that came from farther and farther away. It seemed almost no bird was safe from the Roman palate, though the exceptions betray certain sensibilities. For one, the purple swamphen was not eaten because a purple bird was simply too prestigious to eat. For another, some grumbled about the ethics of eating storks, perhaps showing a sentimental attachment to the birds, or perhaps seeing no sport in gathering up the birds from their nests. Eating a certain type of bird communicated many ideas about status, morality, and wealth, and there were many factors that could add nuance to, or change, this picture.

Like consumption, bird ownership was a powerful communication tool. Elites tended to covet rare, talented, and beautiful birds, making a show of the fact that they were able to invest resources in the simple act of deriving pleasure from birds. Bird ownership was not only motivated by cynical, social factors, however, as in many cases we see a real sentimentality emerging from Roman relationships with companion birds. A cobbler might dote on pet raven and teach it to speak; a person of middling success might dedicate precious space and funds to housing fancy pigeons; a young man might love his prize-fighting rooster and weep when it loses a match. Illogical, emotional factors governed the impulse to keep birds, whether one enjoyed their companionship, loved to hear them sing, or merely liked looking at them. Pet birds offer great insight into the Roman childhood, as we see that children were expected and encouraged to keep or play with birds. These expectations were split along gender lines, as boys were permitted to indulge in rough play and cockfighting, while girls had gentler relationships with hens and pigeons, birds associated with the domestic sphere. In addition, expectations were split along class lines, and certain birds were given to highborn children as indicators of prestige. It is fascinating to consider the social dimension alongside the more intangible emotional one, and consider how Romans felt and thought about birds as much as how they related to them in a physical sense.

This work only scratches the surface of what birds can tell us about the Romans and their values. While it is easy to overlook birds, they are essential to the expression of culture. Societies interact with birds on multiple levels and form practical as well as emotional and spiritual attachments to them. From the mighty eagle standard to the augural hens, the vultures of Romulus to the woodpecker of Mars, the Capitoline geese to Lesbia's sparrow, it is clear that birds held a special and vibrant place in Roman life and myth.

Notes

1 Gill (1994) 587–601.
2 Cocker (2013) 64.
3 Shrubb (2003) investigates how modern farming has caused a collapse in bird populations in Britain, compared to the stability of populations despite intensive farming in the eighteenth and nineteenth centuries.

Bibliography

Adams, J.N. (1982), *The Latin Sexual Vocabulary*. London.

Akerström-Hougen, G. (1974), *The Calendar and Hunting Mosaics of the Villa of the Falconer in Argos: A Study in Early Byzantine Iconography*. Stockholm.

Albarella, U. (2005), 'Alternate Fortunes? The Role of Domestic Ducks and Geese from Roman to Medieval Times in Britain', in G. Grupe and J. Peters (eds), *Feathers, Grit and Symbolism: Birds and Humans in the Old and New Worlds* (Documenta Archaeobiologiae 3). 249–258. Rahden.

Albarella, U., P. Baker, E. Browaeys, C. Corbino, J. Mulville, G. Poland, and F. Worley (eds) (2020), 'The Archaeology of Human-Bird Interactions: Essays in Honour Of Dale Serjeantson Part I', *Quaternary International* 543, 1–148.

Albarella, U., P. Baker, E. Browaeys, C. Corbino, J. Mulville, G. Poland, and F. Worley (eds) (2022), 'The Archaeology of Human-Bird Interactions: Essays in Honour Of Dale Serjeantson Part II', *Quaternary International* 626–27, 1–142.

Albarella, U., and R. Thomas (2002), 'They Dined on Crane: Bird Consumption, Wildfowling and Status in Medieval England', *Proceedings of the 4th Meeting of the ICAZ Bird Working Group Kraków, Poland, 11–15 September, 2001, Acta Zoologica Cracoviensa* 45, 23–38.

Aldrete, G. (2004), *Daily Life in the Roman City: Rome, Pompeii and Ostia*. Westport, Conn.

Alföldi-Rosenbaum, E. (1972), *Notes on Some Birds and Fishes of Luxury*. Bonn.

Allen, B. (2009), *Pigeon*. London.

Anderson, T.R. (2006). *Biology of the Ubiquitous House Sparrow: From Genes to Populations*. Oxford.

Anderson, R. (2018), 'A Story of Blood, Guts and Guesswork: Synthetic Reasoning in Classical Greek Divination', in R. Evans (ed.), *Prophets and Profits: Ancient Divination and its Reception*. 50–64. London.

Anderson, R. (2022), '"Work with the god": Military Divination and Rational Battle-Planning in Xenophon', in C. Addey (ed.), *Divination and Knowledge in Greco-Roman Antiquity*. 84–109. New York.

Ando, C. (2000), *Imperial Ideology and Provincial Loyalty in the Roman Empire*. Berkeley.

André, J. (1967), *Les Noms des oiseaux en latin*. Paris.

André, J. (1998), Essen und Trinken im alten Rom. Stuttgart.

Andreoni, M. (2016), 'Vultures: Exegesis of a Symbol', *Journal of Ancient History and Archaeology* 3:4, 5–9.

Angelini, L.G., L. Ceccarini, and E. Bonari (2005), 'Biomass Yield and Energy Balance of Giant Reed (*Arundo donax L.*) Cropped in Central Italy as Related to Different Management Practices', *European Journal of Agronomy* 22:4, 375–89.

Appadurai, A. (1981), 'Gastro-Politics in Hindu South Asia', *American Ethnologist* 8:3, 494–511.

Arbuckle, B.S., and S. McCarty (2014), 'Animals and Inequality in the Ancient World: An Introduction', in B.S. Arbuckle and S. McCarty (eds), *Animals and Inequality in the Ancient World*. 1–10. Colorado.

Armstrong, E.A. (1958), *The Folklore of Birds: An Enquiry into the Origins and Distribution of Some Magico-Religious Traditions*. London.

Arnott, W.G. (2007), *Birds in the Ancient World from A to Z*. London; New York.

Ashby, T., and R.A.L. Fell (1921), 'The Via Flaminia', *JRS* 11, 125–90.

Attenborough, D. (1998), *Life of Birds*. London.

Audoin-Rouzeau, F. (1995), 'La taille des animaux d'élevage à l'époque romaine et leur exportation', in Hommes et animal dans l'antiquité romaine, Actes du colloque de Nantes. 79–100. Tours.

Babbitt, F.C. (1936), *Plutarch. Moralia, Volume IV: Roman Questions. Greek Questions. Greek and Roman Parallel Stories. On the Fortune of the Romans. On the Fortune or the Virtue of Alexander. Were the Athenians More Famous in War or in Wisdom?*. Loeb Classical Library 305. Cambridge, MA.

Baillieul-LeSuer, R. (2012), *Between Heaven and Earth: Birds in Ancient Egypt*. Chicago.

Balme, D.M. (trans.) (1991), *Aristotle. History of Animals, Volume III: Books 7–10*. Loeb Classical Library 439. Cambridge, MA.

Barth, F. (ed.) (1969), *Ethnic Groups and Boundaries: The Social Organization of Culture Difference*. Boston.

Bartosiewicz, L. (2005), 'Crane: Food, Pet and Symbol', in G. Grupe and J. Peters (eds), *Feathers, Grit and Symbolism. Birds and Humans in the Ancient Old and New Worlds*. 259–69. Rahden/Westfalen.

Beagon, M. (2014), 'Wondrous Animals in Antiquity', in G.L. Campbell (ed.), *The Oxford Handbook of Animals in Classical Thought and Life*. 414–41. Oxford.

Beard, M. (1986), 'Cicero and Divination: The Formation of a Latin Discourse', *JRS* 76, 33–46.

Beard, M. (2007), *The Roman Triumph*, Cambridge.

Beard, M., J. North, and S. Price (1998), *Religions of Rome Vol. I*. Cambridge; New York.

Belmonte, J.A. (2015), 'Solar Alignments – Identification and Analysis', in C.L.N. Ruggles (ed.), *Handbook of Archaeoastronomy and Ethnoastronomy*. 483–93. New York.

Bendlin, A. (2000), 'Looking beyond the Civic Compromise: Religious Pluralism in Late Republican Rome', in E. Bispham and C. Smith (eds), *Religion in Archaic and Republican Rome and Italy: Evidence and Experience*. 115–36. New York.

Bennett, C.E., and M.B. McElwain (trans.), (1925), *Frontinus. Stratagems. Aqueducts of Rome*. Loeb Classical Library 174. Cambridge, MA.

Bentini, M., and R. Martelli (2013), 'Giant Reed (Arundo donax L.) Harvesting System, an Economic and Technical Evaluation', *Journal of Agricultural Engineering*, XLIV:s2:120, 607–9.

Bergmann, B. (2002), 'Art and Nature in the Villa at Oplontis', *JRA*, Supplementary Series no. 47, *Pompeian Brothels, Pompeii's Ancient History, Mirrors and Mysteries, Art and Nature at Oplontis, and the Herculaneum,* 'Basilica', 87–120.

Bergmann, B. (2008), 'Staging the Supernatural: Interior Gardens of Pompeii Houses', in C. Mattusch (ed.), *Pompeii and the Roman Villa*. 53–69. London; New York.

Berthelet, Y. (2015), *Gouverner Avec Les Dieux*. Paris.

Birkhead, T.R. (2011), *The Wisdom of Birds: An Illustrated History of Ornithology*. London.

Birkhead, T.R. (2012), *Bird Sense: What It's Like to Be a Bird*. London.

Birkhead, T.R. (2014), *The Red Canary: The Story of the First Genetically Engineered Animal*. London.

Birkhead, T. (2016), *The Most Perfect Thing: Inside (and Outside) a Bird's Egg*. London.

Bodson, L. (1983), 'Attitudes toward Animals in Greco-Roman Antiquity', *International Journal for the Study of Animal Problems* 4:4, 312–20.

Bodson, L. (2014), 'Zoological Knowledge in Ancient Greece and Rome', in G.L. Campbell (ed.), *The Oxford Handbook of Animals in Classical Thought and Life*. 556–79. Oxford.

Boehrer, B.T. (2004), *Parrot Culture: Our 2500-Year-Long Fascination with the World's Most Talkative Bird*. Philadelphia.

Bond, S.E. (2016), *Trade and Taboo: Disreputable Professions in the Roman Mediterranean*. Ann Arbor.

Bonner, C. (1925), 'Ornithiaka', *CPhil.* 20:3, 210–5.

Bouché-Leclerq, A. (1879–82), *Histoire de la Divination dans l'Antiquitè*. Paris.

Bowe, P. (2004), *Gardens of the Roman World*. Los Angeles.

Bowman, A., and A. Wilson (2013), 'Introduction: Quantifying Roman Agriculture', in A. Bowman and A. Wilson (eds), *The Roman Agricultural Economy: Organization, Investment, and Production*. 1–32. Oxford.

Boyd Ash, H., and W.D. Hooper (trans.) (1934), *Cato, Varro. On Agriculture*. Loeb Classical Library 283. Cambridge, MA.

Bradley, K. (1998), 'The Sentimental Education of the Roman Child: The Role of Pet-Keeping', *Latomus* 57.3, 523–57.

Braund, D.C. (1985), *Augustus to Nero: A Sourcebook on Roman History 31 B.C.–A.D. 68*. London; Sydney.

Braund, S.M. (trans.) (2004), *Juvenal, Persius. Juvenal and Persius*. Loeb Classical Library 91. Cambridge, MA.

Brenk, F.E. (1980), '*Non Primus Pipiabat*: Echoes of Sappho in Catullus' *Passer* Poems', *Latomus* 39:3, 702–16

Brennan, T.C. (2014), 'Power and Process under the Republican 'Constitution', in H. Flower (ed.), *The Cambridge Companion to the Roman Republic* (2nd edn). 19–54. Cambridge.

Buechley, E.R., and C.H. Sekercioglu (2016), 'Vultures', *Current Biology* 26, R543–76.

Bussata, S. (2007), 'Good to Think: Animals and Power', *Antrocom* 4:1, 3–11.

Calder, L. (2007), 'Pet and Image in the Greek World: The Use of Domesticated Animals', in T. Fögen and E. Thomas (eds), *Interactions between Animals and Humans in Graeco-Roman Antiquity*. 61–88. Berlin.

Campbell, B. (1994), *The Roman Army, 31 BC–AD 337*. London; New York.

Capponi, F. (1979), *Ornithologia Latina*. Genova.

Carroll, M. (2015), 'Contextualizing Roman Art and Nature', in B.E. Borg (ed.), *A Companion to Roman Art*. 533–51. Chichester.

Cary, E. (trans.) (1937), *Dionysius of Halicarnassus. Roman Antiquities, Volume I: Books 1–2*. Loeb Classical Library 319. Cambridge, MA.

Castle, W. (1958), 'Observations on Sappho's *To Aphrodite*', *TAPA* 89, 66–76.

Catalano, P. (1960), 'Contributi allo studio del diritto augurale, Vol. I', in G. Giappichelli (ed.), *Università di Torino, Memorie del Istituto Giuridico, ser. 2, mem. 107*. Turin.

Chandezon, C. (2015), 'Animals, Meat and Alimentary By-Products: Patterns of Production and Consumption', in J. Wilkins and R. Nadeau (eds), *A Companion to Food in the Ancient World*. 135–46. Chichester.

Chapman, G.T.L., and M.N. Tweddle (eds) (1995), *A New Herball by William Turner, Part 2 = 1562*. Cambridge.

Clark, G. (2007), 'Philosophers' Pets: Porphyry's Partridge and Augustine's Dog', in T. Fögen and E. Thomas (eds), *Interactions between Animals and Humans in Graeco-Roman Antiquity*. 139–58. Berlin.

Clay, J.S. (1993), '*Providus auspex*: Horace, Ode 3.27', *CJ* 88:2, 167–77.

Cobb, R. (2003), 'Chickenfighting for the Soul of the Heartland', *Text, Practice, Performance* 4, 69–83.

Cocker, M. (2013), *Birds and People*. London.

Collins, D. (2002) 'Reading the Birds: Oionomanteia in Early Epic', *Colby Quarterly* 38, 17–41.

Cool, H.E.M. (2006), *Eating and Drinking in Roman Britain*. Cambridge.

Cooley, A., and M.G.L. Cooley (2014), *Pompeii: A Sourcebook*. London; New York.

Corbino, C., C. Minniti, J. de Grossi Mazzorin, and U. Albarella (2017), 'The Role of the Chicken in the Medieval Food System: Evidence from Central Italy', *TMA* 56, 50–8.

Corbino, C., C. Minniti, J. de Grossi Mazzorin, and U. Albarella (2022), 'The Earliest Evidence of Chicken in Italy', *Quaternary International* 626–7, 80–6.

Corcoran, T.H. (trans.) (1971), *Seneca. Natural Questions, Volume I: Books 1–3*. Loeb Classical Library 450. Cambridge, MA.

Cornell, T.J. (1995), *The Beginnings of Rome*. London; New York.

Cornish, F.W., J.P. Postgate, and J.W. Mackail (trans.) (1913), *Catullus. Tibullus. Pervigilium Veneris*. Revised by G.P. Goold. Loeb Classical Library 6. Cambridge, MA.

Crawford, R. (2003), *Poultry Breeding and Genetics*. Oxford.

Dahl, G., and A. Hjort (1976), *Having Herds: Pastoral Herd Growth and Household Economy*. Stockholm.

Dalla Rosa, A. (2011), 'Dominating the Auspices: Augustus, Augury, and the Proconsuls', in J.H. Richardson and F. Santangelo, *Priests and State in the Roman World*. 243–71. Stuttgart.

de Cupere, B. et al. (2005), 'Ancient Breeds of Domestic Fowl (Gallus gallus f. domestica) Distinguished on the Basis of Traditional Observations Combined With Mixture Analysis', *Journal of Archaeological Science* 32, 1587–97.

de Grossi Mazzorin, J. (2001), 'Archaeozoology and Habitation Models: From a Subsistence to a Productive Economy in Central Italy', in J.R. Brandt and L. Karlsson (eds), *From Huts to Houses: Transformations of Ancient Societies*. 323–30. Stockholm.

de Grossi Mazzorin, J. (2005), 'Introduzione e diffusione del pollame in Italia ed evoluzione delle sue forme di allevamento fino al Medioevo', in I. Fiore, G. Malerba, and S. Chilardi (eds), *Atti del 3° Convengo Nazionale di Archeozoologia.* (Siracusa, 3–5 Novembre 2000. Studi di Paletnologia II, Collana del Bullettino di Paletnologia Italiana). 351–60. Rome.

de Grummond, N.T. (2006), 'Prophets and Priests', in N.T. de Grummond & E. Simon (eds), *The Religion of the Etruscans.* 27–45. Austin.

de Grummond, N.T. (2013), 'Haruspicy and Augury: Sources and Procedures', in J.M. Turfa (ed.), *The Etruscan World.* 539–56. London; New York.

de Melo, W. (trans.) (2011), *Plautus: Amphitryon. The Comedy of Asses. The Pot of Gold. The Two Bacchises. The Captives.* Loeb Classical Library 60. Cambridge, MA.

de Puma, R.D. (2013), *Etruscan Art in the Metropolitan Museum of Art.* New Haven; London.

Dembeck, H. (1965), *Animals and Men.* New York.

Dobiat, C. (2013), 'Early Falconry in Central Europe on the Basis of Grave Finds, with a Discussion of the Origin of Falconry', in U.S.O. Grimm (ed.), *Hunting in Northern Europe until 1500 AD. Old Traditions and Regional Developments, Continental Sources and Continental Influences.* 343–56. Wachholtz.

Doherty, S.P., A. Foster, J. Best, S. Hamilton-Dyer, J. Morris, P. Sadler, C. Skelton, R. Smallman, H. Woldekiros, R. Thomas, and N. Sykes (2021), 'Estimating the Age of Domestic Fowl (*Gallus gallus domesticus* L. 1758) Cockerels Through Spur Development', *International Journal of Osteoarchaeology* 31:5, 770–81.

Dohner, J. (2001), *The Encyclopedia of Historic and Endangered Livestock and Poultry Breeds.* Connecticut.

Donahue, J.F. (2015), 'Roman Dining', in J. Wilkins and R. Nadeau (eds), *A Companion to Food in the Ancient World.* 253–65. Chichester.

Donahue, J. (2019), 'Roman Meals in Their Domestic and Wider Settings' in P. Erdkamp and C. Holleran (eds), *The Routledge Handbook of Diet and Nutrition in The Roman World.* 93–100. New York.

Driediger-Murphy, L.G. (2019), *Roman Republican Augury. Freedom and Control.* Oxford Classical Monographs, Oxford.

Duff, J. (trans.) (1934), *Silius Italicus. Punica, Volume I: Books 1–8.* Loeb Classical Library 277. Cambridge, MA.

Duff, J., and A.M. Duff (trans.) (1934a), *Avianus, Hadrian, Florus, Nemesianus, Reposianus, Tiberianus, Phoenix, Rutilius Namatianus. Minor Latin Poets, Volume II: Florus. Hadrian. Nemesianus. Reposianus. Tiberianus. Dicta Catonis. Phoenix. Avianus. Rutilius Namatianus. Others.* Loeb Classical Library 434. Cambridge, MA.

Duff, J., and A.M. Duff (trans.) (1934b), *Aetna, Calpurnius Siculus, Publilius Syrus, Laus Pisonis, Grattius. Minor Latin Poets, Volume I: Publilius Syrus. Elegies on Maecenas. Grattius. Calpurnius Siculus. Laus Pisonis. Einsiedeln Eclogues. Aetna.* Loeb Classical Library 284. Cambridge, MA.

Dundes, A. (1994), *The Cockfight: A Casebook.* Madison.

Dundes, A. (2007), 'Gallus as Phallus: A Psychoanalytic Cross-Cultural Consideration of the Cockfight as Fowl Play', in S. Bronner (ed.), *Meaning of Folklore.* 285–316. Utah.

Durham, E. (2013), 'Symbols of Power: The Silchester Bronze Eagle and Eagles in Roman Britain', *Archaeological Journal* 170:1, 78–105.

Edlund-Berry, I. (2006), 'Ritual Space and Boundaries in Etruscan Religion', in N.T. de Grummond and E. Simon (eds), *The Religion of the Etruscans.* 116–31. Texas.

Edwards, C.H. (1993), *The Politics of Immorality in Ancient Rome*. Cambridge.

Eidinow, J. (1993), 'A Note on Ovid Ars Amatoria 1.117–19', *AJPhil.* 114:3, 413–17.

Elkins, N. (1988), *Weather and Bird Behaviour*. Calton; England.

Epstein, H.J. (1943), 'The Origin and Earliest History of Falconry', *Isis* 34:6, 497–509.

Erdkamp, P., and C. Holleran (2019), 'Introduction', in P. Erdkamp and C. Holleran (eds), *The Routledge Handbook of Diet and Nutrition in the Roman World*. 1–14. New York.

Evans, A.H. (ed.) (1903), *Turner on Birds: A Short and Succinct History of the Principal Birds Noticed by Pliny and Aristotle*. Cambridge.

Fairclough, H.R. (trans.) (1916), *Virgil. Eclogues. Georgics. Aeneid: Books 1–6*. Revised by G.P. Goold. Loeb Classical Library 63. Cambridge, MA.

Fairclough, H.R. (trans.) (1926), *Horace. Satires. Epistles. The Art of Poetry*. Loeb Classical Library 194. Cambridge, MA.

Falconer, W.A. (trans.) (1923), *Cicero. On Old Age. On Friendship. On Divination*. Loeb Classical Library 154. Cambridge, MA.

Farrar, L. (1998), *Ancient Roman Gardens*. Gloucestershire.

Favro, D. (2010), 'From Pleasure, to "Guilty Pleasure," to Simulation: Rebirthing the Villa of the Papyri', in M. Zarmakoupi (ed.), *The Villa of the Papyri at Herculaneum*. 155–80. Berlin.

Filean, E.P. (2008), 'A Biometrical Perspective on the Size of Cattle in Roman Nijmegen, the Netherlands: Implications for the Supply of Urban Consumers and the Roman Army', in S. Stallibrass and R. Thomas (eds), *Feeding the Roman Army: The Archaeology of Production and Supply in NW Europe*. 99–115. Oxford.

Fischer, T. (2013), 'Hunting in the Roman Period', in O. Grimm and U. Schmölcke (eds), *Hunting in Northern Europe until 1500 AD. Old Traditions and Regional Developments, Continental Sources and Continental Influences*. Wachholtz.

Flegg, J. (2001), *Birds*. London.

Flory, M.B. (1989), 'Octavian and the Omen of the "Gallina Alba"', *CJ* 84:4, 343–56.

Fògen, T. (2014), 'Animal Communication', in G.L. Campbell (ed.), *The Oxford Handbook of Animals in Classical Thought and Life*. 216–33. Oxford.

Fordyce, C. (1961), *Catullus: A Commentary*. Oxford.

Forster, E.S. (trans.), (1954), *Columella. On Agriculture, Volume II: Books 5–9*. Loeb Classical Library 407. Cambridge, MA.

Forsythe, G. (2005), *A Critical History of Early Rome*. Berkeley.

Foster, B.O. (trans.) (1919), *Livy. History of Rome, Volume I: Books 1–2*. Loeb Classical Library 114. Cambridge, MA.

Foti, G. (2011), 'Funzioni e caratteri del "pullarius" in età repubblicana e imperiale', *Acme* 64, 89–121.

Foufopoulos, J., and N. Litinas (2005), 'Crows and Ravens in the Mediterranean (the Nile Valley, Greece and Italy)', *The Bulletin of the American Society of Papyrologists* 42:1–4, 7–39.

Frayn, J.M. (1993), *Markets and Fairs in Roman Italy*. Oxford; New York.

Frazer, J.G. (1891), 'Swallows in the House', *The Classical Review* 5:1–2, 1–3.

Frazer, J.G. (trans.) (1931), *Ovid. Fasti*. Revised by G.P. Goold. Loeb Classical Library 253. Cambridge, MA.

Fuchs, F. (1962), 'Varros Vogelhaus bei Casinum', *Deutsches archaologisches Institut. Romische Abteilung*. Mitteilungen 69, 96–105.

Gaál, B. (2017), 'King Śibi in the East and the West: Following the Flight of a Suppliant Dove', *International Journal of the Classical Tradition* 24:1, 1–34.

Gaisser, J.H. (2007), *Catullus*. Oxford.

Garnsey, P. (1988), *Famine and Food Supply in the Graeco-Roman World*. Cambridge.

Garnsey, P. (1999), *Food and Society in Antiquity*. Cambridge.

Geike, A. (1912), *The Love of Nature Among the Romans*. London.

Genovese, E.N. (1974), 'Symbolism in the *Passer* Poems', *Maia* 26, 121–5.

Giangrande, G. (1975), 'Catullus's Lyrics on the Passer', *MPL* 1, 37–46.

Gilbert, O.R. (2016), *The Spread and Role of Peafowl in Classical Antiquity*. Unpublished Masters Thesis, Sheffield University.

Gill, F. (1994), *Ornithology*. New York.

Giovannini, A. (1983), *Consulare imperium*. Basle.

Giovannini, A. (1998), 'Les livres auguraux', in C. Moatti (ed.), *La mémoire perdue. Recherches sur l'administration romaine*. 103–22. Rome.

Global Invasive Species Database (2021), Species profile: Passer domesticus. Downloaded from http://www.iucngisd.org/gisd/species.php?sc=420 on 30-04-2021.

Goebel, V., and J. Peters (2014), 'Veterinary Medicine', in G.L. Campbell (ed.), *The Oxford Handbook of Animals in Classical Thought and Life*. Oxford, 589–605.

Goldberg, S.M., and G. Manuwald (trans.) (2018), *Ennius. Fragmentary Republican Latin, Volume I: Ennius, Testimonia. Epic Fragments*. Loeb Classical Library 294. Cambridge, MA.

Gooders, J. (2001), *Birds of Britain and Europe*. London.

Goody, J. (1982), *Cooking, Cuisine and Class: A Study in Comparative Sociology*. Cambridge.

Goold, G.P. (1983) (ed.) *Catullus*. London.

Gordon, R. (1990), 'From Republic to Principate: Priesthood, Religion and Ideology', in M. Beard and J. North (eds), *Pagan Priests: Religion and Power in the Ancient World*. 179–98. Ithaca, NY.

Gorman, G. (2017), *Woodpecker*. London.

Gottarelli, A. (2013), *Contemplatio: Templum Solare e Culti di Fondazione*. Bologna.

Gottlieb, G. (1998), 'Religion in the Politics of Augustus', in H.-P. Stahl (ed.), *Vergil's Aeneid: Augustan Epic and Political Context*. 21–36. London.

Graves, R. (1948), *The White Goddess*. London.

Green, C.M.C. (1997), 'Free as a Bird: Varro de re Rustica 3', *AJPhil.* 118:3, 427–48.

Green, P. (2005), *The Poems of Catullus*. Berkeley.

Green, S.J. (2009), 'Malevolent Gods and Promethean Birds: Contesting Augury in Augustus's Rome', *TAPA* 139:1, 147–67.

Green, A. (2019), 'Cultural Responses to the Migration of the Barn Swallow in Europe', *ANU Historical Journal* 2:1, 87–108.

Green, A. (2022), 'Lesbia's Controversial Bird: Testing the Cases for and against *Passer* as Sparrow', *Antichthon* 55, 6–20.

Groot, M., A. Ervynck, and F. Pigière (2010), 'Vagrant Vultures: Archaeological Evidence for the Cinereous Vulture (*Aegypius monachus*) in the Low Countries', in W. Pummel, J. Zeiler, and D. Brinkhuizen (eds), *Birds in Archaeology*. 241–51. Groningen.

Guidobaldi, M.P., and D. Esposito (2012), *Ercolano*. Verona.

Gulick, C.B. (1896), 'Omens and Augury in Plautus', *Harv. Stud.* 7, 235–47.

Haines, C.R. (trans.) (1920), *Fronto: Correspondence, Volume II*. Loeb Classical Library. Cambridge, MA.

Halliday, W. (1922), 'Picus-Who-Is-Also-Zeus', *The Classical Review* 36:4–5, 110–2.

Halstead, P. (2019), 'The Contribution of Zooarchaeology', in P. Erdkamp and C. Holleran (eds), *The Routledge Handbook of Diet and Nutrition in the Roman world.* 63–76. New York.

Hanfmann, G. (1971), *The Season Sarcophagus at Dumbarton Oaks*, 2 vols. Cambridge, MA.

Hanson, A. (trans.) (1989), *Apuleius: Metamorphoses (The Golden Ass), Volume II: Books 7–11.* Loeb Classical Library. Cambridge, MA.

Harden, A. (2014), 'Animals in Classical Art', in G.L. Campbell (ed.), *The Oxford Handbook of Animals in Classical Thought and Life.* 24–61. Oxford.

Harrison, J.E. (1912), *Themis.* Cambridge.

Harrison, T.P. (1956), *They Tell of Birds: Chaucer, Spenser, Milton, Drayton.* Austin.

Harting, J.E. (1871), *The Birds of Shakespeare.* London.

Havelock, E. (1929), *The Lyric Genius of Catullus.* New York.

Henderson, J. (trans.) (2009), *Longus, Xenophon of Ephesus. Daphnis and Chloe. Anthia and Habrocomes.* Loeb Classical Library 69. Cambridge, MA.

Hingley, R. (2006), 'The Deposition of Iron Objects in Britain during the Later Prehistoric and Roman Periods', *Britannia* 37, 213–57.

Hoffman, R. (2014), *An Environmental History of Medieval Europe.* Cambridge.

Holladay, A.J., and M.D. Goodman (1986), 'Religious Scruples in Ancient Warfare', *CQ* 36:1, 151–71.

Holleran, C. (2012), *Shopping in Ancient Rome: The Retail Trade of the Late Republic and the Principate.* Oxford.

Holmes, M. (2018), 'King of the Birds! The Changing Role of White-Tailed (Haliaeetus albicilla) and Golden Eagles (Aquila chrysaetos) in Britain's Past', *Archaeofauna* 27, 173–94.

Hooper, R.W. (1985), 'In Defence of Catullus' Dirty Sparrow,' *G & R* 32:2, 162–78.

Hopkinson, N. (trans.) (2015), *Theocritus. Moschus. Bion.* Loeb Classical Library 28. Cambridge, MA.

Horn, H.G. (1972), 'Ein Römischer Bronzeadler', *Jahrbuch des Römisch-Germanischen Zentralmuseums Mainz* 19, 63–82.

Hornblower, S., and A. Spawforth (2012), *The Oxford Classical Dictionary.* Oxford.

Horsfall, N. (1981), 'From History to Legend: M. Manlius and the Geese', *CJ* 76, 298–311.

Hough, J.N. (1974), 'Bird Imagery in Roman Poetry', *CJ* 70, 1–13.

Houlihan, P. (1986), *The Birds of Ancient Egypt.* Warminster.

Howe, T. (2014), 'Value Economics: Animals, Wealth, and the Market', in G.L. Campbell (ed.), *The Oxford Handbook of Animals in Classical Thought and Life.* 136–156. Oxford.

Husselman, E.M. (1953), 'The Dovecotes of Karanis', *TAPA* 84, 81–91.

Ingersoll, E. (1923), *Birds in Legend, Fable and Folklore.* London.

Ingleheart, J. (2003), 'Catullus 2 and 3: A Programmatic Pair of Sapphic Epigrams?', *Mnemosyne* 56:5, 551–65.

Ingold, T. (ed.) (2008), *What Is an Animal?* London.

Innes, M. (1952), 'Deliciae Meae Puellae', *G & R* 21:62, 78–85.

Jannot, J.R. (2005), *Religion in Ancient Etruria.* Wisconsin.

Jashemski, W. (1979), *The Gardens of Pompeii, Herculaneum and the Villas Destroyed by Vesuvius.* Vol. 1, Photographs, Drawings and Plans. New Rochelle, NY.

Jashemski, W. (1993), *The Gardens of Pompeii, Herculaneum and the Villas Destroyed by Vesuvius*, Vol. 2, Appendices. New Rochelle, NY.

Jennison, G. (1937), *Animals for Show and Pleasure in Ancient Rome*. Manchester.

Jocelyn, H.D. (1980), 'On Some Unnecessarily Indecent Interpretations of Catullus 2 and 3', *AJP* 101, 421–41.

Johnson, L.R. (1968), *Aviaries and Aviculture in Ancient Rome*. Ann Arbor.

Johnson, M. (2003), 'Catullus 2b: The Development of a Relationship in the *Passer* Trilogy', *CJ* 99:1, 11–34.

Johnston, S.I. (2008), *Ancient Greek Divination*. Oxford.

Johnston, S.I. (2015), 'Oracles and Divination', in E. Eidinow and J. Kindt (eds), *The Oxford Handbook of Ancient Greek Religion*. 477–89. Oxford.

Jones, H.L. (trans.) (1923), *Strabo. Geography, Volume II: Books 3–5*. Loeb Classical Library 50. Cambridge, MA.

Jones, A. (1949), 'The Roman Civil Service (Clerical and Sub-Clerical Grades)', *JRS* 39, 38–55.

Jones, J. (1998), 'Catullus' "Passer" as "Passer"', *G & R*, 45:2, 188–94.

Jones, F. (2016), *The Boundaries of Art and Social Space in Rome: The Caged Bird and Other Art Forms*. London.

Kaster, R.A. (trans.) (2011), *Macrobius. Saturnalia, Volume I: Books 1–2*. Loeb Classical Library 510. Cambridge, MA.

Keller, O. (1920), *Die Antike Tierwelt*. Leipzig.

Keller, W. (1975), *The Etruscans*. Norfolk.

Kellum, B. (1994), 'The Construction of Landscape in Augustan Rome: The Garden Room at the *Villa ad Gallinas*', *The Art Bulletin* 76:2, 211–24.

Keyes, C.W. (trans.) (1928), *Cicero. On the Republic. On the Laws*. Loeb Classical Library 213. Cambridge, MA.

Kindt, J. (2021), 'Animals in Ancient Greek Divination: Oracles, Predictions, and Omens', in J. Kindt (ed.), *Animals in Ancient Greek Religion*. 197–216. New York.

King, A.C. (1988), 'Villas and Animal Bones', in K. Branigan and D. Miles (eds), *Villa Economies. Economic Aspects of Romano-British Villas*. 51–59. Sheffield.

King, A.C. (1999), 'Animals and the Roman Army: The Evidence of Animal Bones', in A. Goldsworthy and I. Haynes (eds), *The Roman Army as a Community*. 200–11. Portsmouth.

King, A.C. (2001), 'The Romanization of Diet in the Western Empire: Comparative Archaeozoological Studies', in S. Keay and N. Terrenato (eds), *Italy and the West: Comparative Issues in Romanization*. 210–23. Oxford.

Kleczkowska, K. (2015), 'Bird Communication in Ancient Greek and Roman Thought', *Maska* 28, 95–106.

Klingender, F. (1971), *Animals in Art and Thought to the End of the Middle Ages*. London.

Kolataj, W., G. Majcherek, and E. Parandowska (2007), *Villa of the Birds*. New York.

Koortbojian, M. (2013), *The Divinization of Caesar and Augustus*. New York.

Koorthojian, M. (2015), 'Roman Sarcophagi', in B. Borg (ed.), *A Companion to Roman Art*. 286–300. Oxford.

Kranz, P. (1984), *Entwicklung und Ikonographie des Motivs der vier Jahreszeiten auf kaiserzeitlichen Sarkophagen und Sarkophagdeckeln*. Berlin.

Krappe, A. (1941), 'Picus Who Is Also Zeus', *Mnemosyne* 9:4, 241–57.

Krauss, F.B. (1930), *An Interpretation of the Omens, Portents, and Prodigies Recorded by Livy, Tacitus, and Suetonius*. Philadelphia.

Kron, G. (2008), 'Animal Husbandry, Hunting, Fishing, and Fish Production', in J.P. Oleson (ed.), *The Oxford Handbook of Engineering and Technology in the Classical World*. Oxford.

Kron, G. (2012), 'Food Production', in W. Scheidel (ed.), *The Cambridge Companion to the Roman Economy*. 156–74, Cambridge.

Kron, G. (2014), 'Animal Husbandry', in G.L. Campbell (ed.), *The Oxford Handbook of Animals in Classical Thought and Life*. 109–36. Oxford.

Kron, G. (2015), 'Agriculture', in J. Wilkins and R. Nadeau (eds), *A Companion to Food in the Ancient World*. 160–73. Chichester.

Kron, G. (2017), 'The Diversification and Intensification of Italian Agriculture: The Complementary Roles of the Small and Wealthy Farmer', in T. de Haas and G.W. Tol (eds), *The Economic Integration of Roman Italy*. 107–135. Leiden.

Kunkel, W. (1995), *Staatsordnung und Staatspraxis der Romischen Republik*. Munich.

Kvium, C. (2011), 'Inauguration and Foundation: An Essay on Roman Ritual, Classification and Continuity', in J.H. Richardson and F. Santangelo (eds), *Priests and State in the Roman World*. 63–91. Stuttgart.

Lamberton, R.D., and S.I. Rotroff (1985), *Birds of the Athenian Agora*. Princeton.

Lanfranchi, T. (2015), Les tribuns de la plèbe et la formation de la république romaine. Rome.

Lattimore, R. (1934), 'Portents and Prophecies in Connection with the Emperor Vespasian', *CJ* 29:6, 441–9.

Laufer, B. (1926), 'Ostrich Egg-shell Cups of Mesopotamia and the Ostrich in Ancient and Modern Times', *Anthropology Leaflet* 23, 1–50.

Laurence, R. (1994), *Roman Pompeii: Space and Society*. London; New York.

Lazenby, F. (1949), 'Greek and Roman Household Pets', *CJ* 44:4, 245–52.

Lévi-Strauss, C. (1963), *Totemism*. R. Needham (trans.). Boston.

Lewis, S., and L. Llewellyn-Jones (2018), *The Culture of Animals in Antiquity*. London; New York.

Lewit, T. (1991), *Agricultural Production in the Roman Economy AD 200–400*. Oxford.

Lewit, T. (2022), 'Young Children in the Roman Farming Economy (Western Mediterranean): Evidence, Problems and Possibilities', in D. Van Limbergen, D. Taelman and A. Hoffelinck (eds), *Divergent Economies in the Roman World*. London.

Lichtheim, M. (1957), *Demotic Ostraca from Medinet Habu*. Chicago.

Linderski, J. (1984), 'Cicero and Roman Divination', *La Parola* del Passato 37 (1982–3) 12–38, reprinted in *Roman Questions 1* (1984). 458–84. Stuttgart.

Linderski, J. (1986a), 'The Augural Law', *ANRW II* 16:3, 2147–312.

Linderski, J. (1986b), 'Review Article: Watching the Birds: Cicero the Augur and the Augural Templa', *CPhil.* 81:4, 330–40, reprinted in *Roman Questions 2* (1986), 485–95. Stuttgart.

Linderski, J. (1990a), 'The Auspices and the Struggle of the Orders', in W. Eder (ed.), *Staat und Staatlichkeit in der frühen römischen Republik*. 34–48, reprinted in *Roman Questions 1* (1990), 560–74. Stuttgart.

Linderski, J. (1990b), 'Review: The Bronze Liver of Piacenza: Analysis of a Polytheistic Structure by L.B. van der Meer', *CPhil.* 85:1, 67–71, reprinted in *Roman Questions 1* (1990), 595–9.

Linderski, J. (2006), 'Founding the City', in S.B. Faris and L.E. Lundeen (eds), *Ten Years of the Agnes Kirsopp Michels Lectures at Bryn Mawr College*. 88–107. Bryn Mawr.

Littlewood, A.R. (1987), 'Ancient Literary Evidence for the Pleasure Gardens of the Roman Country Villas', in E.B. MacDougall (ed.), *Ancient Roman Villa Gardens.* 1–30. Washington DC.

Lulof, P., and I. Van Kampen (2011), *Etruscans: Eminent Women, Powerful Men,* Amsterdam.

MacBain, B. (1982), *Prodigy and Expiation: A Study in Religion and Politics in Republican Rome.* Brussels.

Macdonald, K.C., and R.M. Blend (2000), 'Chickens', in K.F. Kiple and K.C. Ornelas (eds), *The Cambridge World History of Food.* 496–9. Cambridge.

MacKinney, L. (1942), 'The Vulture in Ancient Medical Lore', *Ciba Symposia* 4:3, 1258–72.

MacKinnon, M. (2001), 'High on the Hog: Linking Zooarchaeological, Literary, and Artistic Data for Pig Breeds in Roman Italy', *AJArch.* 105:4, 649–73.

MacKinnon, M. (2004), 'Production and Consumption of Animals in Roman Italy: Integrating the Zooarchaeological and Ancient Textual Evidence', *JRA,* Supplementary Series 54. Portsmouth.

MacKinnon, M. (2007), 'Osteological Research in Classical Archaeology', *AJArch* 111.3, 473–504.

MacKinnon, M. (2013), 'Fauna of the Ancient Mediterranean World', in G.L. Campbell (ed.), *The Oxford Handbook of Animals in Classical Thought and Life.* Oxford.

MacKinnon, M. (2014), '"Tails" of Romanization: Animals and Inequality in the Roman Mediterranean Context', in B.S. Arbuckle and S. McCarty (eds), *Animals and Inequality in the Ancient World.* 315–34. Colorado.

MacKinnon, M. (2018), 'Zooarchaeology: Reconstructing the Natural and Cultural Worlds from Archaeological Faunal Remains', in W. Scheidel (ed.), *The Science of Roman History.* 95–122. Princeton.

MacMullen, R. (2011), *The Earliest Romans: A Character Sketch.* Ann Arbor.

Magli, G. (2015), 'Etruscan Divination and Architecture' in C.L.N. Ruggles (ed.), *Handbook of Archaeoastronomy and Ethnoastronomy.* 1637–1642. New York.

Maltby, M. (1984), 'Animal Bones and the Romano-British Economy', in C. Grigson and J. Clutton-Brock (eds), *Animals and Archaeology, Vol. 4. Husbandry in Europe.* 125–38. Oxford.

Maltby, M. (1997), 'Domestic Fowl on Romano-British Sites: Inter-Site Comparisons of Abundance', *International Journal of Osteoarchaeology* 7, 402–14.

Maltby, M. (2010), *Feeding a Roman Town: Environmental Evidence from Excavations in Winchester, 1972–1985.* Winchester.

Maltby, M. (2015), 'Commercial Archaeology, Zooarchaeology and the Study of Romano-British Towns', in N. Holbrook and M. Fulford (eds), *The Towns of Roman Britain: The Contribution of Commercial Archaeology Since 1990.* (Britannia Monograph 27). 175–93. London.

Markandya, A., T. Taylor, A. Longo, M.N. Murty, S. Murty, and K. Dhavala (2008), 'Counting the Cost of Vulture Decline – An Appraisal of the Human Health and Other Benefits of Vultures in India', *Ecological Economics* 67, 194–204.

Martin, E.W. (1914), *The Birds of Latin Poets.* California.

Marvin, G. (1984), 'The Cockfight in Andalusia, Spain: Images of the Truly Male', *Anthropological Quarterly* 57:2, 60–70.

Marzano, A. (2013), 'Agricultural Production in the Hinterland of Rome: Wine and Olive Oil', in A. Bowman and A. Wilson (eds), *The Roman Agricultural Economy: Organization, Investment, and Production*. Oxford, 85–106.

Masseti, M. (2022), 'Representations of Birds in Etruscan Art (6th – late 4th century BC)', *Quaternary International* 626–7, 87–94.

Mattingly, H. (1967), *Roman Coins: From the Earliest Times to the Fall of the Western Empire*. London.

McDonough, C.M. (2003), 'The Swallows on Cleopatra's Ship', *The Classical World* 96:3, 251–8.

Meadows, K. (1994), 'You Are What You Eat: Diet, Identity and Romanization', in S. Cottam, D. Dungworth, S. Scott, and J. Taylor (eds), *TRAC 1994: Proceedings of the Fourth Theoretical Roman Archaeology Conference*. 133–40. Oxford.

Mignone, L.M. (2016), 'The Augural Contest at Rome: The View from the Aventine', *CPhil.* 111:4, 391–405.

Momigliano, A. (1984), 'The Theological Efforts of the Roman Upper Classes in the First Century BC', *CPhil.* 79:3, 199–211.

Morgan, G. (1975), 'Three Non-Roman Blood Sports', *CQ* 25, 117–22.

Morley, N. (2007), *Trade in Classical Antiquity*. Cambridge.

Morris, D. (2009), *Owl*. London.

Morris, J. (2011), *Investigating Animal Burials: Ritual, Mundane and Beyond*. BAR British Series 535. Oxford.

Morrison, J. (1981), *The Classical World: Divination and Oracles*. London; Boston.

Mozley, J.H. (trans.) (1929), *Ovid. Art of Love. Cosmetics. Remedies for Love. Ibis. Walnut-Tree. Sea Fishing. Consolation*. Revised by G.P. Goold. Loeb Classical Library 232. Cambridge, MA.

Mullin, M.H. (1999), 'Mirrors and Windows: Sociocultural Studies of Human-Animal Relationships', *Annual Review of Anthropology* 28:1, 201–24.

Mulroy, D. (2002), *The Complete Poetry of Catullus*. Wisconsin.

Mynott, J. (2009), *Birdscapes: Birds in Our Imagination and Experience*. Princeton.

Mynott, J. (2018), *Birds in the Ancient World: Winged Words*. Oxford.

Nadeau, Y. (1984), 'Catullus' Sparrow, Martial, Juvenal and Ovid', *Latomus* 43:4, 861–8.

Nagy, G. (2020.12.18), 'From the Heavenly to the Earthly and Back, Variations on a Theme of Love-on-Wings in Song 1 of Sappho and Elsewhere', *Classical Inquiries*. http://nrs.harvard.edu/urn-3:hul.eresource:Classical_Inquiries

Nagy, G. (2020.12.25), 'Back and Forth from General to Special Kinds of Erotic Love, Further Variations on a Theme of Love-on-Wings in Song 1 of Sappho and Elsewhere', *Classical Inquiries*. http:// nrs.harvard.edu/urn-3:hul.eresource:Classical_ Inquiries

Neudecker, R. (2015), 'Art in the Roman Villa', in B. Borg (ed.), *A Companion to Roman Art*. 388–405. Oxford.

Oakley, S. (1985), 'Single Combat in the Roman Republic', *CQ* 35:2, 392–410.

Obermaier, S. (2019), 'You Are the Animal That You Eat', in T. Schmidt and J. Pahlitzsch (eds), *Impious Dogs, Haughty Foxes and Exquisite Fish*. 133–65. Berlin.

Oggins, R.S. (2004), *The Kings and Their Hawks*. Yale.

Pagan, V. (2016), 'Horticulture and the Roman Shaping of Nature', in *Oxford Handbook Online*. Oxford.

Pallottino, M. (1956), 'Deorum sedes', *Studi in Onore di Aristide Calderini e Roberto Paribeni* 3, 223–34.

Palmer, R.E.A. (1970), *The Archaic Community of the Romans*. Oxford.

Parker, A.J. (1988), 'The Birds of Roman Britain', *OJA* 7:2, 197–226.

Parrish, D. (1984), *Season Mosaics of Roman North Africa*. Rome.

Parrish, D. (1994), 'Variations in the Iconography of the Winter Season in Roman Mosaics', *La mosaique greco-romaine* 4, 39–46.

Parrish, D. (2003), 'A Few Aspects of the Imagery of Winter in Roman and Late Antique Art', *Mouseion: Journal of the Classical Association of Canada* 3:3, 237–57.

Paschall, D. (1936), 'The Origin and Semantic Development of Latin Vitium', *TAPA* 67, 219–31.

Paton, W.R. (trans.) (1916), *The Greek Anthology, Volume I: Book 1: Christian Epigrams. Book 2: Christodorus of Thebes in Egypt. Book 3: The Cyzicene Epigrams. Book 4: The Proems of the Different Anthologies. Book 5: The Amatory Epigrams. Book 6: The Dedicatory Epigrams*. Loeb Classical Library 67. Cambridge, MA.

Pernigotti, A.P. (2019), 'A Contribution to the Study and Orientation of Etruscan Temples', in G. Magli, A.C. González-García, J.B. Aviles, and E. Antonello (eds), *Archaeoastronomy in the Roman World*. Cham.

Perry-Gal, L., A. Erlich, A. Gilboa, and G. Bar-Oz (2015), 'Earliest Economic Exploitation of Chicken Outside East Asia: Evidence from the Hellenistic Southern Levant', *PNAS* 112:32, 9849–54.

Peters, J. (1998), *Römische Tierhaltung und Tierzucht: Eine Synthese aus archäozoologischer Untersuchungen und schriftlich-bildlicher Uberlieferung*. Rahden.

Petrucci, A. (1996), *Il trionfo nella storia costituzionale romana dagli inizi della repubblica ad Augusto*. Milano.

Pieraccini, L.C. (2014), 'The Ever Elusive Etruscan Egg', *Etruscan Studies* 17:2, 267–92.

Pittenger, M.R.P. (2008), *Contested Triumphs. Politics, Pageantry, and Performance in Livy's Republican Rome*. Los Angeles; London.

Platner, S., and T. Ashby (1929), *A Topographical Dictionary of Ancient Rome*. London.

Pollard, J. (1977), *Birds in Greek Life and Myth*. Colorado.

Pollini, J. (1987), *The Portraiture of Gaius and Lucius Caesar*. New York.

Pomeroy, A.J. (2003), 'Heavy Petting in Catullus', *Arethusa* 36:1, 49–60.

Poole, K. (2010), 'Bird Introductions', in T. O'Connor and N. Sykes (eds), *Extinctions and Invasions: A Social History of British Fauna*. Oxford.

Popkin, M.L. (2016), *The Architecture of Roman Triumph*. New York.

Porstner, L. (2020), 'Boundaries, Magic, and Popular Religion in two Mosaics from Ancient Thysdrus (El Jem in Tunisia)', *New Classicists* 2, 1–69.

Postgate, J.P., F.W. Cornish, and J.W. Mackail (trans.) (1913), *Catullus. Tibullus. Pervigilium Veneris*. Revised by G.P. Goold. Loeb Classical Library 6. Cambridge, MA.

Potter, T. (2004), *A Companion to the Roman Empire*. Oxford.

Purcell, N. (1983), 'The Apparitores: A Study in Social Mobility', *Papers of the British School at Rome* 51, 125–73.

Putz, B. (2014), 'Good to Laugh With: Animals in Comedy', in G.L. Campbell (ed.), *The Oxford Handbook of Animals in Classical Thought and Life*. 61–73. Oxford.

Rackham, H. (trans.) (1940), *Pliny. Natural History, Volume III: Books 8–11*. Loeb Classical Library. Cambridge, MA.

Rackham, H. (trans.) (1945), *Pliny. Natural History, Volume IV: Books 12–16*. Loeb Classical Library 370. Cambridge, MA.

Rackham, H. (trans.) (1950), *Pliny. Natural History, Volume V: Books 17–19*. Loeb Classical Library 371. Cambridge, MA.

Radice, B. (trans.) (1969), *Pliny the Younger: Letters, Volume I: Books 1–7*. Loeb Classical Library. Cambridge, MA.

Rafferty, D. (2019), *Provincial Allocations in Rome 123–52 BCE*. Stuttgart.

Rask, K.A. (2014), 'Etruscan Animal Bones and Their Implications for Sacrificial Studies', *History of Religions* 53:3, 269–312.

Rasmussen, S.W. (2003), *Public Portents in Republican Rome*. Rome.

Rawson, B. (1974), 'Religion and Politics in the Late Second Century B.C. at Rome', *Phoenix* 28:2, 193–212.

Rawson, B. (1985), *Intellectual Life in the Late Roman Republic*. London.

Rawson, B. (2003), *Children and Childhood in Roman Italy*. Oxford.

Reeder, J.C. (1997), 'The Statue of Augustus from Prima Porta, the Underground Complex and the Omen of the Gallina Alba', *AJPhil.* 118:1, 89–118.

Reeder, J.C. (2001), *The Villa of Livia Ad Gallinas Albas*. Rhode Island.

Reitz, E., and E. Wing (2008), *Zooarchaeology*. Cambridge; New York.

Rolfe, J.C. (trans.) (1914a), *Suetonius. Lives of the Caesars, Volume I: Julius. Augustus. Tiberius. Gaius. Caligula*. Loeb Classical Library 31. Cambridge, MA.

Rolfe, J.C. (trans.) (1914b), *Suetonius. Lives of the Caesars, Volume II: Claudius. Nero. Galba, Otho, and Vitellius. Vespasian. Titus, Domitian. Lives of Illustrious Men: Grammarians and Rhetoricians. Poets (Terence. Virgil. Horace. Tibullus. Persius. Lucan). Lives of Pliny the Elder and Passienus Crispus*. Loeb Classical Library 38. Cambridge, MA.

Rose, H. (1974), *The Roman Questions of Plutarch*. New York.

Rosenstein, N. (1990), *Imperatores Victi: Military Defeat and Aristocratic Competition in the Middle and Late Republic*. Berkeley.

Rouse, W.H.D. (trans.) (1924), *Lucretius. On the Nature of Things*. Revised by M.F. Smith. Loeb Classical Library 181. Cambridge, MA.

Rowan, C. (2012), *Under Divine Auspices: Divine Ideology and the Visualisation of Imperial Power in the Severan Period*. Cambridge; New York.

Rowland, B. (1978), *Birds with Human Souls: A Guide to Bird Symbolism*. Knoxville.

Rudd, N. (trans.) (2004), *Horace. Odes and Epodes*. Loeb Classical Library 33. Cambridge, MA.

Ruggles, C.L.N. (2015), 'Analyzing Orientations', in C.L.N. Ruggles (ed.), *Handbook of Archaeoastronomy and Ethnoastronomy*. 411–27. New York.

Rüpke, J. (2007), *Religion of the Romans*. Cambridge.

Rüpke, J. (2011), 'Different Colleges – Never Mind!?' in J.H. Richardson and F. Santangelo (eds), *Priests and State in the Roman World*. 25–39. Stuttgart.

Rüpke, J. (2014), 'Roman Religion', in H. Flower (ed.), *The Cambridge Companion to the Roman Republic* (2nd edn). 213–33. Cambridge.

Rüpke, J. (2016), *On Roman Religion: Lived Religion and the Individual in Ancient Rome*. New York.

Ruxton, G.D., and D.C. Houston (2004), 'Obligate Vertebrate Scavengers Must Be Large Soaring Fliers', *Journal of Theoretical Biology* 228:3, 431–6.

Sax, B. (2003), *Crow*. London.

Scheid, J. (2003), *An Introduction to Roman Religion*. Edinburgh.

Scheid, J. (2005), 'Augustus and Roman Religion: Continuity, Conservatism, and Innovation', in K. Galinsky (ed.), *The Cambridge Companion to the Age of Augustus*. 175–93. Cambridge.

Scheid, J. (2007), 'Sacrifices for Gods and Ancestors', in J. Rüpke (ed.), *A Companion to Roman Religion*. 263–73. Malden, MA.

Scheid, J. (2012), 'Le rite des auspices à Rome: quelle évolution? Réflexions sur la transformation de la divination publique des Romains entre le IIIe et le Ier siècle avant notre ère', in S. Georgoudi, R.K. Piettre, and F. Schmidt (eds), *La raison des signes: présages, rites, destin dans les sociétés de la Méditerranée ancienne*. 109–30. Leiden.

Scheid, J. (2016), *The Gods, the State, and the Individual: Reflections on Civic Religion in Rome*. Philadelphia.

Schlesinger, A.C. (trans.) (1959), *Livy, Julius Obsequens. History of Rome, Volume XIV: Summaries. Fragments. Julius Obsequens. General Index*. Loeb Classical Library 404. Cambridge, MA.

Schmeling, G. (trans.) (2020), *Petronius, Seneca. Satyricon. Apocolocyntosis*. Loeb Classical Library 15. Cambridge, MA.

Scholfield, A.F. (trans.) (1958), *Aelian. On Animals, Volume I: Books 1–5*. Loeb Classical Library 446. Cambridge, MA.

Scott, K. (1925), 'The Identification of Augustus with Romulus-Quirinus', *TAPA* 56, 82–105.

Scullard, H.H. (1981), *Festivals and Ceremonies of the Roman Republic*. London.

Serjeantsen, D. (2000), 'Bird Bones in Late Iron Age and Roman Silchester: Excavations on the Site of the Forum Basilica 1977, 1980–86', in M. Fulford and J. Timby (eds), *Society for the Promotion of Roman Studies*. 484–500. London.

Serjeantsen, D. (2009), *Birds*. Cambridge.

Serjeantsen, D., and J. Morris (2011), 'Ravens and Crows in Iron Age and Roman Britain', *Oxford Journal of Archaeology* 30:1, 85–107.

Shackleton Bailey, D.R. (trans.) (1993a), *Martial. Epigrams, Volume I: Spectacles, Books 1–5*. Loeb Classical Library 94. Cambridge, MA.

Shackleton Bailey, D.R. (trans.) (1993b), *Martial: Epigrams, Volume II: Books 6–10*. Loeb Classical Library 95. Cambridge, MA.

Shackleton Bailey, D.R. (trans.) (1993c), *Martial: Epigrams, Volume III: Books 11–14*. Loeb Classical Library 480. Cambridge, MA.

Shackleton Bailey, D.R. (trans.) (2000), *Valerius Maximus. Memorable Doings and Sayings, Volume I: Books 1–5*. Loeb Classical Library 492. Cambridge, MA.

Shackleton Bailey, D.R. (trans.) (2001), *Cicero. Letters to Friends, Volume II: Letters 114–280*. Loeb Classical Library 216. Cambridge, MA.

Shackleton Bailey, D.R. (trans.) (2010), *Cicero. Philippics 1–6*. Revised by John T. Ramsey and Gesine Manuwald. Loeb Classical Library 189. Cambridge, MA.

Shackleton Bailey, D.R. (trans.) (2015), *Statius. Silvae*. Revised by Christopher A. Parrott. Loeb Classical Library 206. Cambridge, MA.

Sheasley, B. (2008), *Home to Roost: A Backyard Farmer Chases Chickens through the Ages*. New York.

Shipley, F.W. (trans.) (1924), *Velleius Paterculus. Compendium of Roman History. Res Gestae Divi Augusti*. Loeb Classical Library 152. Cambridge, MA.

Shrubb, M. (2003), *Birds, Scythes, and Combines: A History of Birds and Agricultural Change*. New York.

Skutch, A.F. (1996), *The Minds of Birds*. Texas.

Skutsch, O. (1968), 'Enniana IV: *Condendae urbis auspicia*', in O. Skutsch (ed.), *Studia Enniana*. 62–85. Oxford.

Skutsch, O. (1985), *The Annals of Q. Ennius*. New York.

Small, J.P. (1982), *Cacus and Marsyas in Etrusco-Roman Legend*. Princeton.

Smith, H.W. (1971), 'The Epizootiology of Salmonella Infection in Poultry', in R.F. Gordon and B.M. Freeman (eds), *Poultry Diseases and World Economy*. 37–46. Edinburgh.

Spivey, N. (1997), *Etruscan Art*. London.

Stewart, R. (1997), 'The Jug and Lituus on Roman Republican Coin Types: Ritual Symbols and Political Power', *Phoenix* 51:2, 170–89.

Struck, P. (2014), 'Animals and Divination', in G.L. Campbell (ed.), *The Oxford Handbook of Animals in Classical Thought and Life*. 310–24. Oxford.

Sutherland, C. (1974), *Roman Coins*. New York.

Sykes, N. (2012), 'A Social Perspective on the Introduction of Exotic Animals: The Case of the Chicken', *World Archaeology* 44:1, 158–69.

Sykes, N. (2014a), *Beastly Questions: Animal Answers to Archaeological Issues*. London.

Sykes, N. (2014b), 'The Rhetoric of Meat Apportionment: Evidence for Exclusion, Inclusion and Social Position in Medieval England', in B.S. Arbuckle and S. McCarty (eds), *Animals and Inequality in the Ancient World*. 335–53. Colorado.

Szemler, G.J. (1971), 'Religio, Priesthoods and Magistracies in the Roman Republic', *Numen* 18:2, 103–31.

Tammisto, A. (1997), *Birds in Mosaics: A Study on the Representation of Birds in Hellenistic and Romano-Campanian Tessellated Mosaics to the Early Augustan Age*. Rome.

Taran, M. (1975), 'Early Records of Domestic Fowl in Judaea', *Ibis* 117, 109–10.

Taylor, R. (2000), 'Watching the Skies: Janus, Auspication, and the Shrine in the Roman Forum', *Amer. Acad. Rome* 45, 1–40.

Taylor, R. (2003), *How to Read a Church*. London.

Thomas, R.F. (1988), 'Vergil's "White Bird" and the Alexandrian Reference', *CPhil.* 83:3, 214–17.

Thomas, R., and A. Wilson (1994), 'Water Supply for Roman Farms in Latium and South Etruria', *Papers of the British School at Rome* 62, 139–96.

Thompson, D.W. (1936), *A Glossary of Greek Birds*. London.

Thomsen, R. (1961), *Early Roman Coinage*, Vol. 3. København.

Thulin, C.O. (1912), 'Haruspices', *RE* 7.2 col. 2431–69.

Thurmond, D.L. (2006), *A Handbook of Food Processing in Classical Rome: For Her Bounty No Winter*. Leiden; Boston.

Torelli, M. (1966), 'Un templum augurale d'età repubblicana a Bantia', *RAL* 21, 293–315.

Torelli, M. (1969), 'Contributi al supplemento del CIL IX', *RAL* 24, 39–48.

Torelli, M. (1995), *Studies in the Romanization of Italy*. Edmonton.

Toynbee, J.M.C. (1973), *Animals in Roman Life and Art*. Ithaca, NY.

Trentacoste, A. (2013), 'Faunal Remains from the Etruscan Sanctuary at Poggio Colla (Vicchio di Mugello)', *Etruscan Studies*, 16:1, 75–105.

Trentacoste, A. (2014), *The Etruscans and Their Animals: The Zooarchaeology of Forcello di Bagnolo San Vito (Mantova)*. Unpublished PhD Thesis. The University of Sheffield.

Trentacoste, A., A. Nieto-Espinet, and S. Valenzuela-Lamas (2018), 'Pre-Roman Improvements to Agricultural Production: Evidence from Livestock Husbandry in Late Prehistoric Italy', *PLoS ONE* 13:12, e0208109.

Tucker, C.W. (1976), 'Cicero, Augur, De Iure Augurali', *The Classical World* 70:3, 171–7.

Vaahtera, J. (2001), *Roman Augural Lore in Greek Historiography: A Study of the Theory and Terminology.* Stuttgart.

Valenzuela, A. (2018), 'Urban Consumption of Thrushes in the Early Roman City of Pollentia (Mallorca, Western Mediterranean)', *9th ICAZ Bird Working Group Meeting 2018*, Sheffield (Conference Poster Presentation).

Valenzuela-Lamas, S., and U. Albarella (2017), 'Animal Husbandry across the Western Roman Empire: Changes and Continuities', *European Journal of Archaeology* 20:3, 402–15.

Valeton, I.M.J. (1890), 'De modis auspicandi Romanorum II, III', *Mnemosyne* 18, 208–63, 406–56.

van Buren, A.W., and R.M. Kennedy, 'Varro's Aviary at Casinum', *JRS* 9, 59–66.

van der Veen, M. (2018), 'Archaeobotany: The Archaeology of Human-Plant Interactions', in W. Scheidel (ed.), *The Science of Roman History.* 53–94. Princeton.

van der Vliet, E. (1990), 'Early Rome and the Early State', *Staat und Staatlichkeit in der Fruhen Romischen Republik: Akten eines Symposiums*, 12–15 Juli 1988, Stuttgart.

Van Haeperen, F. (2012), 'Auspices d'Investiture, Loi Curiate Et Légitimité Des Magistrats Romains', *Cahiers Glotz* 23, 71–112.

Vervaet, F. (2010), 'The Secret History: The Official Position of Imperator Caesar Divi filius from 31 to 27 BCE', *Anc. Soc.* 40, 79–152.

Vervaet, F. (2014), *The High Command of the Roman Republic: The Principle of the summum imperium auspiciumque.* Stuttgart.

Vervaet, F. (2015), 'The Lex Curiata and the Patrician Auspices', *Cahiers du Centre Gustave Glotz* 26, 201–24.

Veyne, P. (1961), 'Vie de Trimalchion', *Annales: Economies, Sociétés, Civilisations* 16, 213–47.

Vinson, M.P. (1989), 'And Baby Makes Three? Parental Imagery in the Lesbia Poems of Catullus', *CJ* 85.1, 47–53.

Vishnia, R.F. (2012), 'A Case of "Bad Press"? Gaius Flaminius in Ancient Historiography', *Zeitschrift für Papyrologie und Epigraphik* 181, 27–45.

Wallace-Hadrill, A. (1994), *Houses and Society in Pompeii and Herculaneum.* Princeton.

Walters, H.B. (1926), *Catalogue of Engraved Gems and Cameos, Greek, Etruscan and Roman in the British Museum.* London.

Warden, P.G. (2016), 'Communicating with the Gods: Sacred Space in Etruria', in S. Bell and A. Carpino (eds), *A Companion to the Etrsucans.* 163–77. West Sussex.

Wardle, D. (2006), *Cicero on Divination.* Oxford.

Wardle, D. (2011), 'Augustus and the Priesthoods of Rome: The Evidence of Suetonius', in J.H. Richardson and F. Santangelo (eds), *Priests and State in the Roman World.* 271–91. Stuttgart.

Watson, G.E. (2002), 'Birds: Evidence from Wall paintings, Mosaics, Sculpture, Skeletal Remains, and Ancient Authors', in W.F. Jashemski and F.G. Meyer (eds), *The Natural History of Pompeii.* 357–400 Cambridge.

Weinstock, S. (1946), 'Martianus Capella and the Cosmic System of the Etruscans', *JRS* 36:1–2, 101–29.

Wheye, D. (2008), *Humans, Nature, and Birds: Science Art from Cave Walls to Computer Screens*. New Haven.

White, K.D. (1970). *Roman Farming*. London.

White, R.J. (1975), *The Interpretation of Dreams: Oneirocritica by Artemidorus*. Park Ridge, NJ.

Wilkins, J.M., and S. Hill (2006), *Food in the Ancient World*. Oxford.

Wills, S. (2017), *A History of Birds*. South Yorkshire.

Wissowa, G. (1896), 'Augures', *RE* 2, 2313–44.

Wissowa, G. (1912), *Religion und Kultus der Römer* (2nd edn). Munich.

Woolf, G. (2012), *Rome: An Empire's Story*. Oxford.

Yardley, J.C. (trans.) (2019), *Livy. History of Rome, Volume V: Books 21–22*. Loeb Classical Library 233. Cambridge, MA.

Yonge, C.M.A. (1882), *Pictorial History of the World's Great Nations: From the Earliest Dates to the Present Time*. New York.

Zanker, P. (1990), *Augustus und die Macht der Bilder*. Munich.

Zeiler, J. (2013), 'Birds for the Elite? Fowling in the Northern Netherlands in the Roman Period and the Early Middle Ages', *International Journal of Osteoarchaeology* 24, 378–83.

Zeitlin, F. (2013), 'Landscapes and Portraits: Signs of the Uncanny and Illusions of the Real', in M. Paschalis and S. Panayotikas (eds), *The Construction of the Real and the Ideal in the Ancient Novel*. 61–88. Barkhuis.

Zellner, H. (2008), 'Sappho's Sparrows', *The Classical World* 101:4, 435–42.

Zeuner, F.E. (1963), *A History of Domesticated Animals*. London.

Zhao, D.Q. (2018), *Foreigners and Propaganda: War and Peace in the Imperial Images of Augustus and Qin Shi Huangdi*. Unpublished Masters Thesis. The University of Melbourne.

Ziolkowski, A. (1993), 'Between Geese and the Auguraculum: The Origin of the Cult of Juno on the Arx', *CPhil.* 88:3, 206–19.

Zwierlein-Diehl, E. (1980), 'Simpuvium Numae', in H.A. Cahn and E. Simon (eds), *Tainia*. 405–22. Mainz.

Index

9 781032 162867